Sir Robert Ho Tung

Sir Robert Ho Tung, 1930

Sir Robert Ho Tung

Public Figure, Private Man

May Holdsworth

HKU
PRESS
香港大學出版社

Hong Kong University Press
The University of Hong Kong
Pokfulam Road
Hong Kong
https://hkupress.hku.hk

ISBN 978-988-8754-24-3 (*Hardback*)

British Library Cataloguing-in-Publication Data
A catalogue record for this book is available from the British Library.

(Front cover)
A portrait of Sir Robert Ho Tung was painted by Sir Oswald Birley in 1949 for presentation to Jardine Matheson & Co. Eric Hotung subsequently commissioned a copy, which is reproduced on the cover of this book. The copy diverges from the original in its use of a different colour for the background. Photograph courtesy of Andrew Tse.

10 9 8 7 6 5 4 3 2 1

Printed and bound by Hang Tai Printing Co., Ltd. in Hong Kong, China

Contents

Romanisation

The reader will notice discrepancies of romanisation in this book. These arise from the different systems of transliterating Chinese names and places phonetically into the Latin alphabet, all of them concocted from sounds of the original as perceived by foreigners who visited, worked, and lived in China. Ho Tung (later Sir Robert Ho Tung) and his English-speaking correspondents in the late nineteenth and early twentieth centuries usually rendered place names according to the so-called 'Post Office system', which was generally and illogically based on Chinese dialects prevailing in the southern treaty ports. Later, the Wade-Giles system, based on Mandarin, became popular. In 1958 (two years after Sir Robert Ho Tung's death), Communist China officially adopted the Hanyu pinyin romanisation system. A mixture of Post Office romanisation and the Wade-Giles scheme nevertheless continued to be used for many years afterwards.

Original romanisations have been retained in quotations; otherwise I use pinyin. Thus individual names appear in different versions; for example, Chang Tso-lin and Zhang Zuolin, Chang Hsueh-liang and Zhang Xueliang, and K'ang and Kang for the same surname. Sometimes Chinese names were spelt as pronounced in Cantonese; these notably included romanisations of the Chinese names of Sir Robert's relatives: his eldest son, for example, is Ho Sai-kim, and his son-in-law is Lo Man-kam. Referring to his gift to the British Museum of a fine ivory screen, Sir Robert described it in his will in 1955 as being 'fashioned in the time of the Emperor Kien Lung'. 'Kien Lung' is how a Cantonese would pronounce the imperial title; in pinyin it would be transliterated as 'Qianlong'.

We also have Peking and Beijing for China's capital city, and Kwangchow and Canton for the southern city which is now Guangzhou in pinyin. I am not sure if it lessens confusion, but I provide the Chinese characters in the family trees and in the glossary at the back of the book.

Unless otherwise specified, the amounts of money mentioned in this book are in Hong Kong dollars.

Acknowledgements

This biography of Sir Robert Ho Tung has had a long gestation. The late Eric Hotung, Sir Robert's eldest grandson, commissioned me to write it in 1997. More than twenty years on, I am delighted the book is to be published at last.

In Hong Kong, London, and McLean, Virginia, Eric Hotung showed me every courtesy and made himself available to answer questions. This biography would not therefore have been written without his generosity, and to him I owe my special thanks. Grateful acknowledgement is also owed to the late Mrs Diane Woo, who recommended me to Eric Hotung. It is impossible to imagine how I could have embarked on the project at all without the encouragement and many kindnesses of the late Revd. Carl T. Smith. His signature and message on the title page of *A Sense of History: Studies in the Social and Urban History of Hong Kong*, which I cite in this book, is an evocative reminder to me of my debt to him. Over many years of friendly collaboration, I benefited greatly from the knowledge and insights of Christopher Munn, deeply steeped as he is in the history of colonial Hong Kong. For help and support in various ways, I should also like to thank Jeremy Brown of Matheson & Co.; John M. Carroll; Vanda Cole; Peter Daniell, publisher of Hong Kong University Press; Sean Hotung; Fionnuala McHugh; James Watkins; and Runhua Wu. Most of all I am grateful to Andrew Tse, for his belief in me and for his constant support of this book. A descendant of Ho Kom-tong (Sir Robert's half-brother) through his father and of Ho Fook (Sir Robert's younger brother) through his mother, and third cousin several times removed to Sir Robert Ho Tung, Andrew is the family historian and keeper of the extensive Ho genealogical tree—in his head as well as on charts. He kindly provided most of the photographs in this book.

Preface

Sir Robert Ho Tung is a towering figure to many people in Hong Kong, invoked frequently in the press and on television as the first Chinese to live on the Peak, as the greatest philanthropist and the wealthiest man in Hong Kong in his day, the 'J.P. Morgan of the East', and, towards the end of his life, the 'Colony's Grand Old Man'.

When we speak of Hong Kong's birth and development as a marvel of British enterprise and Chinese industry we often forget that something else was created: a community of Eurasians who, as interpreters, compradores, and merchants, participated just as—if not more—keenly in that extraordinary journey from fishing village to gleaming city. Sir Robert, no less than several of his peers, owed his prosperity partly to the conjunction of historical moment, place, and opportunity,

Ho Tung as a young man

but also to his being Eurasian. Like many of his Eurasian peers, he had a good command of both Chinese and English. Of course he was identified—and he identified himself—as Chinese for most of his life; 'no man amongst the Chinese has borne his part in local, commercial and social life with more conspicuous ability, or with greater credit to himself and his nationality than Mr. Ho Tung, J.P.', as his entry in *Twentieth Century Impressions of Hongkong, Shanghai, and Other Treaty Ports of China* claimed. Yet there is no doubt of the ease with which he straddled Chinese and European commercial traditions, or that he profited brilliantly from this facility. Today, of all the old Hong Kong Eurasian families from Anderson to Zimmern, the Ho and Hotung family remains the most renowned and the most compelling.

In his last will, Sir Robert entreated his children to be 'diligent, do good and exhibit modesty and willingness and public spiritedness', in short to follow 'in the ways that have enabled me to establish my reputation and to build up my financial position from nothing'. His rags-to-riches story has often been told—in books and articles, and indeed by himself. Several memoirs were written and published by members of his family. A fuller picture is provided by Zheng Hongtai and Wong Siu Lun in their book *Xianggang dalao: He Dong*. Scrupulously researched from public sources and narrated in Chinese, this is the most comprehensive coverage of the life so far; it examines, in particular, Sir Robert's spectacular commercial successes through the lens of Chinese family business networks and structures. What I offer here shifts the balance a little: if thin on business dealings and public benefactions, my account tries not merely to locate Sir Robert in his place and time but also to show glimpses of him within a social world of family, friends, and the mercantile and political elites of colonial Hong Kong, Great Britain, and China. He encountered a vast number of people in his long life; it became second nature to him to maintain links to most of them.

I believe this will be the first full-length biography in English. To write it I was privileged to have been given the run—all too brief, unfortunately—of a cache of letters and notes left by Sir Robert Ho Tung and then in the possession of his grandson Eric Hotung. When Eric commissioned me in 1997 to write a life of his grandfather, the initial sight of some of those papers made his offer utterly irresistible: at the time the higgledy-piggledy records were mouldering in tea chests in an unfurnished and damp though air-conditioned tenement storeroom in Hong Kong's Wanchai; in a battered suitcase in one of Eric's Mid-Levels apartments; and in a number of files in the basement of his house in McLean, Virginia, near Washington DC.

Sir Robert Ho Tung was nothing if not meticulous, and it is highly likely that business records and copies of correspondence were all carefully maintained. In the pre-digital age, there was no question for Sir Robert's clerks and secretaries that original handwritten letters received would be kept, and carbon copies of outbound letters filed. The attrition of time and war has inevitably eroded many of these. I was not alone among researchers to find frustrating instances of missing pages in paper trails that simply petered out. However, what remained still ran to three or four chests of account books and about fifty standard-size files of letters and notes. While those papers consist mainly of business correspondence, minutes of board meetings, deeds and promissory notes, enough letters have survived to provide illuminating glimpses of the broad directions of Sir Robert's financial, political, and social ambitions; his relations with the colonial authorities of Hong Kong and London; his fastidious care of his own health; and the rather formal contacts between him and some of his children. These uncatalogued papers are referenced in the endnotes as 'Hotung Papers'.

There is, in addition, several years' correspondence between Sir Robert and his son Edward Sai-kim (known in the family circle as 'Eddie'). Through the 1930s and early 1940s, when Eddie looked after Sir Robert's business interests in Shanghai, father and son wrote to each other about property and financial matters nearly every day; at the end of each week a list of all the cables sent was typed out for the record.

A few diaries covering the years 1941, 1942, 1948, 1949, 1952, 1954, and 1956 have been saved. Written in Chinese and English, and frustrating for the biographer (though perhaps revealing of the subject), they are no more than records of appointments, sleeping patterns, diet, medication, and the performance of bodily functions; they give no hint of his emotions or state of mind. In fact, he rarely committed private feelings to paper; what he did express about his experiences or acquaintances were usually perfunctory remarks which added little to what was generally known.

Sometime after the late 1960s, Sir William Teeling made a start on a biography, probably invited to do so by Eric Hotung. According to his Wikipedia entry, Sir William (1903–1975) was an Irish writer, traveller, and Conservative member of parliament for Brighton. A strong supporter of Taiwan and friend of Madame Chiang Kai-shek, he was in Asia for extended periods and very likely visited Hong Kong. A fragment of his typescript remains among what I reference as 'Hotung Papers'. Sir William Teeling's account is marked by fluent writing and wit of presentation, but he clearly used only the material Eric had to hand at the time; it is journalistic in tone and far from finished.

Sir Robert himself made an attempt at writing his memoirs while waiting out the Japanese occupation of Hong Kong in Macau; some of his typed notes are extant. He left details of his early schooling—before he enrolled in the Central

School—and the first years of what he called his 'business career'. Had he completed the memoir, it would have been almost entirely about his public life, with a veil drawn over most personal details, including his parentage.

A biographer's dearest wish, on the other hand, is to unearth more of the subject's personal life than the public one (which would, in any case, be broadly known to anyone who cares to search for it), to excavate something surprising, intimate, dramatic, and perhaps even embarrassing or scandalous—provided, of course, that sources denied to previous biographers became available. My research has been less arduous, since Eric Hotung made free to me all the documents and family papers that have been preserved.

In 2010, the late Eric Peter Ho, Sir Robert Ho Tung's great-nephew, said in the course of what he called his own 'delving' into his family's past that it was a matter for regret that no one had yet published an authoritative biography of Sir Robert's life and work:

> This all the more so as two of his daughters, Irene Cheng and Jean Gittins, were no mean authors with the ability and the inclination to write. Furthermore, as he had been served by secretaries for a long time up until his death in 1956, and his own children's accounts that their requests of, and proposals to, him had to be put in writing, there must be a wealth of material for a biographer to work on, especially as his principal residence, Idlewild, was not looted during the Japanese Occupation of Hong Kong, from 1942 to 1945. His papers must be largely intact. Although I am most grateful to Sir Joseph Hotung [Sir Robert Ho Tung's grandson; Edward Sai-kim's younger son; Eric Hotung's brother] for sharing with me the file he has assembled about his grandfather, we both realise this is only a minute part of the whole archive. Thus this pithy coverage of the most distinguished member of our clan is no more than the cobbling together of such available information, personal knowledge, and other bits and pieces I have been able to collect in the course of my family research.[1]

I make no claim to having produced an authoritative biography, but I did have access to the 'archive' which, if not as intact or voluminous as E. P. Ho suspected, was still indispensable to me in my attempt to liberate Sir Robert Ho Tung out of the legend, so to speak, and, without diminishing him, to reveal the private man, with all his human frailties and contradictions, behind the public figure.

1
Longevity

A group photograph recalls the event. It is Monday 22 December 1952.[1] Seventy faces, including four of babes in arms, are caught in the frame. Here, seated in the centre, resplendent in silk robe and jacket, is the patriarch Sir Robert Ho Tung. He is undoubtedly of a great age, but the eyes peering out of the pale, emaciated face are still wonderfully bright. Around him are his sons, daughters, in-laws, grandchildren, and great-grandchildren. He is flanked by his two sons (Edward Sai-kim and Robert Shai-lai), two daughters-in-law (Hesta and Kitty), his eldest daughter Victoria, to his far right, and her husband, Lo Man-kam, to his far left.

This photograph commemorates Sir Robert Ho Tung's ninetieth birthday. As he recounted afterwards, those of his children and grandchildren who were not already in Hong Kong flew back from all over the world specially for the occasion: seven from England, three from New York, four from Los Angeles, four from Melbourne, and one from Taipei.

In preparation for this occasion, Victoria had counted a total of seventy-five family members. Five were missing from the family reunion and from the photograph, including his grandsons Eric and Joseph, unavoidably detained in the United States.

When the photographer had finished, the family group reassembled opposite the seated patriarch and bowed deeply before him. They should perhaps have dropped to their knees, on this his ninetieth birthday, but he had not wished for that. For days beforehand, an unceasing stream of congratulatory messages was delivered to his house, Idlewild, at 8 Seymour Road on Hong Kong Island—from Governor and Lady Grantham, the bishop of Hong Kong, the colonial secretary, Sir Arthur Morse of the Hongkong and Shanghai Banking Corporation, the Chinese members of the Executive and Legislative Councils, the Tung Wah Group of Hospitals, the Chinese Chamber of Commerce, the Po Leung Kuk, and hundreds of others. If he thought this the crowning moment of his life—a moment to savour the culmination of his efforts and achievements—he did not show it. Those luminous eyes merely lingered benignly on the gathering as a warm wave of affection and reverence washed over him.

People had been coming and going all day. Idlewild was decked with flowers, bunting, and fairy lights. In anticipation, his staff had alerted police traffic control of possible jams along Seymour Road. There were onlookers enough, craning their necks to catch a glimpse of Hong Kong's elite as callers arrived to offer their good wishes or leave their cards. As each car stopped at the gate, musicians stationed at the entrance struck up a tune to announce the new arrival. Nobody was allowed to leave without sampling the traditional refreshments of longevity buns, noodles, sweet soup, lotus seeds, and nuts. Servants, including several extra ones engaged for the day, hovered at the entrance and busied themselves in the kitchen. Guests milled about the covered garden at the back. It was such a crowd that two sittings for each meal had to be provided just for those in the house. To add to the hubbub and clatter, staccato bursts of firecrackers occasionally filled the air, as was only proper on a grand and auspicious occasion such as this.

Shadows were deepening on the flowers in their earthen pots before Sir Robert could leave the garden to go to his room for a rest. There was to be a great, festive Chinese dinner in the evening, though he himself would have none of the roast meats and suckling pig. For the good of his health, he rarely deviated from his diet of sour milk and boiled rice or noodles. That he had been spared death for so long was a wonder to him, for he never expected to reach his tenth decade. There was a time in his late forties when ill health confined him to bed for three whole years and his doctors gave him up for lost. His telegraphic address had been 'Longevity' (later changed to 'Hotung Hongkong'), but he really thought the attainment of venerable old age, a blessing cherished by all Chinese, would elude him.

For such a notable occasion as the ninetieth birthday of Sir Robert Ho Tung, the initial preparations had been signally restrained. He wished to keep the event as quiet as possible, with no ostentatious display, and no expensive presents. So he informed his daughter-in-law Hesta by letter as early as September 1952 and all his children by a memo circulated in October. He would mark it only with his family, he said, and offered to pay passage for those members who were abroad.

This generous offer was warmly welcomed by his children. Victoria Lo, his eldest daughter, immediately telephoned her husband, Sir Man-kam Lo or M. K., as he was informally known, to tell him the splendid news. M. K. (then fifty-nine years old) sent a long letter of thanks the following day:

> To my father-in-law who is one generation older than myself, I know that according to any Chinese standard of decorum it is improper for me to talk about my own old age, but I hope you will forgive me if I say that I have attained an age when to me there can be no greater joy than to be able to be with my children . . . Your generosity will enable Vic and myself to have a family reunion of our children and grandchildren in December, an event which was utterly beyond my dreams and expectations.[2]

Sir Robert's hope of a modest celebration was, however, a vain one; he was too prominent a figure in Hong Kong for his anniversary to pass without commemoration. In fact, the many public organisations which he supported had been collecting subscriptions for weeks. It was all his children could do to decline or return those laudatory scrolls, embroidered banners, carved ivory images, silver tripods, and other engraved objects that threatened to flow in to do him honour.

There was a beautiful scroll from three old friends from Jardine, Matheson & Company, however, which he did not have the heart to send back. It was addressed to him by 'David Keswick, W. J. Keswick and John Keswick, the three sons of the late Henry Keswick, the grandsons of the late William Keswick'. 'The association of Sir Robert with the Keswick family stretches over three generations,' the scroll reads, 'through the amazingly active life of a young man to the peaceful serenity of old age . . . It is the privilege of good friends to pay tribute to the sagacity, wisdom, understanding, energy and spirit which carried him and his family to distinction, fortune, benevolence, and high regard among his fellow men.'

Sir Robert wrote to John Keswick in grateful acknowledgement of this tribute:

Birthday tribute from Jardine, Matheson and Company Limited

I am deeply touched at this further demonstration of affectionate regard from your family—a regard which, I am proud to repeat, it has been my privilege to enjoy for over 60 years. To you in particular, I owe an old man's gratitude for a brimming cup of happiness.[3]

Indeed his cup was about to overflow, for Jardines wished to do more—marking his anniversary with the establishment of a 'Sir Robert Ho Tung Bursary' at the University of Hong Kong. John Keswick, on behalf of the 'Princely House', wrote:

The members of Jardine Matheson & Co. Ltd are anxious to mark the auspicious occasion of your ninetieth birthday, and to offer some expression of the high regard and sincere esteem in which you are held by all of us.

To this end it is proposed, and we hope you will signify your assent, that a Bursary shall be established by the Firm in the Hongkong University to be known as 'The Sir Robert Ho Tung Bursary'.[4]

All these expressions of esteem could not go unacknowledged. He had already begun the tradition of making large charitable donations to mark his major anniversaries; in the next few days cheques would be sent to the Young Women's Christian Association, St John's Ambulance Brigade, and the Welfare League. And since it was hardly possible to ask all his well-wishers to dinner, they must be thanked by the presentation of a souvenir. Good Chinese manners required no less. The souvenir, Victoria proposed, could be a gold ornament in the shape of a peach—a Chinese symbol of longevity. It could be ordered in two sizes: a large one (five grams) for family members, and a smaller one (1.5 grams) for friends and acquaintances. A quotation from the goldsmith, she reported, would be based on the price for pure gold on the day of the order, plus a standard charge for the engraving. Sir Robert was happy to agree to this, and more than 500 gold ornaments in the form of pendants were struck. One side carried the Chinese character for 'longevity', the other was inscribed with the dates '1852–1952' and four words (*qiyi jinian*) which translated as 'souvenir of a century'. Sir Robert explained their significance to L. N. Shaw, an American friend who was presented with one:

According to old Chinese custom, when a person is over 80, ten years will be added to his age. Therefore, although I was only celebrating my 90th birthday, it meant that I was celebrating my 100th birthday.[5]

Nor did he forget Sir Winston Churchill, met in 1924, when he and Lady Ho Tung represented Hong Kong at the Wembley Empire Exhibition. Sir Winston's accumulation of honours and medals surpassed his own. When news that the queen had made Sir Winston a Knight of the Garter reached him in the spring of 1953,

The two sides of the gold peach pendants

Sir Robert seized the opportunity not only to write a letter of congratulations but also to send Sir Winston a pair of the peach pendants, giving the same explanation as he had done to his American friend Shaw about the characters for 'longevity' and 'souvenir of a century'. Despite the British customs authority's insistence on charging £5. 2s. 3d. for them, and Lady Churchill's instruction to return the pendants to customs, Sir Robert had the gratification of a letter of thanks from Downing Street for the 'gifts which my Wife and I are happy to receive', signed with the initials 'WSC' in Winston Spencer Churchill's own hand. Even in old age, Sir Robert could still relish being in awe of a great man.[6]

If Sir Robert claimed the experience and wisdom of a centenarian, who could blame him? He had risen with the high tide of history from extreme poverty to spectacular riches. When he was born, China was an empire and the colony of Hong Kong was in its adolescence. His ninety years had spanned two Chinese revolutions, two world wars, and a thousand other events that changed people's lives forever. In an interview for the *South China Morning Post*, he reminisced about three events which evoked the strongest memories: the extension of the colony by a ninety-nine-year lease on the New Territories in 1898; the harrowing Japanese occupation in 1941–1945; and his tour of Europe and America in 1948 and 1949, when he was entertained by royalty and leading statesmen made a fuss of him.[7] Nor did he forget the very special concession by Charles Ford, superintendent of gardens and plantations at Hongkong,[8] which allowed him, weak from a bout of pneumonia some sixty years earlier, to be carried in a chair into the Botanical Gardens, to breathe in its fresh, scented air. He had come a long way since his birth in a dingy corner of the clamorous city which lay golden in the light of a setting sun that December afternoon.

2

A Beginning in the East

A man's life begins with his ancestors and is perpetuated by his sons. Ho Tung barely knew who his ancestors were, and remained sensitive about his parentage all his life.

One would never guess this from the impressive grave of his mother at the Eurasian cemetery, the Chiu Yuen, off Mount Davis Road in Hong Kong. The headstone, set up on 'an auspicious day in September, the twenty-third year of Emperor Guangxu's reign' (1898), is carved with the names of fifteen dutiful descendants. At the centre, two lines of characters define the dedication. They read, 'Conferred by imperial mandate, high-ranking lady, deceased mother, surnamed Sze' and 'Conferred by imperial mandate, senior mandarin, deceased father Sze-man, noble gentleman of the house of Ho'.[1] The preamble is perfectly in keeping with the traditional high-flown eulogies etched on Chinese graves; but the implication that the noble deceased father is buried here is a fiction, since he lies far away on another continent. The name on the headstone merely satisfies his descendants' need to make offerings at the graves of their forebears.

Mount Davis is named after Sir John Davis, the second governor of the British colony of Hong Kong. This subtropical island off the southern coast of China was a sleepy settlement inhabited by fishermen and farmers before it became a possession of the Victorian empire. It was signed away in perpetuity when the hapless Qing empire, defeated in the Opium War, signed the Treaty of Nanking (Nanjing) in 1842. Neither of the signatories—Britain and China—realised at the time what large historical forces were being unleashed by the treaty. Besides Hong Kong, five other ports on the China coast—Guangzhou, Xiamen, Fuzhou, Ningbo, and Shanghai—were to be thrown open to foreign trade and residence. These 'treaty ports', the first cracks in the fabric of the closed Chinese world, would witness the fateful meeting of East and West, old and new, the Confucian order and the capitalist system.

The grave of Ho Tung's mother in the Chiu Yuen Eurasian Cemetery

European, especially British, penetration of China quickened in the next twenty years. Until compelled to open her markets by the Treaty of Nanking, China was exclusive and kept foreign traders at arm's length, insisting firmly on her own self-sufficiency and consistently repelling their overtures. After 1843 everything changed. Now clippers began to throng harbours where previously only coastal junks anchored. These ships loaded the tea, silk, and porcelain so coveted by the West, and discharged a growing torrent of opium from British India. Opium was the one foreign commodity, it seemed, that China could not resist.

Soon, not content with the colony of Hong Kong and the five treaty ports, European merchants began agitating for access to the entire interior of China. They also pressed for more favourable tariffs, a diplomatic presence in Beijing, and legalisation of the opium trade. By the straightforward means of sending gunboats up the China coast, the British succeeded in wresting more concessions from the

Qing government. In 1858, under the terms of the Sino-British Treaty of Tientsin (Tianjin), more ports, including several on the Yangtze River, were opened. It took another British campaign, however, to enforce its terms on the intransigent Chinese. By the Convention of Peking (Beijing) which terminated this round of hostilities in 1860, the Kowloon peninsula, opposite Hong Kong, was also ceded to Britain.

The opportunities offered by treaty ports drew hordes of Chinese from their impoverished villages. Of course, since they were created to ease the conduct of foreign 'mercantile pursuits', the treaty ports also brought to China's shores seamen, traders, soldiers, administrators, doctors, and lawyers, not only from Britain but also America, France, and other countries of Europe. That some of these men took Chinese girls as mistresses is hardly to be wondered at, since few Western women followed in their wake. Robert Hart, the renowned inspector-general of the Chinese Imperial Maritime Customs, was a junior consular officer when he first arrived in Hong Kong in 1854. Appointed to the customs service in 1859, he was eventually to sire three children by his Chinese mistress. He later explained that it was 'common practice for unmarried Englishmen resident in China to keep a Chinese girl, and I did as others did'.[2]

It was no different in Hong Kong. An overwhelmingly masculine society, the new settlement at first harboured a handful of Westerners and a much larger, floating population of labourers and artisans from the Chinese mainland. In the latter half of the nineteenth century it became a transit point for ships that dispersed increasing numbers of Chinese 'coolies' and emigrants to Central and South America, Southeast Asia, the gold fields of Australia and California, and the plantations of Hawaii. Unaccompanied by their womenfolk, these men would find brief solace in brothels which not surprisingly proliferated apace. Because of the shortage of women locally, the brothels kept themselves supplied with girls kidnapped or bought in China.

Human trafficking was nothing new in China, where it was not uncommon for destitute families to dispose of their young daughters by selling them for adoption as *mui tsai* (literally 'little sisters') to rich households. Mui tsai were owned, and could therefore be resold for a profit or married off at their patrons' discretion. In some cases they stayed as unpaid domestic servants and were kindly treated; in others they were taken as concubines by the head of the house; in still others they were tricked into providing sexual services for money. Prostitutes in Hong Kong were sought out by both Chinese and Western settlers. Occasionally a woman would be taken under the wing of one of her regular clients and a longer-term liaison evolved. If she cohabited with a foreigner she fell into a group known in the language of bureaucrats as 'protected women'.

As an official publication had it, this class of women had 'no parallel either in China, outside the Treaty Ports, or in Europe'. Such a woman 'resides in a house rented by her protector, who lives generally in another part of town, [and] receives a fixed salary from her protector . . . the offspring of such a liaison are not recognised by the father beyond making such allowance or settlement for the children's maintenance and education as his means may afford.'³ The Rev. E. T. Moncreiff of the London Missionary Society called them 'the offspring of sin'. Nevertheless, these children constituted 'a very promising class', endowed as they were with 'a portion of European energy'.⁴ As for their mothers, they were 'as a general rule, a happy, contented, and remarkably quiet sort of people, specially noted for their devotion to the rites and ceremonies of popular Buddhism and Taoism. They consider themselves infinitely above a common prostitute, and congratulate themselves that they are far better off, and far better treated by their foreign protectors, than the legitimate first wife of a well-to-do Chinaman is treated by her husband or her mother-in-law.'⁵

Ho Tung's mother, whose family name was Sze, and whose given name is believed to be 'Tai', was sold to a bordello around 1855, when she was around thirteen years old. Trafficking in female children was a thriving business by then, with rich rewards for kidnappers, sellers, and brokers through whose hands the girls often passed. In poor Sze's case, it had obviously been worth someone's while to bring her across what would have been in those days a very long distance to the recently founded colony of Hong Kong. Her story is as poignant as it is appalling—like a piece of chattel, she was sold to discharge gambling debts allegedly incurred by her brothers. The habit of gambling ruined many a family. Two of Sze's nephews were apparently degenerate gamblers; Sze herself became inordinately fond of playing mah-jong.

Sze had exchanged one island for another. Her own village was located on Chongming, a long, flat expanse of land at the mouth of the Yangtze just above Shanghai. Chongming began life as a cluster of sandbars built up over centuries by the river's stupendous loads of silt. As the Yangtze meets the sea, its tumbling flow becomes more sedate; it is at this point that much of the silt is deposited. By the middle of the seventeenth century, the largest of the sandbars had coalesced into an island of considerable size. Here some people settled, scratching a living out of saltpans and fish.

In time the land was harnessed for the planting of cotton and a variety of fruits and vegetables. Three centuries later, despite development of some light manufacturing in the towns, Chongming is still the market garden of its neighbouring metropolis, Shanghai. While there is no way of discovering when the Sze family first settled on Chongming, we do know that the name remains one of the most

common on the island today. A connection of Sze's tells us that the family, originally from Suzhou in Jiangsu Province, fled to Chongming some time after the
outbreak of the Taiping Rebellion in the early 1850s.[6] There were two orphaned
daughters, Sze Tai and an older sister: the older sister married a widower, Zhu Pu,
who had three grown sons. Sze Tai was taken into his household as well, but it
was not a happy arrangement; the girls, maltreated by Zhu Pu's sons, ran away to
Shanghai, where they found work as domestics. It was presumably from Shanghai
that Sze was spirited to Hong Kong. Her sister eventually returned to her husband
on Chongming, and she, too, had three sons. Sze remained close to her sister, and
tried to help the Zhu family when she could. Years later, two of her nephews were
given work by Ho Tung as rent collectors in Shanghai. Sir Robert Ho Tung also
provided for his mother's 'poor relations on Chongming' through a bequest in his
will.[7]

What did the girl Sze make of Hong Kong? In some ways it would have looked
familiar: its waterfront, the Praya, thronged with hawkers and coolies; its fishing
villages hugging the southern shore; its wild rural areas; even its noise and smells;
were reminiscent of Chongming. Unlike Chongming, though, it appeared brown
and rocky, with many hills—an altogether different terrain to the flat green island
she had left behind. In the new town of Victoria, the buildings stood dazzlingly
white in the fierce sunlight reflected back by the swirling waters of the crowded
harbour. They were very grand compared to the low, grey-roofed dwellings and
untidy matsheds of home, for many were large, solid, brick-and-granite structures
encircled by spacious verandas. A few houses nestled in the hills behind, some of
them more imposing than the rest, boasting as they did of two or three storeys.

Running along Queen's Road, the main thoroughfare parallel to the waterfront, a line of shipyards and warehouses straggled towards the west. In the network
of streets behind, cheek by jowl with coal sheds, cooperages, lumber merchants,
and carpenter shops, were markets, boarding houses, and taverns. It is not recorded
where Sze spent her first few years in Hong Kong, nor how she became the protected woman of a Dutchman, but we do know that it was in Peel Street, up the hill
from Queen's Road, that her second child was born.

Racial prejudice in those early days was as prevalent in Hong Kong as elsewhere in the British empire; since it originates in fear, interracial unions were
seen as especially threatening. In fact, such alliances were so deplored that the
women were kept in decent obscurity in a part of town where their presence was
least likely to give rise to comment. Peel Street, running steeply down to Queen's
Road, was within the invisible boundaries of this neighbourhood. To the east lay
the predominantly European settlement; on the west was Taipingshan, a 'native'
quarter created when the colonial authorities moved Chinese inhabitants out of

the central district in 1844. In between, and almost exactly marking the line of segregation, was Peel Street. Characterised by terraced houses in which well-off Chinese and Portuguese merchants lived in close proximity to Indians and Parsees, it was a twilight zone 'neither exclusively European nor exclusively Chinese'.[8]

The father of Sze's second child was a Charles Henry Maurice Bosman, at one time running a commission agency, Koopmanschap & Bosman, on Queen's Road.[9] Of Dutch and Jewish origin, he is assumed to have changed his name from Mozes Hartog Bosman to Karel Hendrik Bosman, and later to have anglicised the first two names to Charles Henry.[10] Born in Rotterdam in 1839, he arrived in Hong Kong probably in 1859 and set up a business with Cornelius Koopmanschap to charter and run ships between Hong Kong and San Francisco and ports in Southeast Asia. Cornelius Koopmanschap, a native of Weesperkarspel, near Amsterdam, who fetched up in California at the time of the gold rush, had established himself in San Francisco as a commission merchant dealing mostly in Chinese goods.

Koopmanschap & Bosman was initially very successful, acting as agent for six ships out of a total of twenty-five that plied the route between Hong Kong and San Francisco. Its business steadily increased, for in 1861 the company accounted for half of the traffic crossing the Pacific (sixteen ships from a total of thirty).[11] Around that time Henry F. Edwards joined as a third partner; in the autumn of 1862 (two months before Ho Tung was born) the twenty-three-year-old Bosman was sending out a printed circular to his clients:

> to advise you that the business of the undersigned will henceforth be carried on under the name and style of Bosman & Co.
>   Calling your attention to signatures at foot,
>   We are,
>   Dear Sir,
>   Your obedient Servants,
>   Koopmanschap & Bosman
>   Mr C. H. M. Bosman, will sign (signed)
>   Mr C. Koopmanschap, will sign (absent)
>   Mr H. F. Edwards, will sign (absent)[12]

By this arrangement C. Koopmanschap and C. H. M. Bosman, respectively based in San Francisco and Hong Kong, hoped to carve out an even greater slice of the transpacific shipping business, not only by consigning ships to each other but also taking on the chartering themselves. In this way they could earn a percentage as both charterer and agent. In fact, their aim was nothing less than control of the route, but as the 1860s wore on their attempt to set up a regular shipping service began to unravel. Nevertheless, as a merchant of some standing, Bosman was well regarded enough to be appointed consul for the Netherlands in Hong Kong for a time.

Bosman clearly had more than one string to his bow. There were other ways to cash in on the shipping traffic crossing the Pacific in those days: besides chartering vessels, we hear of him arranging consignments of quicksilver for Jardine, Matheson & Company, and, from routine correspondence in 1862, entering into exchange operations between Mexican silver dollars (the currency of trade) and gold bars:

> Referring to the conversation held with our Mr Bosman we now beg to inform you that we can employ about twenty thousand dollars in advance to be made against goods shipped to the consignment of our house in San Francisco.
>
> In regard to returns from there we beg to advise you that we have been reliably informed that all Chinese exporters have ordered remittances to be made in Mexican Dollars—it is in consequence fair to presume that Gold Bars will be the preferable Bullion to select.
>
> We shall thank you to inform us at what premium in Mex. Dollars you are willing to take our 90 days sight draft on Messrs Koopmanschap & Co. in San Francisco?
>
> We are,
> Gentlemen,
> Your Obedient Servants,
> Bosman & Co.[13]

Bosman tried his hand at other business ventures. These included the import and export of such commodities as rice and flour: the company is recorded to have shipped flour to Calcutta, for example.[14] He advertised himself as an insurance agent in the early 1860s. His name, with the description 'Merchant' after it, appears among those who signed the original memorandum and articles of association of the Hongkong Hotel on 2 March 1866.[15] At the new hotel's inauguration in March 1868, Bosman, as chairman of the hotel company, toasted Governor and Lady MacDonnell before entertaining them and 150 other guests to tiffin. They sat down to eat at tables set with sparkling monogrammed china, in a dining room gaily decorated with flags.[16] Bosman also became a director of the Hongkong and Whampoa Dock Company, which was incorporated later that same year.

Despite all these interests, it was not a business record that smacked of steady progress or long-term success. Too prone to taking risks, Bosman overstretched himself; indeed a story has come down suggesting that Bosman's company was on the brink of failure on three occasions. The *coup de grâce* came in the late 1860s: Bosman and Koopmanschap fell out, most likely over losses incurred by the shipping business, and their relationship ended. Bosman did go bankrupt in 1869

C. H. M. Bosman

and left Hong Kong that year. For his part, Koopmanschap became engaged in another trade—the import of Chinese labourers on contract into America.[17] We may assume that Bosman had been similarly engaged from the report of a lawsuit in 1869, in which Bosman & Co. was plaintiff in a case against one Tam A-foo involving the supply of labourers to work on the Pacific Railway in California.[18] Koopmanschap petitioned for bankruptcy in 1872.

There was a semblance of stability in his private life, though, for Bosman maintained a relationship with Sze for some years, judging from the births of their children. By the time Bosman came on the scene, Sze already had a daughter with an unknown foreigner. This girl, Pak-ngan (then or later given the surname Ho) was born in 1861, a year before Ho Tung was born. To a woman imbued with Chinese beliefs, the appearance in the world of her first son must have been regarded as significant, especially as the omens could not have been better. His birthday, 22 December, fell on the winter solstice, the time of year when the sun appears to stand still, the cosmic negative force of *yin* is at an extreme point, and the masculine force of *yang* is supposed to be returning to ascendancy.[19] If a fortune-teller had been around to cast the baby's horoscope, he would have approved of the name Kai-tung ('a beginning in the east'). The association with sunrise is reinforced by the child's alternative name (some say his 'business' name, adopted somewhat later), Hiu-sang ('born at dawn').

In later years he tended to drop 'Kai', the generational name he had in common with his younger brothers. At school he was called Ho A-tung, with the typically southern Chinese prefix 'A' or 'Ah' attached to his given name. When writing in English, he always signed his name simply as Ho Tung or, after he was knighted, R. (for Robert) Ho Tung. It was his children who used Ho Tung as a surname, with or without a hyphen. Some have reverted to Ho, and one branch is now known as Hotung.

Kai-tung became one of nine children born to Sze. There remain some unsolved questions about Sze's life, the most puzzling being the father of some of her children. Not having an entirely prosperous time of it in Hong Kong, and involved as he was in seaborne trade, Bosman must have left Sze for extended periods which, in some cases, lasted as long as a year. After Kai-tung two more boys, Kai-fook and Kai-mun, came in quick succession (Kai-mun, according to the memoir of her mother by Ho Tung's daughter Irene, was given away for adoption by a childless family). Then Bosman went away, and during his absence Sze bore another son, Kai-tong (later known as Kom-tong), possibly by a lodger named Ho. While this might not have been the result of a lasting relationship, it seems the name Ho stuck and was adopted for all her offspring—or so one story goes. Another story associates the name with a homophone of the 'Ho' in 'Ho Lan', the Cantonese romanisation of 'Holland', Bosman's place of origin. Afterwards, on Bosman's return, a fifth son, Kai-gai, was born. In due course the family increased by two more daughters and another son, who died young; they were evidently neither Bosman's children nor Ho's, but believed to be fathered by a Kwok Hing-yin, alias Kwok Chung, a cattle merchant who took Sze as his concubine some time around 1868.

Bosman left Hong Kong for good in 1869. He did not drop totally out of sight, however, for he would be sidetracked by another commission at least once, in Yokohama, shortly after he left Hong Kong. Ever the agent, he was reported to have acted for no less a personage than the emperor of Japan. Sailing to the United States in November 1869, he was tasked by the emperor to accompany 'four natives of Japan, two being of royal blood and two of the nobility' to New Brunswick, NJ, to attend a university located near the city: when he had delivered them over 'to the safe keeping of the president of the college his duty will be accomplished.'[20]

We next hear of him settling in London. He took British nationality, swearing an oath of allegiance to HM Queen Victoria in November 1888. He continued to operate as an Eastern agent and was associated with James Whittall (a former partner of Jardines) at the time of his death in 1892.[21] He died at home, presumably in the bosom of his second family, which consisted of his American wife, Mary, whom he had married in the United States in 1877, four sons, and a daughter. Etched on the back of his gravestone in Brompton Cemetery, London, are these words: 'Distinguished China Merchant / Netherlands Consul at Hong Kong 1866–69'. There is no mention, unsurprisingly enough, of his family in Hong

Kong; yet from our present viewpoint that is, without a doubt, his most significant legacy.

With pregnancies occurring so closely together, Sze's child-rearing must have been rather haphazard at times. She was fond of gambling; at the mah-jong table she could lose herself and her troubles, hardly a prudent pastime in the light of Bosman's business record and her frequently straitened circumstances. Perhaps Kai-tung's older half-sister Pak-ngan showed him tenderness (he referred to her as his 'beloved elder sister' in his last will); it is more likely that he learnt to armour himself against any expectation of intimacy.

One wonders, also, what effect his mother's situation had on him. All doors to European society would have been firmly closed to her; from the Chinese community she would have received, at best, indifference or pitying tolerance. It was a time when colonial bigotry against miscegenation revealed itself in moral disapproval; in most cases it was the 'native' women who were censured. The children of such unions, with their fairer skin and Eurasian features, must have lived with the painful awareness of many a curled lip, averted look, or wounding remark. To any child, a mother and a father represent security, the normal scheme of things. But the Ho children were bereft of the steadying presence of both father and mother. By the time Ho Tung and his brother Ho Fook reached their teens, Sze

Ho Tung's half-sister, Kwok Sui-ting, in middle age. She changed her surname from 'Kwok' to 'Ho' before her marriage.

This photograph of Charles Henry Maurice Bosman, found among the 'Hotung Papers', may have been the one taken 'between 1885 and 1890', when Bosman would have been in his late forties or early fifties.

had become Kwok Hing-yin's concubine; she would bear three more children, the eldest of whom, Kwok Sui-ting, adopted the surname Ho before her marriage, perhaps because of a wish to ally herself with a more respectable branch of the family. One story attributes the switch to Ho Tung, who is said to have offered a dowry if she changed her name from Kwok to Ho.

Years later, when Ho Tung and Bosman met in London, the son had some difficulty acknowledging Bosman as father.[22] The inability to feel affection for his father is hardly surprising, since Bosman had been a largely absent parent who abandoned his Hong Kong family without so much as a backward glance. He did not make financial provisions for his 'protected woman' or their children, as some foreigners did by the creation of a trust or by a gift of property. He had, after all, filed for bankruptcy and would have had to pay his creditors before anyone else. In a more mellow mood many years later—too late, perhaps, since Bosman had long died—Ho Tung did try to retrieve something of the relationship by at least making contact with his half-brother, Alec Bosman. From an exchange of letters after the Second World War in 1946 Ho Tung obtained a photograph of his father, taken, according to Alec, 'between 1885 and 1890'.

The infant grew into the child, the child into the boy. While he played among the ragtag of Parsee, Chinese, and other Eurasian children around Peel Street, there was little reason to predict his great destiny. A Eurasian and born out of wedlock (the two things were practically synonymous in those days), he was doubly disadvantaged. All the same he distinguished himself early. One story goes that when he first went to school and the fees were found to be rather more than his mother could afford, his tutors offered to teach him for nothing. Some carbon copies of an incomplete and undated typescript found among the 'Hotung Papers' provide a more detailed account of his early schooling:

> 1868 – began schooling at the school kept by Li King Chow. Stayed there for one-and-three-quarters years. Cost of fees $12 a year. School was at Wo On Lane (near Wellington Street). Li was an inveterate opium smoker and never got up for classes until 2 pm or 3 pm. When he started to teach he would begin to beat the boys and treat them rough, so that when he began to come to class, the students would make pretended excuse to go to the lavatory. In the morning... the lessons were taken by one Ti Kor ... Very little was learned in this school.

> 1869 – This second school was run by a Lai Sum Woon. Fee was $18 a year. I began to grow a pig-tail. Better school, but still not much improvement because though we learned much parrot-wise, yet there was very little explanation of what we learned. Stayed there two years.

> 1871 – Moved to the third school in the summer. Run by Yeung Yung Chuen, this school was situated opposite to the Central School (Queen's) ... Paid only $6 a year for fees. The teacher liked me so much that sometimes he would give me 20 cash to buy myself some congee for lunch when he sent me down to buy the same lunch for him. I was head student in that school and stayed 2 years.

His teachers were not all so kind; from one cruel master he received so many swingeing clouts on the ear that his hearing was permanently impaired. Kai-tung learnt well enough, though, to read and write Chinese with ease all his life. The classical texts, with their emphasis on duty and personal virtue, were at the core of the traditional curriculum. His mind was opened to the civilisation of China and the proprieties expected of a gentleman; his sense of the exact degree of courtesy and deference to extend to his elders and betters became finely tuned. He absorbed all he could whenever he could, buying time by working late into the night and nearly ruining his health in the process. If he had a full bowl of rice, he ate half to save the rest for another meal. It was the same with his daily allowance, part of which he always put by rather than spend on food. These habits of frugality, which persisted even when he became reputedly the richest man in Hong Kong, aggravated a digestive problem that would plague him in middle age.

Before his twelfth birthday, Kai-tung entered the Government Central School in Gough Street, not far from his home. His four years there would be the making of him. Eurasian children, noted E. J. Eitel, the inspector of schools in 1880, 'are invariably sent to school'. Their mothers

> understand the value of education and prize it far more than respectable Chinese women do. The boys are invariably sent to the Government Central School where they generally distinguish themselves, and as a rule these boys obtain good situations in Hong Kong, in the open ports and abroad. The girls crowd into the schools kept by Missionary Societies. These children are generally provided with a small patrimony by their putative fathers. They dress almost invariably in Chinese costume and adopt Chinese customs.[23]

The Central School represented the triumph of politics over religion in the sphere of education. In Hong Kong's early years as a colony such educational provisions as there were consisted of a few vernacular and missionary schools, as well as small tutorial set-ups such as the three Ho Tung attended. Then voices began to be raised in support of government intervention in public education. It was time, many felt, that the domination of education by churchmen was brought to an end. Other factors were also at work: economic progress and the increasing demand for clerks and translators made the acquisition of English by the local Chinese highly desirable. All this culminated in the decision to establish an institution with a British headmaster who would not only introduce English classes but also superintend other government schools.

A young man from Aberdeenshire, Frederick Stewart, was appointed to the post of headmaster and inspector of schools. He arrived in Hong Kong in early 1862, some ten months before Kai-tung was born. Stewart had decided views on how the school was to be conducted: the education it would furnish should develop all the faculties of the mind without stripping the boys of their own language and culture. From the beginning he insisted on giving equal weight to the teaching of English and Chinese. Moreover, the knowledge imparted was to be an end in itself, not just a necessary qualification for a job or a practical means of achieving commercial success.

The Central School rapidly gained favour with parents, most of whom found no difficulty in meeting the fee of one dollar a month for the English classes, though the alacrity with which they paid owed more to expectations of lucrative jobs for their sons than any high-minded aspirations for good scholarship. Besides Chinese merchants' sons, who were in the majority, there were Macanese, Portuguese, Indian, English, Japanese, American, and Eurasian pupils. More than 500 pupils were on the register when Ho A-tung enrolled. With the mix of nationalities and faiths, Bible study was not imposed, much to the chagrin of the church authorities. Bishop Alford (whose son Edward became Ho A-tung's manager at Jardines) arraigned the 'godless education' the school provided. The curriculum did include, however, chemistry, geography, algebra, geometry, and mathematical drawing. Since Ho A-tung was trying hard to learn a foreign language, he needed to put in a full day's work, which included four hours of Chinese lessons in the morning and four hours of English in the afternoon.

Shortly after the founding, a second English master was recruited; another assistant master, Alexander Falconer, was engaged in 1869. Falconer's teaching, as well as Stewart's, left its mark on Ho A-tung. In the school list of awards, Ho A-tung was shown to have won the second class prize on 1 February 1874 (he remembered receiving a magnifying glass from the governor, Sir Arthur Kennedy, on speech day), and the first on 27 January 1877.[24] In 1876 the school played host to Guo Songtao, a member of the first Chinese mission to England (and later the first Chinese ambassador to the Court of St James), whose recollections conjure up a picture of Ho A-tung's school days for us. There were five halls, Guo observed, in three of which the children were instructed in the Five Classics and the Four Books—the authoritative ancient texts of Confucianism—along with contemporary literature. European literature was also taught, since there were European boys at the school, too, among them Frank Hazeland (Francis Arthur Hazeland), who was to be appointed first police magistrate in 1909 and to act as judge on several occasions. The classes were large—a hundred pupils, all sitting in rows at long desks, were supervised by two masters, one in front and a second in the middle of the class: 'The idea is that he can see and hear everything; so not a single boy can escape from or gloss over his work . . . The rules are well thought-out and severe, and the viewpoint [of those who made them] is farsighted.'[25]

The rules also required boys to be presentable when they came in the morning, with clean face and hands and shaven forehead, wearing shoes and stockings. No hawking, spitting, or pulling of pigtails was allowed in class. It was not very orderly outside, however. With the windows thrown wide open during the hot weather, the boys were frequently disturbed by the loud cries of hawkers peddling their wares in the street outside—'No less than twenty-nine vociferous hawkers have been known to pass in the short space of two hours,' noted Mr Falconer.[26] Even more of a nuisance was a shantytown behind the school, cluttered with about eighty pigsties and as many dilapidated huts sagging into the mud. Men of dubious character inhabited this slum in shifts. Gamblers huddled there during the day, swearing loudly and getting into fights from time to time. At night, pedlars took over to prepare the congee that they would sell the next morning. Fetid in the humid summer, the slum was positively dangerous in a typhoon, when many of the flimsy dwellings would simply collapse into a pile of rotten timber and rubble.

These shabby conditions did not distract Ho A-tung unduly. He worked hard and was mentioned in the *Government Gazette* in 1878, having proved himself in a test the only Chinese to have reached a competent standard in speaking and writing English. By then he had to look out for his younger brother, Ho Kai-fook or Ho Fook, who also did well, winning the prize (a gold pencil case) for Class 2 the same year.[27] Prize days, always exciting events in the school calendar, were often dignified by the presence of the incumbent governor and, perhaps of more immediate interest to the boys, heralded the Chinese New Year holidays.

Ho A-tung's honours were gained despite privations at home. 'I was a poor boy and had to work hard when school hours were over . . . carrying firewood and laundry . . . and sometimes scrubbing floors', he later recalled.[28] Perhaps his academic performance was an exception, for overall standards were apparently not high. On a visit to the school in 1878, the newly appointed governor, John Pope Hennessy, was unimpressed by the limited extent to which instruction was being given in English, or so he informed the colonial secretary. Like Guo Songtao, he visited a large classroom where

> there must have been a hundred and fifty Chinese youths who were being instructed by three Chinese teachers. They were reading the Chinese classics. I found that the three Chinese teachers who were instructing them in the Chinese classics had themselves no knowledge whatever of the English language . . . During the whole of the year we have had six hundred and ten pupils attending the school. I asked Mr Stewart this morning how many of these were able to speak English, and he said under fifty or sixty, and this small number very imperfectly.[29]

This was in Hennessy's view a lamentable state of affairs, believing as he did that political and commercial interests would be best served if the study of English was made a priority in government schools. His determination to improve standards provoked a conflict with Stewart, still adamant that vernacular education was as important as English-language instruction. It was a battle that Hennessy eventually won. Meanwhile, there appeared a slight lapse in Ho A-tung's usually excellent examination scores. At a test for a student teaching post at Wongneichong Government School, although all seven candidates 'did remarkably well in English parsing and dictation, also in Chinese reading and memoriter writing, and all, with the exception of Ho A-tung, were ignorant of the art of asking questions in English', the first prize passed him by and he came only fifth.[30] Ho A-tung later explained that this was no aberration but a deliberate ploy. It seemed teaching held no allure and he wished to save himself for the more rigorous entrance examination to join the Chinese customs service, which regularly recruited candidates from the school.

In March 1878 Ho A-tung was still some nine months away from his sixteenth birthday but considered nearly seventeen by Chinese reckoning. Like many other boys who attended the school for only as long as it took them to acquire enough English to find jobs in the European trading firms or in government service, he was not going to stay the full course of seven years. His love of learning gave way to the realities of having to earn his keep; he left school for good shortly after Stewart's departure for home leave. The fulsome vote of thanks presented to the headmaster by parents of boys at the school—even allowing for the flowery language customarily used by Chinese in such addresses—reflects the touching esteem in which he was held:

> Excellent indeed are your manifold virtues! Your fame has spread throughout the Middle Kingdom. Your erudition is broad, and your influence is felt in parts remote... You have set an example for the whole colony; your kindness, like the dew which falls from heaven, is felt everywhere.[31]

Ho A-tung felt no less grateful. Later he took upon himself the filial obligations of a son, a step which leaves us in no doubt of the strength of Stewart's influence. The headmaster had clearly been regarded as a father figure, a role model in whom the qualities of intellect, ambition, diligence, and humility were combined. At least until a year or so after the Japanese occupation of Hong Kong (1941–1945), Ho Tung paid for the upkeep of the graves in the Colonial Cemetery at Happy Valley of three men he admired: Frederick Stewart (died 1889), Alexander Falconer (died 1888), and William Young (died 1898, of whom more later). In his last will he gave to his executors and trustees a sum of money the income from which was to be spent on maintaining the family graves as well as that of Dr Stewart 'in good order and condition' and to 'keep the lettering thereon legible and cause the same to be re-cut from time to time for that purpose.'[32]

The bottom rung of the career ladder for Ho Tung was a school in Wanchai, east of Victoria, where he was able to make himself useful as a pupil teacher for six months before travelling up to Canton (Guangzhou) to sit the entrance examination for China's customs service. There was no denying that his chances were slim, for he was the youngest of the twelve candidates. When the papers were marked, however, it became clear that he had acquitted himself better than the others. Only one offer was made, and it went to Ho Tung.

When Ho Tung joined it in October 1878, the Imperial Maritime Customs was already a powerful institution with nearly 2,000 employees serving in all the treaty ports. Of these, Chinese outnumbered foreigners by about four to one. They were divided into 'Outdoor' staff, deployed at the harbours, on patrol boats, and in various sorts of coastal surveillance work, and 'Indoor' staff, which comprised the executive and clerical branches. Most of the Chinese employees on the Indoor staff worked in quite lowly positions; around 300 of them were clerks and interpreters. Ho Tung was first asked to join as interpreter on board a customs cruiser, but as he was a bad sailor, he excused himself. He was then appointed to the 'Indoor' staff, at a salary of twenty taels a month—equivalent to about thirty Hong Kong dollars. At that time, he recalled years later, thirty-five to forty catties of rice, or a hundred eggs, could be bought for one dollar. But he would soon discover that the top salary for a principal clerk after twenty-five years of service amounted to no more than 125 taels, while the most senior principal clerk earned only 200 taels. He made up his mind, he noted in a few undated sheets of typescript tucked in with other 'Hotung Papers', to change to 'other occupation with rosier prospects'.

In 1946, when looking into the fate of four houses and a piece of land he owned over the Chinese border in Samshui (Sanshui), near the city of Guangzhou, Ho Tung wrote to the commissioner of Chinese customs in Kowloon. The houses, he said, were on the right-hand side of the private residence of the commissioner of the Imperial Maritime Customs. He asked if the houses had survived the ravages of several years' war with Japan, and, before closing, he added a postscript: 'Perhaps the Commissioner of Customs at Canton may be interested to know that I was employed as one of the clerks in the Indoor Staff of the Customs during the years 1878 till the beginning of 1880 and I still have very good reminiscences of my days in Canton.'[33]

The young Ho Tung found himself in the midst of an efficient and cosmopolitan staff and enjoyed the independence that his monthly salary of $30 provided. He could have lived in the 'mess' for Chinese clerks but chose to go into lodgings, 'to prevent myself from falling into temptations and bad habits.'[34] The company of others like himself was irresistible, nevertheless, and since gatherings of Chinese were all too prone to pass time together gambling, Ho Tung would go to the mess and end up taking part in *pai kau* (*paijiu*), a game of chance played with tiles like dominoes. It was just as well that he was soon able to channel his penchant for a wager, which he shared with his mother, into business ventures.

As a clerk on the Indoor staff, he was unlikely to find his duties as varied as one would expect in a service responsible for collecting duties on China's foreign trade. It did not take him long, though, to be struck by the fact that the institution was run by foreigners. In 1854, the foundation for a foreign-run customs service had emerged out of the disruptions of a rebellion in Shanghai, when a temporary inspectorate to collect duties from Western merchant ships on behalf of the Chinese authorities was hurriedly put in place by three foreign consuls, each of whom nominated an inspector. Though initially hostile to such interference, Chinese officials found that, shorn of all the fraud and corruption that had formerly characterised it, the service worked remarkably well, with higher revenues as a result. Five years later the inspectorate was extended to the other treaty ports; Horatio Nelson Lay, who had succeeded the British inspector in 1855, was confirmed as the first inspector-general. He had a lofty idea of his office: 'My position was that of a foreigner engaged by the Chinese government to perform certain work *for* them but not *under* them. I need scarcely observe in passing that the notion of a gentleman acting under an Asiatic barbarian is preposterous.'[35]

Robert Hart, who transferred from the consular service in 1859 when he was offered the post of deputy commissioner of customs in Guangzhou, was more circumspect. Rising to the post of inspector-general in 1863, he advised each member of the service 'to conduct himself towards Chinese, people as well as officials, in such a way as to avoid all cause of offence and ill feeling,' and to remember that 'he is the paid agent of the Chinese government.'[36] Although his subsequent posting was to Shanghai, then Beijing, he made inspection tours of the treaty ports and it was probably on one of these, to Guangzhou, that Ho Tung encountered him.

The effect of this Irishman, so slim, so young (he was then forty-three years old), and yet so powerful, was not lost on Ho Tung. But admirable though Hart was, Ho Tung was still uneasily conscious of the anomaly of working for the Chinese

Robert Hart shown as a Chinese mandarin and scholar: caricature in the British magazine Vanity Fair, *1894. The three Chinese characters at top left—jiang haiguan, referring to the customs service—are inadvertently reversed.*

government and taking his orders from a European. This contradiction awakened him to China's feeble state; he saw how economic weakness, corrupt officials, and lack of government initiative had served to deliver the country into foreign hands. He would have sympathised with the Self-Strengthening Movement spearheaded by progressive-minded Chinese, which urged salvation for China through relief of poverty and the development of Western-style, profit-oriented enterprises. China's need to advance materially mirrored his own ambitions. To be able to hold up his head among his fellow men, he, too, must first become rich.

3

Compradore

Before he could achieve anything like wealth, the young Ho Tung looked around him, for he had first to ascertain what it was possible to achieve given the opportunities available to him at the time. For the moment he had to be content with his humble clerkship in the Imperial Maritime Customs, where he took his orders from European officers not much older than himself. He saw how they lived. Mostly young bachelors, they were accommodated in messes, a sort of extension of boarding school familiar to many an English boy. Their daily routine was punctuated by enormous meals. While in the smaller ports these could be less than appetising, there being much recourse to tinned food, in the northern postings officers could live comfortably on a greater variety of meat, game, fruit, and vegetables. For exercise they rode out or shot. Society was rather confined, but in the larger treaty ports there would be fellow countrymen serving as missionaries or agents of the trading firms. One customs officer came across the Scottish representative of Jardine, Matheson & Company in Tianjin in the early 1860s. This young Scot, Hector Coll MacLean, was 'a good looking, good tempered, rather addlepated fellow with a vast notion of his own importance and of the littleness of other mortals, much given to the cracking of bad jokes and the making of poor puns; and if it were not for the intense amusement which he himself derives from his own jocularity he would be rather a bore.'[1]

As an agent in an important 'outport' such as Tianjin, MacLean led the same sort of life as a customs officer, with his day agreeably marked by breakfast, tiffin, tea, riding, cocktails, and dinner. In the early 1860s Jardines was making an immense amount of money in China, and its European employees could affect 'a lordly indifference to expense . . . the profits are large and the expenditure—*laissez aller*', as a *Times* correspondent claimed.[2] MacLean probably lived in the comfortable company mess in Tianjin and, like others in the firm, alternated each five-year tour of service with a nine-month home leave. Junior members of the firm were not allowed to marry until at least the end of their first tour; even then they had to

Hector Coll MacLean

apply for permission from the senior partners. Married employees sometimes did not fare much better, for the demands of children and schooling often kept their wives in England and entailed long separations. MacLean remained a bachelor but kept a Eurasian mistress by whom he had a daughter, Margaret Mak Sau-ying.

Jardine, Matheson & Company, founded in Guangzhou in 1832, was the leading British firm (*hong* in Chinese) in the trading of teas and silks from China to Europe. It had also been most active in the opium trade until the early 1860s; then, with the business becoming more competitive and less profitable, Jardines quitted it for other enterprises. This new direction was pioneered by William Keswick, a great-nephew of William Jardine, one of the firm's founders. Arriving in China in 1855, when he was only twenty-one years old, Keswick had gone on to open Jardines' first office in Japan and was *taipan* (the Chinese term for the head of a firm) and member of the Hong Kong Legislative Council by the time Ho Tung joined Jardines. He was the first of several generations of Keswicks who would serve the firm and whom Ho Tung would come to know.[3]

Under William Keswick's capable leadership Jardines began riding the wave of technical advance that had started in Europe and America and was spreading to the Far East. Through the 1870s the firm diversified into manufacturing, mining, docks, and railways. A whole new range of goods was suddenly in demand as Asia embarked on industrialisation. Jardines found itself developing an extensive agency business for such European, particularly British, products as ship machinery, armaments, coal, rolling stock, and metals. It also made a profitable move into service operations including banking, shipping, and insurance. The firm had been involved in writing marine risks since the days of the opium trade, either in conjunction with other Guangzhou firms or, as William Jardine did in 1829, on its own account under the name 'Jardine, Matheson and friends'—the 'friends' being the firm's partners, senior staff, and close business associates. In 1838 Jardines established the Canton Insurance Office Ltd, which it later reorganised and incorporated in Hong Kong. Since this specialised in marine risks, a separate establishment, the Hongkong Fire Insurance Company, was founded in 1866 for the purpose, as its name makes plain, of writing fire and accident insurance.

In 1880 Jardines' insurance interests and its former Tianjin agent, Hector MacLean, were about to enter Ho Tung's life. Early that year, Ho Tung resigned from the customs service and joined Jardines as a clerk in the Compradore's Office. In the following year, on little more than his prospects and his first-year bonus of 600 dollars, he married MacLean's daughter, Margaret Mak Sau-ying. Ho Tung later confirmed that Margaret had been born in Tianjin. Sze and Margaret's mother (known only by her surname, Ng) had long planned the match: in fact, when Margaret lost her mother in 1877—she was then barely twelve years old—Sze had taken the girl into her own household to bring up as her son's betrothed. No photograph of the wedding survives, but from contemporary portraits we can be sure that Ho Tung made a handsome bridegroom. He was quite tall, with his wavy brown hair shaved back from his forehead and combed into a pigtail at the nape, deep-set eyes, high cheek-bones, a straight thin nose, and a squarish jaw which made him look determined and purposeful. The writer Austin Coates endowed Ho Tung with 'pink cheeks, piercing blue eyes, ferocious red eyebrows, [and] a shock of red hair'; these attributes seem unlikely, however, in a Eurasian whose mother was Chinese.[4] Margaret, too, was attractive. In the only extant photograph from that period, she appears to have had dark hair framing a round face and slightly almond-shaped eyes. Sixteen years old when she married, she had a short but neat figure (though she was to gain a great deal of weight as time went by). Her dowry from Hector MacLean, said according to one story to be two houses in Mosque Terrace on Hong Kong Island, or $200,000 according to another, financed Ho Tung's first attempts at going into business for himself.[5]

Ho Tung and Margaret would have been punctilious in observing traditional Chinese nuptial rites. Family lore has it that an embarrassment over the wedding

Margaret Mak Sau-ying, around the time of her marriage to Ho Tung

banquet was narrowly avoided. It seems that the prospective mother-in-law, Sze, had been unable to resist raiding the family kitty for stake money to fund her mahjong games. Two weeks before the marriage, she was found on the Praya wringing her hands and contemplating the desperate measure of throwing herself into the harbour, for she had gambled and lost the savings set aside for the wedding celebrations. Then and later, Ho Tung was able to allay her anxieties, to laugh off the loss, and to reassure her that they would muster a decent banquet somehow. Keeping his mother under his eye—and bridling her profligacy at the mah-jong table—was one of the unobtrusive but essential disciplines of his early life. On the eighth day of the tenth moon by the lunar calendar, in 1881, Ho Tung and Margaret were able to marry in some style, holding a banquet for 200 guests in Hung Fa Lau, a large restaurant on Hong Kong Island's main thoroughfare, Queen's Road.

Towards his father-in-law he was equally dutiful. Margaret's adoption of a Chinese surname, Mak, suggests she was never formally acknowledged by MacLean. Yet in 1890 MacLean named Ho Tung as the sole beneficiary and executor of his will; it was Ho Tung who put up the tombstone to MacLean's grave in

Sir Robert Ho Tung left a legacy in his last will to maintain Hector MacLean's grave. Photograph courtesy of Lam Ho Yan.

the Colonial Cemetery in Hong Kong. It seems that by this time neither MacLean nor Margaret minded admitting such connections openly.[6]

To join Jardines Ho Tung actually took a cut in salary from $30 to $15, but he knew he had vastly improved his prospects: Jardines was the most successful and commanding merchant house in China and Hong Kong, and the position of compradore, to which he aspired, would allow him to make his fortune.

It was Tsoi Sing-nam, the husband of his elder half-sister, Pak-ngan, who introduced Ho Tung to the firm. Jardines' compradore in Hong Kong, Tsoi recruited Ho Tung because of his own rather shaky grasp of English. A story goes that on the first day, Tsoi introduced Ho Tung to the manager with the words, 'This man belong muchee cunning'—it was as good a reference as any if true.[7]

By this time the position of compradore in a particular firm was beginning to be something of a family tradition, being transferred from relative to relative or from one generation to the next, though it is impossible to say if Tsoi had Ho Tung in mind as his successor at this stage. In fact, the post passed briefly to a former Jardines compradore at Fuzhou, Ng Wei (or Ng A-wei), before Ho Tung assumed it.

The compradore system itself was a material feature of the China trade, having arisen out of the need to use interpreters to bridge the language gap between foreign and Chinese merchants. In the early days communication was conducted in pidgin English, so that the role of the local go-between could only be a limited one. As English proficiency became more widespread in Hong Kong, thanks to the success of institutions like the Central School, Chinese and Eurasians who joined foreign firms were able to participate more actively in business transactions, and the position of compradore assumed correspondingly greater importance.

Before his formal appointment, a compradore must be guaranteed to his employers by a surety. The amount of surety was usually large; Ho Tung was later to find himself, as his nephew's guarantor, liable for a loss amounting to over a million dollars. It is a measure of the enormous trust placed in the compradore that he would sometimes be called upon to act as banker, not only in having charge of cash and bullion but honouring cheques and orders on occasion when his employer's account was overdrawn.[8]

In his day-to-day dealings the compradore supervised and saw to the hiring and firing of the Chinese staff, servants, and coolies. Outside the firm he was responsible for all commerce with Chinese merchants and suppliers; he negotiated the terms of contract on his firm's behalf—whether for a purchase or a sale or for the rendering of a service—and he had to ensure their fulfilment. His firm allowed him to charge a commission from the Chinese merchants on each deal. A compradore's salary was generally rather low, but that was beside the point, for he stood to earn regular commissions and bonuses. Ho Tung remembered earning $1,000 in commission a year or so after his marriage.

A compradore was thus the right man in the right place at the right time, the nexus of two commercial cultures. Generally proficient in English, as already noted, he was able to absorb Western methods of capitalism and management which, in combination with his innate entrepreneurial skills, often turned him into a more effective businessman than his compatriots. These were considerable advantages; nevertheless, to someone like Ho Tung, the greatest boon of all was the freedom to trade on his own account. His brother-in-law Tsoi brokered in refined sugar, buying from Jardines on behalf of several Chinese companies and supplying customers in Kobe and Yokohama. Tsoi also owned a steamer, bought through Jardines, which he deployed to import rice from Haiphong. His business was on such a scale that it occupied premises in Victoria which stretched the length of Stanley Street (parallel to Queen's Road) from Pottinger Street to Cochrane Street, with a shop and offices on street level and accommodation for his family on the floors above. It was understood between a compradore and his employer that such private trading did not impinge on his role within the firm. Indeed, as long as he possessed or could acquire capital, he was permitted to enter into transactions not only for himself but also on joint accounts with the firm he served. Both parties profited by such an arrangement—time after time, the linked fortunes of master and servant rose together.

Just how fruitful a partnership this could prove may be seen in Ho Tung's case. When he retired from the chief compradoreship of Jardines in 1900 he had savings of two million dollars, according to one account, or $600,000, according to another.[9] Two million dollars sounds a touch exaggerated, but the latter, more credible figure is still impressive: since his first salary was $15 a month he had clearly made good use of the chance to venture what money he had. He was to speak of the importance of money and the virtue of thriftiness again and again as time went on. Money was a social benchmark, the measure of status. For a man who could boast neither a lofty lineage nor even legitimate birth, his path to respectability and prestige would depend solely on his wits and his acquisition of wealth. In later years he also became ambitious for rank and influence. These wishes might well have sprung from the feeling of being an outsider who would gain acceptance largely by the favour of the great and the good—people whom he regarded as being on the *inside*.

Setting up home together in 1881, Ho Tung and Margaret lodged in Stanley Street until they were offered rooms on the top floor of a building that had been the harbour-master's office; Jardines' insurance business occupied the lower floors. They lived modestly in the small social milieu that was familiar to both of them.

Ho Tung's working environment, on the other hand, furnished altogether novel impressions and pressures. One of his earliest duties as a clerk was filling out immigration forms for Chinese emigrants passing through Hong Kong, the convenient port of embarkation for foreign shores. Chinese emigration had continued since the opening of the treaty ports, propelling two million labourers to Southeast Asia, the West Indies, Australia, and the Americas from 1848 to 1888. Fleets of vessels crammed with this human cargo earned lucrative passage fees for shipowners and charterers, not to mention commissions for agents like Koopmanschap. In Koopmanschap & Bosman's day the rush of Chinese was to the mines and railroad construction sites of California; those who stopped in Hong Kong in the early 1880s were largely bound for the rice fields and sugar plantations of Hawaii or the tin mines and rubber estates of Malaya. Jardines' shipping interests were boosted in 1881 by the establishment of the Indo-China Steam Navigation Company to run steamers on the coast and rivers of China to the Straits Settlements and Calcutta. A steamer left Hong Kong every three weeks: if it carried passengers, Ho Tung would be sent to the Harbour Office to take their names down, a duty that invariably kept him at work late into the night, on account of the passage brokers' habit of not submitting their lists until the eve of departure. He recalled decades later that a fifty-cent brokerage was charged for each passenger.

From shipping office to marine insurance was a small step. Not long afterwards a more challenging job presented itself. With an eye on winning business from Chinese merchants, Jardines took the decision to open an insurance branch office in what was then known as 'Chinatown', the area to the west of the Central District on Hong Kong Island. Edward Alford, manager of the insurance department, appointed Ho Tung 'native agent' and put him in charge of drumming up custom.[10] Poised at that critical moment when his life's first adventure was about to begin, Ho Tung had no doubt that the future would be shaped by his own responses and effort. Before long he was calling on the *nam pak hongs*, import-export concerns which sourced and purveyed a huge range of products across China and Southeast Asia. Nam pak hongs clustered along Bonham Strand, not far from Stanley Street, their business conducted in rooms demarcated by commodity and trading centre, whether it was tea from Fuzhou, beancake from Zhifu (now known as Yantai), ginseng from Manchuria, herbal medicine from Sichuan, or rice and seafood from Siam.

Bonham Strand was familiar territory to Ho Tung, though a foray to sell insurance there was not without its terrors. Whenever he called at a nam pak hong he had to run the gauntlet of the staff who manned the counters in the ground-floor reception hall. While he bowed in turn to each one of the men, few returned the courtesy. Such slights were bound to diminish a young man's confidence, but worse was to come. A humiliating episode from the same period obviously left a deep impression, for Ho Tung himself told the story many years later. He had gone to see a Chan Lee-choy, manager of one of the largest Chinese firms, Yuen Fat Hong, about an insurance claim for bags of rice damaged by sea water during shipment from Bangkok to Hong Kong. Yuen Fat Hong, founded by a merchant from Shantou, had been trading in Hong Kong since the early 1850s, its chief business being rice imports from Siam, where it owned several mills. The usual procedure in a claim of this nature was to send a marine surveyor to inspect the damaged goods; so Ho Tung, dispatched by Alford, informed Mr Chan. This incensed the old man so much that he banged the table and shouted, 'Is my word not good enough? Your company is the very worst and I shall tell my agents to give you no more business in future!' It was all rather crushing, and certainly unjust, since the commission involved belonged not to Ho Tung but to the Bangkok office.

All the same, as the story illustrates, Chinese merchants were now more receptive to Western ways of spreading commercial risk. Hong Kong was coming into its own as an entrepôt and reaping the benefits of expanding trade from the treaty ports. Almost half of British exports to China passed through the colony; if Imperial Maritime Customs records were anything to go by, Hong Kong was handling a significant proportion of China's trade as well. With all the coming and going of ships, marine insurance enjoyed good business. Policies were taken out to cover all manner of cargo: apart from rice and other commodities, there was still some opium, besides cotton yarn and bullion (silver being the currency of trade for the region). One can imagine letters similar to this one being passed round the office while Ho Tung was there:

As verbally agreed between your Goodselves & our Senior, we agree to hold you covered on Shipments of Treasure made on behalf of your Bank from San Francisco to Yokohama, Shanghai, Hongkong, Calcutta & Bombay to the extent of $200,000—Two hundred thousand dollars by one Iron Steamer of the Occidental & Oriental or Pacific Mail Companies, the rates of Premium being as follows:

San Francisco to Yokohama 3/8th % nett

Shanghai } ½ .. ..
Hongkong }

Calcutta } ¾ .. ..
Bombay   }

On your side you agree to give us the preference of all such risks, to advise us immediately you are aware of shipments, or intended shipments, from San

Francisco, and in the event of transhipment at Yokohama for Shanghai to inform us thereof prior to the interest leaving the former port.[11]

The vessels themselves were insured: in one case from the 1880s, for instance, the Canton Insurance Office paid out $10,000 in settlement of Messrs Douglas Lapraik & Co.'s claim for total loss on the hull machinery of SS *Douglas*. Vigilance against unnecessary risks also meant that shipping agents occasionally needed to be reminded of their own negligence, as evident in a letter about the steamer *Aegean*, sailing under the auspices of the company Arnhold Karberg, in September 1882:

Dear Sirs,

> We regret to inform you that from information which we have received, we are of the opinion that the above steamer is insufficiently manned, & we consider that she should ship further hands as per memo.
> Memo of hands required—3 more seamen[12]

Like any novice in the early days before vocational courses and training programmes, Ho Tung learnt the underwriting business from paying attention to the correspondence and practices of his seniors. He was also beginning to understand that business gave rise to a complex web of relationships which did not necessarily involve any conflicts of interest; after all, Arnhold Karberg, censured for not shipping enough hands, was itself a shareholder of the Canton Insurance Office. The most affluent of the Chinese merchants were also acquiring stakes in the business as insurance caught on. One of them, Ho A-mei, at various times emigration agent, clerk in the Imperial Maritime Customs, interpreter, investor in mining ventures, and, from about 1877 until 1898, secretary of the On Tai Insurance Company, was a shareholder in the Canton Insurance Office around the time Ho Tung joined. That the shares continued to be in demand, at least until 1884, can be deduced from a lucrative deal Ho Tung executed, with perfect timing, for himself. Largely with borrowed money from a sympathetic bank manager, he bought five Canton shares which he sold a month later for a profit of more than eight per cent.

Hong Kong's rising prosperity brought a greater influx of Chinese immigrants to the colony. By 1881 the population had exceeded 160,000, but public works and services failed to keep pace with the increase; housing, in particular, was woefully inadequate. In overcrowded and makeshift conditions, precautions against fire were often ignored. Although a fire brigade was in existence, a conflagration such as that which occurred at the end of 1878, when 361 houses in the town burnt down, more than showed its shortcomings.[13] The Hongkong Fire Insurance Company was much exercised by the government's delay in tackling the problem. It was just as concerned about the safe storage of flammable goods. The company repeatedly took up the question of the protection of godowns (warehouses) which stored kerosene and matches. Reflecting that concern is a letter from that period, in which Alford asked an expert's opinion on whether 'Bi-sulphate of Lime packed in proper casks' would be likely 'to burst the cask if it got damp in any way?'[14]

Alford was among the eight members of a committee formed to lobby the governor of the day, John Pope Hennessy, on the issue of fire protection and the government's fire-fighting services. Little action followed, however, compelling those most concerned and most at risk to devise their own solutions, such as the establishment of a volunteer fire brigade.

Against this background the insurance branch run by Ho Tung must have been favoured with numerous clients and abundant commissions. His pride and joy in those days was a private sedan chair which the firm put at his disposal when calling on clients. Finding some of them unfamiliar with the ways of modern business, Ho Tung offered his own clerical services, preparing invoices transcribed in English for twenty-five cents a set—an evening job which usefully augmented his income. These were by no means the full extent of his activities. His horizons were expanding: in August 1886 he and Margaret paid a visit to Yokohama, where Jardines had a dominant presence. Occupying the 'Number One House' on the waterfront, the firm was spearheading Japanese trade, shipping an ever greater variety of foreign goods, raw materials, and modern machinery from the West. One of the commodities Jardines shipped in huge quantities to Yokohama from Hong Kong was sugar.

For a time Jardines was merely the landlord to a sugar refinery at East Point operated by a syndicate of merchants, Wahee, Smith & Co. This refinery did not prosper; even more troubling, it caused a nuisance by burning a foul-smelling animal charcoal. When no other solution to these problems presented itself, Jardines took the plant over in 1878 and formed the China Sugar Refinery Company. The business was turned around quite quickly, prompting the *Hongkong Telegraph* to comment approvingly: 'Although its original proprietors failed to reap the benefit of their spirited undertaking, it has been gradually developed by judicious management and the command of unlimited capital into one of the most remunerative undertakings in the commercial history of the Colony.'[15] Raw sugar fed into the plant came out refined, crystallised, or moulded into cubes. The processed variety was then exported to an extensive market: in the 1880s Jardines recorded sugar sales at Sydney, Melbourne, Adelaide, Nagasaki, Yokohama, Kobe, Bombay, Calcutta, Dunedin, and Wellington, in addition to a large number of Chinese ports. Rum, a by-product, was popular in the more remote stations like Moulmein (Mawlamyine today) and Mukden (now Shenyang).

Following the example of his brother-in-law, Ho Tung traded sugar on his own account, importing it from Java and the Philippines and shipping the refined product principally to Shanghai and the northern Chinese ports where, under Jardines' wing, he had developed his own network of contacts. Several Jardines taipans befriended him. John Bell-Irving, for one, gave him considerable leeway by letting him introduce sugar shipments to the Yangtze River and northern Chinese ports without requiring him to put up security.[16] William Keswick also demonstrated faith in him, particularly over the acquisition of the Lee Yuen Sugar Refinery, a Chinese company on the brink of closure. It was a plant Keswick was anxious to get his hands on; powerful competition was expected, however, from several wealthy Chinese merchants. But Ho Tung, screwing up his courage, went to East Point and asked Keswick for an interview. Then, lucidly and politely, he submitted his proposal on how the taipan might proceed. It was lucky that Keswick fell in with his suggestions, for Ho Tung succeeded in acquiring Lee Yuen for Jardines, at a price substantially below what Keswick had considered offering.

Looking back over a period of sixty years to his service at Jardines and continuing association afterwards, Ho Tung in the 1940s acknowledged

> a deep sense of pride in the reflection that throughout this long stretch of time I enjoyed the confidence of every partner of the firm. This trust which I have enjoyed and am still enjoying, as well as the cordiality which was and is still being shown to me by successive generations of managing partners, will always remain one of the treasured recollections of my life.[17]

That trust was fully deserved. He had not approached Keswick about Lee Yuen without careful groundwork and a feeling in his bones that he would succeed. Earlier, he had ascertained who the Chinese bidders were, been to see the principal, and persuaded the gentleman to withdraw—by what cogent or forceful argument we have no way of knowing now. Suffice it to say that the takeover was accomplished. On the satisfactory outcome, Keswick presented Ho Tung with a cheque for $20,000. Instead of pocketing the bonus, Ho Tung chose to distribute the bulk of it to those in the office involved in the purchase, not forgetting the compradore of Jardines' own China Sugar Refinery, Choa Chee-bee. He had already grasped that 'before you can receive you must learn how to give', a maxim he expanded upon years later, in 1933:

> There are many men who have a good idea. That is not enough. A man should have two good ideas in case one fails. A man will tell you such and such a proposition is good but impossible of achievement. I have heard that said of many things I have attempted. My advice is that you should always attempt the impossible. I have made mistakes, but I have never failed. Many men would be rich if they talked less and listened more. My ears have done me more good than my tongue. A man's confidence is worth more than his wealth. Gain his confidence and you

will become rich. An army training is good for any businessman. I plan all my business deals on military lines. I arrange my attack and my defence. Before you can receive you must learn how to give.[18]

He certainly paid careful attention to the burst of enthusiasm for land and property that gripped the Chinese community in the 1880s. It had started in 1881. Although much real estate had already passed into Chinese hands by then, what happened that year was more akin to gambling than prudent investing. A Chinese broker was rumoured to have bought and sold the same house as many as eight times in a day, rushing from buyer to seller and creaming off a commission on each transaction. Ho Tung could not have been unaffected by the 'get-rich-quick' frenzy in the air. But he had no capital, only a willingness to keep his ear to the ground. From the older and more experienced businessmen he learnt the rudiments of property investment. When he had grasped the implications of interest margins, mortgages and re-mortgages, collateral security, equity redemption, and so forth, he launched himself into property broking. His first transaction is believed to have involved five houses owned by Linstead & Davis in Stanley Street, and his boldest a block of offices and godowns on two marine lots between Queen's Road and the Praya, which he bought from Turner & Co. for John Bell-Irving and Catchick Paul Chater, earning a commission from both sides on the deal. It involved a sensational turnover which was only surpassed when the land was resold to a syndicate composed of himself, Ng A-wei and a few friends, on mortgages from Bell-Irving, Chater, and the Hongkong Fire Insurance Company. How intertwined their dealings had become may be seen in a letter from the solicitors acting for Jardines in 1888:

Dear Sirs,

The R.P. of M.10 & 12

We return to you with thanks the mortgage and title deeds etc. of M. Lot No. 10—in mortgage to the Hongkong Fire Insurance Co. Ltd.

And also the mortgage and title deeds etc. of M. Lot 12 in mortgage to ditto. And also

1. Assignment—Ng A Wei to Messrs Bell-Irving & Chater of the R.P. of M. 10, subject to mortgage.

2. Letter of agreement, dated 3rd May 1888, from Mr Bell-Irving to Ho Tung as regards M. 10.

3. Assignment—Ho Tung to Messrs Bell-Irving & Chater of the R.P. of M. 12, subject to mortgage.

4. Letter of agreement, dated 3rd May 1888, from Mr Bell-Irving to Ho Tung—as regards M. 12.

These four documents should not be kept with the mortgages and deeds, but belong to Mr Bell-Irving and Mr Chater, except the letters which belong to the former.[19]

In less than a month the solicitors were writing again, this time about two sections of Inland Lot No. 585 (the area around Mosque Street on Hong Kong Island), on which mortgages were granted by Bell-Irving to Choa Leep-chee and Ho Tung.[20]

It comes as no surprise to find Chater a key player in a marine lot property deal. Though described as a bill and bullion broker in legal documents, Catchick Paul Chater was much more of a financial heavyweight than that suggests. An Armenian from Calcutta who had arrived in Hong Kong, aged eighteen, in 1864, he made a fortune in exchange dealing and then diversified into property development, dock operation, cotton-spinning, and mining. One of his ventures was the Hong Kong and Kowloon Wharf and Godown Company, which he founded with a man called W. Kerfoot Hughes. At the same time that he was backing Ho Tung, Chater was hatching a Central Praya reclamation scheme to push the waterfront further out into the harbour and conjure up sixty-five acres of extra building land. Begun in 1890, the reclamation added three more thoroughfares to the city—Des Voeux Road, Connaught Road, and Chater Road. The prospect of doing very well out of the reclamation could not have been lost on the marine lot owners, all of whom would be offered portions of the newly formed site, on various terms, to develop and build on. Marine lots 10 and 12, traversed by two narrow pathways, Li Yuen Street East and Li Yuen Street West, would change hands again nearly a decade later—and five years before the reclamation was completed—when the Hongkong Fire Insurance Company, Ho Tung, and his brother Ho Fook and half-brother Ho Kom-tong were recorded as vendors.[21]

His brothers' careers closely followed the pattern set by his own. Ho Fook, as we saw, also attended the Central School. He took employment as a clerk and interpreter, first in the registrar general's office and subsequently at a firm of lawyers, Dennys and Mossop. Frederick Stewart had recommended him to the registrar general, confirming in his reference that, having worked hard at Chinese as well as English, Ho Fook was fit for the work which 'many of his countrymen could not accomplish'.[22] From around 1885 Ho Fook worked for Jardines; in 1900 he took over from Ho Tung and assumed the position of chief compradore. Like his brother, he conducted business on his own account as well as the firm's: this included a substantial trade in such commodities as cotton and sugar. Ho Sai-wing or Ho Wing, his eldest son by his wife, Lucy Lo Sui-choi (sister of the Eurasian compradore Lo Cheung-shiu), would be adopted by Ho Tung and Margaret

Ho Fook in Western dress

*Ho Kom-tong in later years,
wearing his decorations*

around 1889 (Ho Fook had, altogether, twelve children with his wife and concubine). Ho Kom-tong, Ho Tung's half-brother by a different father, also attended
Central School and followed his brothers to Jardines, where he became assistant
compradore in 1901. He was if anything even more entrepreneurial: not only did
he build up a prodigious regional trade, he also acquired an interest, with Ho Fook,
in Sun Cheong Fat, a cotton and yarn company, as well as a great deal of real estate.
One of his properties, which he lived in himself, was the Classical Revival–style
mansion Kom Tong Hall in the Mid-Levels on Hong Kong Island, built two years
before he retired from Jardines in 1916. Furnishing it allowed him to indulge his
taste for European and Chinese decoration and antiques.[23] He applied the same
degree of attentiveness to designing his own and his family's burial plot within the
Eurasian cemetery, Chiu Yuen: every care was taken to ensure that it had perfect
fengshui.

Before the end of the 1880s there were echoes of the speculative fever that prevailed at the beginning, only this time it was spilling over into share-dealing and
leading to several dramatic bankruptcies. In the rather crude stock market of the
time, a form of futures was sold on the expectation of ever-rising prices. Anyone

could be a stockbroker, and indeed many who had gambled to their own detriment sometimes took up broking to prey on the cupidity of others. Mining shares were particularly prone to booms and busts. Ho Tung admitted losing a good deal of money in Punjom Mining Company shares, whose price soared to $80 and then slumped to $1. Heavy losses from share-dealing were suffered, he remembered, by the son of Leong On, the compradore of Gibb, Livingstone and Co., who had himself been in the bankruptcy court in 1883. Lo Hok-pang, the Hongkong and Shanghai Bank compradore, also became the talk of the town: he had clearly risked more than he was worth, and when he found himself unable to meet his commitments he allegedly did a moonlight flit in 1892, saddling the bank with a debt of a million dollars. The Hongkong Land Investment and Agency Co., formed by Chater in partnership with the Jardines taipan James Johnstone Keswick (William's brother) in 1889, doubled its share value shortly after its launch but failed to sustain its dizzy ascent. Again, Ho Tung was forced to sell at a loss.

Such eventful times were perhaps not for the financially fainthearted. But Ho Tung remained optimistic. Sir Charles Addis, for many years in the service of the Hongkong and Shanghai Banking Corporation, reminded him of his confidence when writing from England in 1941:

> I remember you saying to me 55 years ago [around 1886], as we walked home together from a dinner at Beaconsfield [Beaconsfield Arcade, opposite the City Hall in the Central District], 'I believe in Hong Kong!' You have lived to see, and indeed are yourself partly responsible, for the fulfilment of your prophecy.[24]

Addis (1861–1945) spent three years in Hong Kong from 1883, after which he was posted to Beijing by the Hongkong and Shanghai Bank and thence all over China for the next two decades. He helped to form the first China Consortium of banks which issued a major loan to Yuan Shikai's government in 1913. Convinced that international foreign loans were also potentially political transactions, he had observed in 1905 that 'an imperial policy is essentially a commercial policy'—an adage which would have resonated with Sir Robert Ho Tung during his involvement in warlord and Chinese nationalist politics (see Chapter 6).

It must have seemed perfectly obvious to Ho Tung that Hong Kong, created for trade in the first place, would always remain a mercantile town. He saw the effectiveness of the joint-stock enterprise operating in an environment where commercial discipline prevailed. Though still describing himself as an 'assistant compradore', he was serving a firm in which his own stake, through purchase of shares, was increasing apace. Untiring in his attendance of shareholders' meetings, he appears through the late 1880s and 1890s in the reports of Hongkong Fire Insurance, Hongkong Land, China Sugar Refinery Co., Hongkong & Kowloon

Wharf and Godown Co., and Hongkong Ice Co.—all Jardines concerns. He was accumulating real estate at quite a clip, too: a godown on Praya East, a house in Old Bailey Street, land in Taipingshan, in addition to the two marine lots already mentioned—there seemed no limit to the spread of his holdings. He was active in turning the properties round as well; in 1899 Lammert the auctioneer sold twenty-one lots for him in Wellington, Peel, Cochrane, and Stanley Streets, offering at the same time to make arrangements for a mortgage on each lot if required.[25] Steadily, through buying and selling, re-mortgaging and assigning, he multiplied his assets and his wealth. Those were heady days. He was to look back upon them as a period of 'remarkable expansion'. When asked to contribute to J. M. Braga's *Hong Kong Business Symposium: A Compilation of Authoritative Views on the Administration, Commerce and Resources of Britain's Far East Outpost*, he cited Governor Sir William Des Voeux, whose report of 1888 is tinged with a sense of excitement. This obscure entrepôt, the report declared, had become a city of closely built houses and home to a large and thriving population, its harbour crammed with shipping: 'some 40 to 50 ocean steamers, including ships of war, large European and American sailing vessels, and hundreds of sea-going junks; while in the space intervening and around, are many thousands of boats, for the most part human habitations, with steam launches rushing in all directions . . . Going ashore, one would see long lines of quays and wharves, large warehouses, shops stocked with all the luxuries as well as the needs of two civilisations; in the European quarter could be seen a fine Town Hall, stately Banks, and other large buildings of stone; in the Chinese quarter one saw houses, constructed after a pattern peculiar to China, of solid materials, packed closely together and thronged so densely as to be, in this respect, probably without parallel in the world'.[26]

By the time he became chief compradore of Jardines in 1894, Ho Tung had outgrown the office and all but delegated his day-to-day responsibilities to Ho Fook. His business interests had spread far beyond the confines of the firm. One of them was the opium farm, an exclusive licence to boil, prepare and sell the drug in Hong Kong which the government auctioned to the highest bidder once every three years. In 1895 the opium farm was granted to Ho Kom-tong and his partner, Lum Sin-sang; Ho Tung, Ho Fook, Lo Cheung-ip, and Lo Cheung-shiu constituted the other members of the syndicate.[27] It was a lucrative monopoly while it lasted, although for Ho Tung the time would soon arrive when the business aroused only aversion and a wish to dissociate himself from it altogether. An occasional opium user at one time, he broke himself of the habit and would eschew even cigarettes and alcohol for the rest of his life. Writing to a Mrs Li Ho Huen Man in 1951, he informed her that he was reducing his bequest to her by over twenty per cent because: 'in spite of the large amount of medical fees which I spent on your behalf in Macao during the Japanese occupation of Hongkong, and the loss of your services for a long time during your illness, you still went on smoking in spite of my telling you seriously not to do so.'[28]

With all those business and financial interests, he had to keep up a prodigious pace, putting in a full day's work which more often than not lasted through dinner. Interrupted meals could hardly have helped his digestive ailment, which subjected him to recurrent bouts of vomiting at night. His doctors thought it was a form of sprue; his daughter Irene Cheng tells us a diagnosis was made years later, when tests revealed that 'his stomach did not secrete hydrochloric acid'.[29]

One might hazard a guess that stress was also a contributory factor. For the moment, though, he lived with the condition, only taking some opium to relieve it. In the midst of it all, he married a second time, to Clara Cheung. Perhaps it was through her urging that he was eventually brought to admit a faltering of his natural energies; a few years later, he resigned his compradoreship of Jardines. Although J. J. Bell-Irving's testimonial was brief, it was to the point:

> Dear Mr Ho Tung,
>
> We have much pleasure in recording your long service with our Firm for the long period of twenty years.
>
> In the year 1880, when you were quite a youth, you joined our Firm as a junior assistant in the Compradore's Office. Hardly within twelve months you were appointed to open a Chinese Branch in Chinatown and to act as Native Agent for the Canton Insurance Office Ltd., and the Hongkong Fire Insurance Co. Ltd., both companies being under your management. A few years later you were asked to be the chief of the Chinese Staff in our Shipping Department in addition to the Insurance duties and to establish branches for the selling of the refined sugar in most Treaty Ports in China. You became Chief Compradore of our Firm in 1894 and it is with the greatest regret that owing to ill health you have to retire from our Firm.
>
> We wish to state that during all these twenty years our relations with you have been extremely cordial and that your exceptional ability, tact, and sound judgement in all commercial matters have been fully appreciated by all the successive partners of our Firm.[30]

4

Family

Some time before December 1894 Margaret Ho Tung came to a remarkable decision. She would give her blessing to a marriage between her husband and her cousin
Clara Cheung Ching-yung. We cannot tell if there had been a struggle in Margaret's
mind before; all we know is that by then she was no longer in any doubt. Too many
barren years had elapsed and her husband should have a second wife. What was
more, she had a suitable candidate in mind. How fortunate it was that Clara had
come to Hong Kong, had been invited to visit, and had caught Ho Tung's eye! She
was, indeed, very pretty and well mannered, and there was a look of intelligence
about her fine eyes. Her antecedents, too, were unexceptionable. Also a Eurasian,
Clara was born on 19 December 1875 the eldest of four children. Her father was
Cheung Tak-fai, an employee of the Imperial Maritime Customs, first in Shanghai
and later in Jiujiang, and her mother, surnamed Yeung, was the daughter of an
American, G. B. Glover. According to Ho Tung's youngest daughter Florence Yeo,
Clara's 'European blood was English and Scottish', there having been an English
grandfather, Thomas Lane, on her father's side to account for the genetic mix.
Although Thomas Lane is known to have been in Hong Kong between 1843 and
1866, the line of descent is unclear. He might have had a Chinese mistress before
marrying Maria Reynell, the daughter of an English mariner in Macau, in 1862.
His legacy in Hong Kong—besides a mixed-race child and a son and daughter by
Maria—is the general store Lane, Crawford & Co., which he established with a
Scottish trader, Ninian Crawford, in 1850. Clara was thus a second-generation
Eurasian. She might even have been a third-generation Eurasian, for, based on Eric
Hotung's research into his family's 'blood ancestry', one great-grandfather is said to
have been 'Spanish-Portuguese'.[1]

    Clara was with her parents in both Shanghai and Jiujiang. Two of her siblings
had died young. When she was eighteen, death struck again—this time it was her
father. And it was because they were bringing his coffin back for burial in Hong
Kong, his native place, that the Cheung family—Clara, her mother, and younger

brother—returned to the colony. There they called on their relations, including Margaret, who saw at once that Clara would make her husband an excellent second wife. In the circumstances, Margaret was all for being magnanimous, so when she canvassed the match with Clara's mother, she offered to welcome Clara not as her husband's concubine but as an 'equal wife', one with an implied higher status than a concubine. Margaret did not concern herself with the fact that, in China, a second wife brought into an existing marriage—even if deemed equal to the first wife by the family—was still a concubine in the eyes of the law. She wrote to her aunt to confirm this unusual arrangement:

> Although we have not seen each other for a long time, you are often in my thoughts. I am now presuming on your affection and kindness to make my importunate and foolish request.
>
> The institution of marriage has been considered important since antiquity. Empresses selected consorts for emperors from respectable women whose honour sprang from their observance of the Three Dependences and the Four Virtues. To the superior man, establishing his virtue is one of the Three Imperishable Qualities he cherishes. When virtue prevails, the family is harmonious and all things prosper.
>
> Since ancient times, and in accordance with precedent, parents have been in charge of their children's marriages. A mother's right to choose her daughter's mate arises from her love of her offspring and her wish to ensure that her child is not ill-treated or forsaken. The dearest hope of parents is to see their children well settled in life.
>
> We have countless historical examples of marriage being a reward for virtue. The *Yijing* compares the perfect union between man and woman with the auspicious harmony of the heavenly and earthly principles. Felicity in marriage is a providential gift, and it is Providence that directs us to our partners in life. We very much hope that your daughter will agree to become such a partner to my husband. In doing so, she will enjoy equal honours, without any distinction of status between us: she will be looked upon as a sister, and may Providence strike me down if she suffers any slight. I hope this vow convinces you of my good faith.
>
> Yesterday we received news of your willingness to give your daughter in marriage to my husband. In case she is still uncertain, I write this letter to assure your daughter further of my earnestness and sincerity. I look forward to receiving good news from you soon, so that we may select an auspicious date for the wedding without delay.[2]

Margaret Mak Sau-ying herself had not long reached child-bearing age when she married Ho Tung thirteen years earlier. As one of a small circle of Eurasians, she had known the Ho family since she was quite young and it is highly probable that the two mothers made the match. Less socially integrated in those days

A studio portrait of Clara Ho Tung, probably taken not long after her marriage

than now, Eurasians tended to marry among themselves. Sze evidently looked with favour upon the marriage, for with the untimely death of Margaret's mother, when Margaret was no more than twelve years old, Sze took the girl under her wing and into her house until the wedding.

Ho Tung and Margaret held a conventional ceremony and celebrated afterwards with a suitably elaborate banquet the cost of which was found somehow, despite Sze's losing streak at mah-jong two weeks before the event. The bride and bridegroom in their embroidered robes went down on their knees to serve tea to the older generation and performed enough kowtows 'to give them housemaid's knees', as Sir Robert Ho Tung quipped at their golden wedding anniversary fifty years later.[3] They had no expectations of romantic love—how could they have?— but they respected the obligations imposed by marriage.

They did, of course, expect to have children; no traditionally minded Chinese would have thought otherwise. Yet the years passed and Margaret did not become a mother. Still, failure to have a son need not be an irretrievable calamity, as convention had devised a solution. Ho Tung's younger brother, Ho Fook, duly fulfilled his part and gave his first son, five-year-old Ho Sai-wing (or Ho Wing), for adoption into the childless family. Tradition also sanctioned the practice of taking a concubine; in the Ho family the choice fell on a Chinese girl, Chau Yee-man, of whom little is known except that for several years she, too, proved infertile.

Ho Wing was sent to his father's alma mater, the Central School, and later served as compradore to the merchant house E. D. Sassoon & Company. Afterwards, guaranteed by his adoptive father to the tune of $300,000, he became the compradore of the Hongkong and Shanghai Bank. But Margaret would make one more attempt, as we noted above, to satisfy what she regarded as the profoundest of human instincts and to help her husband have offspring of his own. She succeeded beyond her hopes, for Clara would produce no fewer than ten children.

It would not be quite accurate to say that Ho Tung took his new wife on honeymoon, but as a letter of reference from the consul-general of the United States indicates, he did make plans to travel a few months after his marriage:

> I hereby certify that Mr Ho Tung is personally known to me and to be a merchant of high financial standing and good repute in the Colony of Hong Kong . . . he is desirous of making a tour through the United States . . . taking along with him his wife and his wife's cousin, Miss Cheung Ching-yung, who has in the past been a member of his family and who is to travel in the capacity of his wife's lady companion. I have to further state that I am also personally acquainted with Mrs Ho Tung and Miss Cheung Ching-yung and I am fully satisfied that this party of three are genuine tourists proceeding to Canada via the United States having no other interest whatever in view but a pleasure trip.[4]

Ho Tung was understandably sheepish about revealing Cheung Ching-yung's relationship to himself: they were, after all, embarking on a visit to a country where polygamy was banned. Yet he was to remain reticent for years, even though concubinage was not abolished in Hong Kong until 1971. In a will drawn up in 1913, Margaret was named as his 'widow' and Clara only his 'cousin-in-law'.

On return this *ménage à trois* lived in an atmosphere, as far as one can tell, that was calm and congenial. The Ho Tungs had long moved from their rooms above the office and now had a house at 1 Seymour Road, in a select district known as the Mid-Levels. This was at a time in Hong Kong when a man's social standing was directly correlated with the altitude of his house. Ho Tung (and his brothers) had now reached the halfway mark; by the turn of the century he would aspire to live on an even higher level, in the exclusive environs of the Peak.

There was no appearance of friction between the two wives, who addressed each other as 'cousin', although Clara was always careful to give Margaret precedence. The marriage was not of her choosing, but it never occurred to Clara to do anything else but make the best of it. She had returned to Hong Kong from Jiujiang with her widowed mother and younger brother. Sad as their mission was—to bury her father in his native place—their prospects had been even more wretched. Without her father Cheung Tak-fai's salary from the Imperial Maritime Customs, they were at the mercy of their own wits and their relatives. Of all those who might have helped them, Ho Tung was by far the most notable. He was the chief compradore of Jardines, a justice of the peace, and a man of considerable means. There would have been no question of Clara resisting the marriage.

Within a year of the wedding, Sze died in Guangzhou while on a visit there. She had endured much in her fifty-four years. Filial as he was, Ho Tung was with her to the last. His daughter Irene has given us this picture of his devotion: 'Long after his mother had died he carried a miniature photograph of her on his travels and set it in a place of honour in his bedroom. He said that she liked roast chicken and when she visited them on Sundays after his first marriage they always had it for her. So every Sunday after her death, roast chicken was offered at her shrine.'[5] The dutiful daughters-in-law, for their part, ordered prayers to be said in her memory at a Guangdong monastery.

The next year brought another great change. On 22 June 1897 Queen Victoria celebrated her diamond jubilee. The pomp and circumstance which marked this event in London were echoed in her imperial possessions; a message from the queen was telegraphed to them all: 'From my heart I thank my beloved people. God Bless them.' Tributes poured in from all four corners of the world, including her colony of Hong Kong, where, on Sunday 21 June, the celebrations began with thanksgiving services in all the churches. The one at St John's Cathedral was

像遺人夫太氏施母何

Formal portrait of Ho Tung's mother, Sze Tai

the most splendid, attended not only by the governor, Sir William Robinson, but all the bigwigs of the colony. They marched to the cathedral through a guard of smartly turned-out policemen; Ho Tung was near the head of the procession, a few steps behind the choir and the clergy. On the day of the anniversary itself, a choir of 300 voices belted out the famous *Hallelujah* chorus from Handel's *Messiah* in Happy Valley, and at nightfall brilliant fireworks discharged by fifty illuminated launches lit up the harbour, to the immense delight of the pressing crowds. At 1 Seymour Road, it was a time of private celebration as well, for in the same month Clara gave birth to Ho Tung's first child. She was named Victoria Jubilee Kamchee (though she would soon become 'Vic' to her family).

The cycle of joy, grief, and revived hope was to continue. Within fifteen months of Victoria's birth, the longed-for son was born. To judge from a portrait, Henry Sai-kan's most obvious inheritance was the good looks of his parents. Perhaps the presence of babies had something to do with it; at any rate, before long Ho Tung's concubine, Chau Yee-man, also became pregnant. Her daughter, Mary Patricia Shun-chee, was born within a few months of Clara's third child, Daisy Wai-chee, who arrived on the last day of the century. If the parents found Daisy slow to develop, they had little time to worry about it, for soon an even darker shadow fell on the household. At six months she contracted pneumonia; Henry caught it as well, but, unlike Daisy, he did not recover and died before his second birthday. Clara was devastated. Going into deepest mourning, she would not lessen the vehemence of her grief until her doctor became alarmed. Eventually, afraid that she would succumb either to tuberculosis or a nervous breakdown, she pulled herself together.

Henry had died at Idlewild, a house at 8 Seymour Road to which the Ho family had moved after the birth of Vic; it would be kept in the family for the next fifty years. A high-rise block of flats now stands in its place, but scores of photographs have preserved for us the lineaments of its famous entrance: the solid pillars framing the extravagantly carved porch; above them, in relief, the white letters 'IDLEWILD.', complete with the full stop that somehow lent the name a touch of stateliness; finally the wide stone stairs flanked by balustrades and two beautiful lanterns at the bottom. The outer walls were painted an auspicious red, a startling colour to cover a building of such gigantic proportions. One could easily get lost in such a house, and, from a description by Clara's fourth daughter Irene, it appears to have been awkwardly designed.[6] In spite of its size, there were few rooms in which its residents could be private and quiet, although in a large family attended by many servants, life was inevitably somewhat communal.

When one entered the house, having passed through the teakwood doors inlaid with stained-glass panels and down the corridor lined with blackwood

Idlewild, the Ho Tung mansion at 8 Seymour Road, Mid-Levels

furniture, one looked up the central staircase to the bedroom suites—Ho Tung's and Clara's on the first floor, Margaret's on the second. How telling this was of the degree of intimacy between Ho Tung and his two wives, one can only guess. At the back of the house, in what was virtually a separate wing, a warren of rooms housed the female staff. The furnishings in the house reflected the two worlds which its denizens straddled. In the formal reception and dining rooms, the straight-backed and ungiving blackwood chairs with their grey marble inlays would have produced an impression of gloom were it not for the embroidered red satin of the cushions. Against one wall was a magnificent opium bed, its polished wooden surface enriched by mother-of-pearl. Above it hung a portrait of the matriarch, Sze. The other sitting room contained Western-style furniture, though even here the most conspicuous objects were Chinese, from scrolls of calligraphy to a decorative cloisonné elephant on a pedestal. For a time Ho Tung kept a chef conversant with Western cuisine, whose kitchen was upstairs; the main Chinese kitchen, a scene no doubt of perpetual cooking on feast days, lay off a central inner courtyard at the back, surrounded by quarters for the menservants.

Like many other houses in the Mid-Levels, Idlewild was built on the side of a hill. It had a terraced garden connected by paved walks and concrete steps. Here the flower beds, ornamental trees, orchids, and potted plants in tidy rows were coaxed into bloom by a team of gardeners year after year. Further at the back was a kitchen garden; on one side there was a tennis court on which, according to Irene, not many games were ever played.

Two months after Henry's death, Margaret and Ho Tung sailed for the United States on the *Empress of China*.[7] The ship's brief docking at Shanghai provided the opportunity for a quiet meeting with the powerful Chinese official Li Hongzhang (of whom more later). Travel plans had been made before the family tragedy; a change of scene might have done everyone some good, but Clara had not felt up to accompanying them. In San Francisco, Ho Tung checked into the Waldeck Sanitarium and subjected himself to a strict regimen. An account he left spells out his symptoms and treatment in detail (this habit of keeping his own medical record persisted to the end of his life, indeed became part and parcel of a grand obsession with his frail constitution, diet, and weight). He was particularly preoccupied with his bowel movements, scrupulously noting the number of times he went to the lavatory, whether he had taken castor oil or some other laxative, and the condition of the stools, correlating all this with what he had eaten. As well as dyspeptic symptoms, his sleep was frequently disturbed by bouts of sweating and rises in body temperature. It may have been on this visit that Margaret also sought medical advice. We are told by Irene that a uterine tumour diagnosed in America probably accounted for her infertility, but her fear of the surgeon's knife put remedy out of the question.[8]

Ho Fook and Ho Kom-tong kept their brother informed of all that passed in Hong Kong by a flow of newspaper cuttings and letters, now reporting on losses of refined sugar they had stored in the warehouses of the Chinese Mining & Engineering Company at Tianjin, now commenting on the fall in Ewo and Hongkong Cottons shares. A few glancing allusions to family appear in the interstices of these letters: Ho Wing and several servants were stricken with malarial fever but had recovered, and Clara (whom her husband continued to refer to as 'my wife's cousin') was still frosty at the suggestion of going abroad.

As the year drew to a close, and prompted by her brothers-in-law and her doctor with his dire warnings of consumption or a breakdown, Clara felt her spirits reviving. But what finally brought her round to the idea of travel was the decision to include her children, so it was a very large party that set off for Europe in the spring of 1901, consisting of Clara, the two little girls, Clara's mother and brother, Ho Wing (carrying with him a Kodak Brownie), and an amah.[9]

April 1901 found Ho Tung and Margaret in New York. Different ages produce different predicaments, so when we find Ho Tung electing to travel under his European name, we need look no further for an explanation than convenience.

Anyway, it was under this name that he registered at the Waldorf-Astoria Hotel, as we are told by a reporter of the *New York Times*:

H. T. Bosman of Hongkong, accompanied by his wife and servant, is staying at the Waldorf-Astoria. No one would suspect Mr Bosman's identity from reading his autograph, which appears in a bold English hand upon the register; indeed, it is hard to realize even after meeting him that he is an Asiatic by blood as well as by birth, although he has all the physical characteristics of the Oriental. At home Mr Bosman is better known as Mr Ho Tung, and he is one of the leading merchants of his native city as well as one of its most extensive property owners.[10]

Though this was not the first time he had been quoted in the American press, the interview was still something of a debut for him on the stage of world affairs. New Yorkers might have found the oriental Mr Bosman exotic, but they took his views on the Boxer indemnity, a topic then in the news, with a seriousness that was highly gratifying (see Chapter 6).

From New York the Ho Tungs went on to London, where they put up at Bailey's Hotel, Gloucester Road. Later, joined by Clara and the children, they rented a house in Bayswater, and from this temporary base they made sightseeing forays to other parts of England. Either then, or on a subsequent visit, they met up with Ho Tung's youngest brother, Kai-gai, who since his school days had been more generally known as Walter Bosman. Walter's story strikes an incongruous note in an account of a family which clung to its Chinese roots. Some five years younger than Ho Tung, he bore a strong resemblance to his elder brother. In a group photograph of 1938, Captain Walter Bosman (as he appears in the caption) is striking for his European looks. That photograph was taken at a dinner attended by fourteen old boys of the Central School, from which Walter, as the first winner of the Government Scholarship in 1884, had progressed to studies in England when he was seventeen. Worth £200 annually, this scholarship was tenable in England for four years.[11] Although Sze was opposed to her son going so far away, it was too good an opportunity to pass up and Ho Tung pressed her to consent. Several decades later Ho Tung had cause to remind his brother, in tones of disappointment and bitterness, of the farewell dinner he had organised and paid for; it was attended, he said, by such eminent men as John Bell-Irving, Stewart Lockhart (assistant colonial secretary at the time), Dr Bateson Wright and Alexander Falconer of the Central School, as well as several of Walter's friends.

In England the scholarship boy acquitted himself as well as expected, coming first in all his examinations at the Crystal Palace Engineering Institute. On graduation, he got an appointment with the railways in Natal. Ho Tung begged him not to go to South Africa and sent money for his return passage to Hong Kong, only to find that Walter had no intention of staying 'to work for China'—his elder brother's fervent wish. Walter settled in Durban, marrying an Englishwoman, Louise Davenport, in 1891. He served as aide-de-camp to Colonel Duncan MacKenzie, commander of the British colonial forces in Natal and Zululand, during the Zulu Rebellion of 1906. An estrangement between the brothers followed Walter's refusal to return to Hong Kong; though it only once boiled over, for Ho Tung it simmered for a long time below the surface of their relationship. He never forgot being applied to for loans and not getting repaid. What he resented most, however, was Walter's attempt to deny his heritage. In London they had gone together to a wholesale firm of diamond dealers at the Holborn Viaduct. A large number of purchases were made by both of them. When the proprietor, a Mr Bonnais, asked Walter what his nationality was, Walter said he was English, unaware that Ho Tung was within earshot.[12] Another instance of Walter's touchiness on the subject of his origins was reported to Ho Tung years later by Alfred Hall, a Hong Kong Eurasian. Travelling in South Africa, Hall had happened to meet Walter at the Durban Club. He was smartly taken aside and asked not to mention the Chinese connection, as Walter passed himself off as an Englishman there.

Something of the brothers' uneasy intercourse can be traced between the lines of Ho Tung's letters, in which we find instances of Walter forcing himself upon his older brother's notice, either when he was short of money and making free with Ho Tung's hospitality, or because his behaviour was embarrassing, as it had been at the Durban Club. (Ho Tung did not seem to have reflected on how embarrassing it would have been for *Walter* if his origins were discovered; Walter had, after all, made a life for himself in a society where racial discrimination against Chinese and other Asian immigrants was widely prevalent.) For all that, there is no denying that Walter remains an intriguing figure, at one moment publishing a book on the Natal uprising (*The Natal Rebellion of 1906*), at another travelling overland from Europe to Asia with his wife, Louise, in 1937:

> We travelled no less than 18,200 miles by autocar with a caravan (trailer) attached. Traversed 18 countries from West to East . . . Our entry into Persia was at Krouswie, the Custom House. First our gun was confiscated and our movie camera securely sealed. Everything was unpacked, and we were kept there for four and a half hours. We were escorted by a Persian soldier whose sole object was to eat our food . . . After two days we were allowed to proceed . . . Then we ascended the great Kurdistan and had to plough through three feet of snow . . . [At Ban] we prepared ourselves for a stretch of 280 miles across the Great Salt Desert . . . By day we had to push the caravan walking barefooted, and we all got sand sores.[13]

Walter resurfaces in 1939, when Foreign Office and South Africa House memoranda record a visit to South Africa House in London a year earlier by 'a certain William (or Walter) Bosman', a Union national, announcing his intention to return to the Union and to raise funds for the purchase of arms for China. To the civil servants there and the honorary trade commissioner for the Union of South Africa in Shanghai who made enquiries about him, Bosman appeared to be 'a wanderer and an original character'. One report contains, by its own admission, 'conflicting information'; it also contains several errors of fact, such as the claim that Walter had made the great journey from West to East with his wife and child:

> Bosman is a man of about 70 years of age, and looks like a Chinaman. Enquiries made have resulted in conflicting information. One source alleges that Bosman is the brother of Sir Robert Ho Tung, a well known personality in Hong Kong: that Bosman settled in Natal as a child and adopted the name of Bosman: that he has travelled extensively in China and Russia and is alleged to be well known there: and that recently he with his wife, child and a nurse, travelled by motor caravan through Russia, Persia, India and China.
>
> On the other hand, he is stated to have resided for the last five years in the Union where he is known as Walter Bosman, and is believed to be a European with the features of a Chinaman: that he is an engineer, a man of considerable means and interested in the Natal Coal Industry: and that he is also an artist and paints pictures of the country he visits on his travels.[14]

Nothing on the dénouement of Walter's attempt to buy 'arms for China' has been found so far, nor can we throw any light on his apparent change of heart; having declined to 'work for China', was he now interested in helping the country, caught in a confused political and military situation with Chiang Kai-shek's armies being challenged by Japanese invaders on the one hand and by communist guerrilla forces on the other? Or was his avowed intention to raise funds merely hypothetical, a dream that fizzled out after he left Hong Kong in 1938?

After the death of Louise, Walter married a second time, to Gladys Steyn, in 1942. He died in Bloemfontein, South Africa, in 1946.

Back in Hong Kong in the spring of 1902, the arrival of babies continued unabated. In March the birth of a second son, Edward Samuel Sai-kim, was greeted with tremendous joy. From his first conscious moment Edward (or Eddie) must have been aware of his parents' relieved affection being concentrated on him. And not only his parents, but all the family and servants were intensely attentive. Yet, in spite of all this care, in spite of the material comforts of home, his infancy was

Walter Bosman (Ho Kai-gai)

marred by a strange tropical illness which took hold when he was about six or seven months old, and which was aggravated by the humid heat of Hong Kong. Beside herself with worry and dread, Clara got it into her head that unless the baby was removed to another place he would die, so she took him to Macau. Here Ho Tung found a charming site at the side of Strada da Bela Vista to buy and erect a house on.[15] He would buy another house in Macau, in Largo de Santo Agostinho, in 1918 (see Chapter 8).

In November Ho Wing married Catherine Hung, the seventeen-year-old daughter of Hung Kam-ning, a Eurasian.[16] It was entirely fitting that the eldest son of Ho Tung should be given a dazzling wedding. At noon, the governor's wife and daughter

> Lady and Miss Blake took [the] opportunity of witnessing an interesting specta-
> cle . . . It was the most brilliant wedding procession ever seen in Hong Kong. The
> decorations of kingfishers' feathers and the chairs and other paraphernalia were
> all brought from Canton. Youths dressed in armour and children on horseback
> in archaic costume are an uncommon spectacle . . . The procession was about a
> quarter of a mile in length.[17]

That night and on the following Sunday, a thousand guests sat down to dinner, 'the ladies at Idlewild and the gentleman at the Hung Fa Lau Hotel' (the same restaurant that had catered the wedding banquet of Ho Tung and Margaret twenty years earlier).

The wedding was only a brief respite from anxiety for Clara, as Eddie remained delicate. Come the spring rains, he fell ill again, necessitating another move, this time into Ho Fook's house. Clara probably believed it had a more benign atmosphere, since her sister-in-law had brought nine children successfully into the world within its walls.[18] By then Clara was pregnant again. As soon as the next child, Eva, was safely delivered, Clara left her with a wet nurse and took Eddie to Japan for its cooler temperatures, a change which seemed to suit him very well. In the next few years summers in Japan became a ritual for Eddie; perhaps because he spent long periods alone—or only in the company of his mother—he grew up with a gravity beyond his years and extraordinary will power, driving himself to the limit in whatever endeavour he happened to be engaged.

The family steadily grew: the fourth daughter, Irene, was followed by a son, Robert Shai-lai (whom his family called Robbie), and, at two-year intervals, by Jean and Grace. Clara was a good mother. Her children absorbed far more of her time and attention than usual in a household with a plenitude of domestics. It is not hard to evoke a cosy picture of the family at meal-time: the children teasing or bickering with each other, servants hovering and bringing dishes to the table, Clara telling this one to sit up and helping that one to a spoonful of food, and in between imparting a homily or recounting a recollected anecdote. She encouraged English conversation at the table; the two daughters who wrote about their childhood—Irene Cheng and Jean Gittins—both mention that, though Cantonese was spoken at home, the children grew up bilingual and slipped effortlessly from one language to another. As with language, the habits of everyday life were also Chinese rather than Western. Two shrines were kept at Idlewild for daily burning of incense at the altars of the deities and ancestors; twice a year the dead and buried were remembered by offerings of sacrificial foods and libations of wine on their graves. All the traditional foods were served at the lunar new year, an occasion for paying respects to Margaret at Idlewild. The children called Margaret 'Mother' and Clara 'Mamma'.

Ho Tung was not always in evidence at these gatherings, a lack for which Clara tried hard to compensate. Fathers were often remote from their children in old-fashioned Chinese families and tended to be represented—or idealised—by their wives as superior, worthy authoritarian figures to whom filial respect and gratitude were due. It was no different for the Ho Tungs. That Clara occasionally felt the strain of lone parenthood can be gauged from her daughter Jean's account of her impatience:

Curly-haired Edward Sai-kim as a schoolboy

I used to take hours over my meals . . . Mother decided to take me in hand and her disciplinary measures were so rigid that I became terrified of her. Whenever she showed the slightest sign of impatience, or even when she called me to her without any thought of reprimand, I would burst into tears. This further aggravated her irritability and unkind people made things worse by telling her that this constant weeping in a child was a bad omen and Father was doomed to die. Poor, misguided Mother, instead of giving me the comfort and understanding one might have expected of her, she became more impatient still. It was a vicious circle and although as I grew older the tears became less frequent, the fear remained.[19]

Clara had good reason to be visited by superstitious premonitions of her husband's death. Jean is referring to the time when Ho Tung's digestive disorder confined him to bed from 1910 to 1913 and left him debilitated. It was impossible not to think that he was doomed to be a chronic invalid when one doctor after another came and departed, baffled by the ailment and unable to effect a cure. Meanwhile, not far away in Caine Road, his concubine Chau Yee-man really was dying, a victim of tuberculosis, but the fact of her death in 1911 would be concealed from Ho Tung until he had recovered. It was during the period of his illness that K. T. ('Katie') Archee came into his life, as a nurse and companion, and later as the mother of George (born 1918). Although it became common knowledge that George, who took the surname 'Ho', was Ho Tung's son, he was never formally recognised as such. As the child of Ho Tung's middle age, nevertheless, George was in some ways closer to his father than his much older half-siblings had been. Much of his childhood was spent with his mother in one of Ho Tung's houses on the Peak. Mother and son were generously remembered in Ho Tung's will—Katie for her 'long faithful and devoted service' as his 'secretary', and George for being his 'friend'.

It was just as well that when Ho Tung became ill the family had already moved from Idlewild, a house not suited to an invalid needing tranquillity and seclusion. In 1906 Ho Tung set a precedent by taking himself and his family to live in properties he had bought on the Peak, the most socially rarefied residential area of Hong Kong, barred to any Chinese who was not a servant living in quarters provided by the employer. To do so required special exemption from a provision of the Peak District Reservation Ordinance. Originally passed to make the Peak an absolutely exclusive enclave for Europeans, the ordinance proved unpopular with the few Chinese whose opinions mattered; by way of a sop a clause was incorporated sanctioning exceptions to be granted at the discretion of the 'Governor-in-Council'. When approval was bestowed on this basis to Ho Tung, he acquired not one but three houses—two for his large family and one for himself.

The houses carried names—Dunford, The Chalet, and The Neuk—which probably evoked homes left behind in Europe by their first owners rather than the bracing cold of the Alps and the Scottish Highlands; all the same, the fact that the Peak's lower temperatures made the muggy summers more bearable recommended it to Clara, who thought it healthier for the children, particularly her beloved Eddie. As the houses were not very big, the children had to be dispersed between The Chalet and Dunford, which were close enough together to make this practicable, being separated only by a pair of tennis courts. Fifteen minutes away by footpath was The Neuk, which Ho Tung kept for his own use. Clara, it seems, spent time in all three, while Margaret remained at Idlewild.

In some ways the Peak houses were extremely inconvenient, handicapped as they were by primitive plumbing (absence of running hot water) and difficulty of access. Since there was as yet no motor road, the children had a tortuous journey to school, involving a donkey or sedan chair ride to the funicular railway station, another sedan chair or rickshaw at the bottom, and, since the girls attended school in Kowloon, a ferry and a third rickshaw before reaching their final destination. On the other hand, there was an unhampered outdoor life when the weather was fine, and they could keep a large number of pets. From all accounts they had a carefree childhood. Above all, they lived with the constant and happy awareness of numerous siblings, cousins, uncles, and aunts. The convolutions of the family tree were complicated by the multiple wives of various uncles. Their uncle Ho Fook, for example, had nine children by his wife Lucy Lo Sui-choi (their eldest son Ho Wing was adopted by Ho Tung and Margaret) and a further three by his concubine. Ho Kom-tong had five children with his wife Edith and a further twenty-three with his twelve concubines. Another dynasty was founded when his eldest daughter, Elizabeth, married Simon Tse Ka-po, son of Francisco Tse, a prominent merchant of both Macau and Hong Kong. Ho Kom-tong also had a mistress in Shanghai, a Eurasian believed to be of Russian and Chinese descent. To everyone's distress, one of her daughters eloped with a Cantonese opera singer, Lee Hoi-chuen, who took the young woman with him to San Francisco, where he had been engaged to perform. Their first son, born in San Francisco's Chinatown in 1940, would become the famous martial arts actor and film star Bruce Lee. Such a ramified genealogical network would have been utterly confusing were it not for the sensible Chinese system of designating relatives in sequential terms—as second maternal aunt or sixth paternal uncle and so on. In the Ho Tung household there was also an endless stream of nannies, Chinese and English tutors, piano teachers, and swimming coaches—the houses were always full of servants. For the children it was a private kingdom in which life seemed unchangeably secure.

Seven of the Ho Tung children: Victoria (carrying baby Jean in her arms), Eva, Eddie in a sailor suit, Daisy (far left), Irene (sitting on the ground), and Robbie to her left. Jean was born in 1908, so the photograph would have been taken some time after her birth.

Even so, harsh reality would intrude every now and then, however inapprehensible it was to young minds at the time. Jean describes afternoon walks with her sister Grace and their English governess Miss Hecht, who would

> meet other governesses and, sitting at some shaded seat, they would knit and chat whilst we played with the other children at hopscotch or some other game. This was the highlight of a normal day except, on occasion and without any apparent reason, the others might suddenly refuse to play with us because we were Chinese, or they might tell us that we should not be living on the Peak. Racial discrimination had extended even to the children and children can be so cruel.[20]

It is clear that the family's high social position, buttressed by wealth, was still precarious. Racial bigotry could not be whittled away overnight. The whole question of their living on the Peak would flare up anew during Ho Tung's attempt to rent a house called The Eyrie, in the course of which some quite discourteous personal remarks were made by the governor behind his back. While Ho Tung lost that round, he did succeed in establishing the right to send his children to the English-medium Peak School. To Clara it was patently obvious that the best way to protect her children from the snubs and barbs of bigots was to make them strong and confident in themselves. This could be achieved, in her view, by arranging for them to be well educated. She was determined that her sons and daughters would distinguish themselves in their chosen fields, and not fritter their lives away as the offspring of rich men sometimes did.

Doubtless Ho Tung, a self-made man who owed much to his masters at the Central School, supported Clara in her aspirations. With his dislike of emotional display, he had his own odd way of teaching his children and showing his approval of them. As his daughter Jean Gittins recounts:

> Because of . . . his indifferent health, we saw little of Father during these years. He would sometimes send for us on a Sunday and, when we had assembled in the drawing room of The Neuk, he would come in and, in single file, we would approach him, to be gently shaken by the hand and given a parental kiss. At these meetings he would accord us the same courtesy that he would give to visitors and would, if he felt well enough, have 'tiffin', the midday meal, with us. I can still recall the slim, elegant figure of the early days, the frailness of his physique, his long blue Chinese gown over which he wore a short black jacket with jade stud buttons, and his delicate and very smooth hands. If at any time he was displeased with us he would not show it but would give Mother the responsibility of correcting us: when our behaviour did not become us, we were 'her' children; if, as in later years, we did well at school, we took after him![21]

In the matter of their schooling, he apparently deferred to Clara. With the boys it was easy, for naturally they would go to the Central School, now renamed Queen's College. At Clara's insistence, the girls were sent to the Diocesan Girls' School in Kowloon, which she had chosen for its excellent English instruction. It rankled with Ho Tung, all the same, that the Peak School, only a short walk away from their home, was reluctant to accept Chinese children. How he overturned the school's unwritten policy is not on record. We do know that some time before April 1914, during Ho Tung's absence from Hong Kong, his representative Ho Fook was informed that the children would be admitted for the term shortly commencing. Then Ho Tung apparently changed his mind. Subsequently Ho Fook called on the governor, Sir Henry May, and, as reported in a dispatch from Government House to the secretary of state for the colonies,

> told me [Sir Henry May] that as Mr Ho Tung had established his right to send his children to the School, he [Ho Fook] would advise him to let them remain under the tuition of a private governess. He said that he recognised that if Mr Ho Tung exercised his right, many if not all the European children at the School would be withdrawn.
>
> Recently, on the day before the new term began, Mr Ho Tung himself called upon me and said that he had decided not to send his children to the School. I told him that I thought he was right in so doing as the School was not really intended for the children of rich parents who can afford to send their children abroad for their education or to engage private teachers for them in the Colony.[22]

The resolution was no doubt of great relief to all concerned. Yet the subtext of the governor's letter seems clear: the attendance of the Ho Tung children at an exclusively European school would cause an outrage. Ho Tung could hardly have wanted to expose his children to such mortification; why, then, had he applied? Was it because, since he had chosen Chinese identity against integration with the colonial ruling class (of course there was always a question mark over whether the latter would wholeheartedly admit him), he had decided to put himself forward as a test case in each assault on racial injustice? Though he had a Chinese mother and a Dutch father, he had very early on decided where he stood; his attempt first to live on the Peak and then send his children to the Peak School suggests that, over and above the stated reasons of seeking the healthy air or taking advantage of the proximity, he might have had some thought of battling racial prejudice in mind.

No wonder we find him eager to know China better and to offer his allegiance to that country. In 1913, still shaky from his long illness, he visited Beijing, taking Vic and the two boys. Northern China must have appeared almost exotic to these visitors from the subtropical south, and the cold winter was certainly a novelty. Clara and the children went to Shanhaiguan the following year, and Ho Tung would have joined them were it not for the crisis in Europe—then throwing itself into war—cutting short the holiday for everyone. Shanhaiguan, at the point on the coast of northeast China where the Great Wall reaches the Gulf of Zhili, had been a strategic pass for the route from Beijing into Manchuria in imperial times. By the early twentieth century the traffic had declined and Shanhaiguan's importance had correspondingly dwindled, but it possessed a pleasant beach and, what was more exciting, a vacant Buddhist temple which could be rented. Clara, having set her heart on spending the summer there, first had the temple cleaned and whitewashed. Then a massive operation was launched to move a dozen children (including a couple of cousins), sundry servants, a hundred pieces of luggage, not to mention furniture as well as a piano, by boat and train and trolley car to the rented temple.[23] The children must have found it a magical place. The cool, dark temple halls where they slept on camp beds under sweeping yellow roofs; a shimmering sea nearby to dive into for a pre-breakfast swim; the top of the Great Wall, like a wide, arching mountain road, just perfect for donkey rides—all would long remain in their memories.

The war in Europe turned out not to be immediately disruptive for Hong Kong. There was increased traffic to mainland China, always seen as a refuge during times of trouble or danger by Chinese in the colony. By 1915 Ho Tung was well again and once more on the move. On this occasion he took Clara and Vic to Qingdao, a port with an eventful history. Towards the end of the previous century, at the time of foreign depredations on China, it had been occupied by Germany (the British, for their part, took over Weihaiwei in northern Shandong and exacted a ninety-nine-year lease on the hinterland of Kowloon, which came to be known as the New Territories). As a result Qingdao had a distinctly German look: wander down some of its cobbled streets and one came face to face with white stucco houses roofed in red tiles, a turreted church or two, and fancy gables in all shapes and sizes. And around its lovely sandy bay one would find enough villas and hotels to give credence to Qingdao's one-time claim as the 'Riviera of the Far East'. In 1914 Japan, entering World War I on the side of the Allies, seized the German territory around Qingdao, but under Japanese control the port continued to attract visitors, many from Hong Kong. Whether or not there was a link between Ho Tung's recovery and Clara conceiving after a gap of five years must be a matter of speculation; at all events, it was in Qingdao that their last child, Florence, was born. For Clara at least the family was now complete.

5

The Public Man

By the time he was thirty-two Ho Tung had attained not only considerable wealth and property but distinction, too: he had been made a justice of the peace in 1891 and appointed Jardines' chief compradore in 1894. Through the 1880s and early 1890s, he had been single-minded in his pursuit of material success. Although this continued, other preoccupations were beginning to burgeon. He started taking an interest in the social world and the way he and others like him lived in it. He realised he could no longer remain impervious to the demand of some of his peers for change, for a setting which was more just, flexible, and free.

For most Chinese in late nineteenth- and early twentieth-century Hong Kong the social distance between a bungalow on the Peak and a room above the office was the difference between heaven and earth. It could not have been crossed without a marked amelioration of rigid racist attitudes, and that could hardly be achieved without antagonisms and desires erupting to change the way things were.

Until then, segregation between the Europeans and the Chinese was all but absolute. An anonymous resident did not mince his words in a letter to a newspaper in 1878:

> That we Chinese in this Colony are despised individually, collectively, and socially, and that we are ignored as a community (except in a few instances) there cannot be the least doubt. Individually we have imposed on us certain burdens peculiar to our nationality and we receive uncivility and indignity even at the hands of the police, to whom we contribute to pay largely for our protection. In European society we particularly have no status. To correspond socially with Europeans with whom we are daily brought into contact, to be admitted as favoured guests at their dinner table, to have the privilege of counting them as personal friends, are things which no Chinese, however ambitious he may be in other respects, would ever aspire to obtain. As a political body we are unknown. We are unrepresented, and it would be easier to find a fish climbing up a tree, as

our adage says, than to see a Chinese Justice of the Peace, or a Chinese member of the Legislative or Executive Council in Hongkong.[1]

Of all the manifestations of official discrimination, the light and night pass regulations were thought to be the most pernicious. An ordinance in 1857 imposed a curfew on Chinese inhabitants should they be 'at large in the City of Victoria' between eight o'clock and sunrise unless they obtained a night pass from the superintendent of police. In 1870 they were further required to carry lanterns at night; in 1888 these provisions were confirmed in a new ordinance entitled 'Regulation of the Chinese'. When caught, offenders were fined or summarily locked up for the night. The regulations were harshly enforced in times of insecurity, though less frequently invoked when crime rates were down. Not surprisingly calls for the abolition of these repugnant rules became a recurrent theme in dealings between Chinese community leaders and the government. The colonial control system extended at the same time to brutal punishment of criminals who, if they were not deported or imprisoned, would be publicly flogged. Since the gaol was often crowded, sentences were sometimes remitted by banishing the prisoner after branding to discourage his return to the colony, or by whipping, with up to a hundred lashes by rattan cane or the cat-o'-nine-tails.

John Pope Hennessy, the same governor who expressed disquiet about the standard of English among Central School pupils, was appalled by such treatment of Chinese inhabitants. Intent on promoting racial equality, he suspended public flogging and looked about for other abuses to abolish. None of this endeared him to the foreign merchants, who believed only that his pro-Chinese and over-liberal attitude was encouraging crime and damaging British imperial interests. In response to several cases of barefaced burglary, robbery, and murder during 1878, the merchants, led by Jardines taipan William Keswick, called a meeting. Ostensibly to discuss 'public insecurity', the meeting was in reality to protest in the strongest terms against the governor's 'undue leniency towards the criminal class'—by implication, the Chinese.

What happened on 7 October 1878 was the first significant confrontation between the races. The Chinese reaction took Keswick and his fellow merchants totally by surprise: they had advertised the meeting at the City Hall, turned up at the appointed hour, and found the place already filled with Chinese—not (as one of the leaders Ho A-mei later pointed out) 'shop coolies and the like', but men who 'belonged to the better classes' holding 'large stakes in the welfare of the colony'.[2]

In the commotion that broke out, such distinctions were lost on the gentlemen who shouted, 'D . . . d Chinamen, turn them out!' and 'Let us have the meeting

elsewhere to prevent the Chinese coming'. Appropriately, the meeting was recon-
vened at a place close to British hearts—the cricket ground. Forming themselves
into a tight circle, the foreign merchants succeeded in shutting out the Chinese
who had followed; when Ng Choy, a Chinese barrister, asked for an interpreter
to be present so that the other Chinese would understand what was being said,
they paid no attention. This was not a snub that could be borne; Ng Choy led his
group off the pitch, leaving the meeting to pass its several resolutions, one of which
asserted, 'what is needed is firm and unfettered administration. Flogging in public
is the only means of deterrent. It should be reinstated.'[3]

The most vociferous Chinese participants at this confrontation were, predict-
ably enough, Ho A-mei and Ng Choy, who stood at the very top of 'the better
classes'. The former, who had spent some ten years in Australia, was at the time secretary of the On Tai Insurance Company and a community leader of some conse-
quence.[4] The latter had recently been admitted to the bar and was to be appointed
by Hennessy as a temporary legislative councillor in 1880, the first Chinese to be
so honoured; he was also the first Chinese magistrate and would later offer his
services to the Chinese imperial government and be sent, under his other name,
Wu Tingfang, as envoy to the United States. Ho Tung's and Wu Tingfang's paths
would cross in 1901 (see Chapter 6). Where Ng Choy and Ho A-mei led, the
younger Ho Tung would follow in due course.

Despite their efforts, however, the light and pass regulations were not repealed,
though they were enforced with a lighter hand. Then, in 1895, again in response to
an outbreak of robberies, they were once more invoked and applied by the police in
a most offensive manner. 'To force respectable Chinese to go to the Police Station
and stop there until bailed out is unpleasant enough, but it makes the ordeal ten
thousand times more exasperating when half-a-dozen or more of these alleged law-
breakers are tied together by their queues and driven like a flock of sheep to the
nearest lock-up', ran an editorial in the *Hongkong Telegraph*.[5]

From the crusade of words launched by the press over this issue we may infer
that Ho Tung had been so treated by the police. But he reacted with characteristic
moderation. Conscious as he must have been of the authorities' discriminatory
practices, he was nevertheless a realist, not a revolutionary. He believed that more
could be achieved for his compatriots by negotiation than by confrontation. He
first solicited the views of other merchants like himself; then, armed with their
signatures, he presented a petition to the government. Still in this circumspect
vein, he joined forces with Ho A-mei and invited the Chinese community to a
meeting so that others might air their views. The meeting took place at the Tung
Wah Hospital on 22 December 1895. Nominated to the chair by Ho Tung, Ho
A-mei began by reviewing the operation of the light and pass ordinance, reminding

This cartoon from Illustrated London News *shows a Sikh policeman grabbing a Chinese offender by his queue prior to making an arrest—a not infrequent sight in the streets of nineteenth-century Hong Kong. Courtesy of gwulo.com.*

his audience that though it had previously fallen into abeyance, its recent strict enforcement was intolerable. 'What is to be particularly deplored,' he said, 'is that the system is intended against the Chinese only, and for this reason it must be condemned on principle . . . Why are we singled out?'

Quite apart from its discriminatory nature, the law was bad for business: 'Considerably fewer people visit the eating houses at night, and, of course, as the business decreases so the sale of sharks' fins, etc., by the Nam Pak Hongs decrease; in fact, there is a general deadlock in every branch of trade.'

As he warmed to his theme, Ho A-mei became more strident and daring: if the government refused to act, he intimated, he and his fellow Chinese would not scruple to lay the matter directly before the secretary of state for the colonies. He was at pains, however, to point out that the petition was not 'an agitation on the part of Mr Ho Tung. He has taken part in the matter simply out of public spirit.'

Indeed, Ho Tung sounded admirably temperate when he rose to address the meeting. Allowing for the possibility that perhaps Chinese were too passive, he said, 'If a thing is unreasonable we can always appeal to the Government to have it modified or repealed, otherwise the Government is not in a position to know our hardships.' Young as he was, he was too shrewd not to grasp the difficulty of getting Chinese to unite over any matter of public concern. It was as well to realise, he reminded his audience, that the light and pass legislation affected only the Chinese. Citing the case of Chinese theatres, which had to be closed at 11 p.m., he said, 'If the play goes on after that time a policeman steps on the stage and puts a stop to it. In the City Hall, however, they are allowed to go on until one o'clock in the morning. That shows the distinction between Chinese and Europeans. The Government encourages all sorts of recreation for the European community. What have they done for the Chinese? They gave them a recreation ground in Taipingshan. What kind of a place is that for recreation, while latrines and urinals are there? We are the principal ratepayers in Hongkong; we pay more taxes than the Europeans, and derive the least advantage.' He then urged his audience to express their views without having been 'influenced in any degree by Mr Ho A-mei or by myself, and you must not think you have been influenced by wealth or position.' The meeting ended on a vote by a show of hands; for once it seemed the Chinese were unanimous, for no one opposed the motion.[6]

A furore in the press followed this meeting. Ho Tung's stand was so outrageous, claimed the *China Mail*, that he should be removed from the roster of justices of the peace forthwith. 'Apart from the absurdities in which he wallowed, he gave utterance to sentiments which can have no other effect than that of inciting his hearers to defy any law in the Colony,' wrote the editor in affronted and pompous tones. It was a privilege for the likes of Ho A-mei and Ho Tung to live in Hong Kong, he continued, for 'they would not be allowed to talk such screeching rubbish in any other country . . . Let Mr Ho Tung go to Canton and try to hold a public meeting and say what he thinks of the officials of his own country and state his reasons for not trusting himself and his business in their grasp . . . and if he does not care to go, it would do this Colony no harm to send him there.'

A milder contributor—who signed himself 'Brownie'—mitigated the picture of Ho Tung as a rabble-rouser by giving him the benefit of the doubt: 'I am inclined to exonerate that gentleman from any seditious leanings, and can only marvel at his appearance and attitude at the Tung Wah's meeting.'[7] The *Telegraph*, too, weighed in on Ho Tung's side, making a mockery of the ineptitude of the governor, who had

got out of his depth in a perfect torrent of assumed righteous indignation, because forsooth, a Chinaman had dared to speak in public against a galling ill-considered

Government measure. Because a Chinese gentleman of the highest standing had the unparalleled audacity to object to being imprisoned and treated with all the indignities a clumsy policeman, dressed in a little brief authority, delighted to inflict on him for just taking a stroll in the cool of the evening, and because the above mentioned wicked and seditious Chinese arrogated to himself the right of thinking for himself like a man—which the Government could not do if it tried—and because this celestial reprobate was so hardened in crime as to actually say what he thought with due moderation, for which under the circumstances, he should have had the highest credit as becomes a man who strives for the right and fights the cause of his unfortunate countrymen, and seeks to protect even the humble coolie from the tyrannical minions of the 'lor!' [law].[8]

With the storm clouds gathering all around, His Excellency Sir William Robinson finally bowed to popular feeling. He did not yield wholeheartedly, but he did at least go so far as to instruct the police to suspend the regulations except in the case of persons abroad after midnight who might be suspected of criminal intent. It would be another two years before the curfew system was repealed in its entirety.

The whole episode showed some progress, albeit very small, in narrowing the communication gap between government and people. As for members of the Chinese community, Ho Tung had given them much food for thought. Unless they spoke up for themselves with one voice, it was all too easy for officialdom to ignore their grievances.

In fact a forum for Chinese to express their views did exist, for hadn't Ho A-mei and Ho Tung held their meeting at the Tung Wah Hospital? If anything symbolised the emergence of social and political consciousness among Hong Kong's Chinese population, it was the Tung Wah, the first significant attempt at community organisation. Though not set up to be a representative body, that was what it became. By the closing years of the 1800s the path to public life for Chinese in colonial Hong Kong was well established, and its chief signposts were the committees of the Tung Wah Hospital and its associate, the Society for the Protection of Women and Children or the Po Leung Kuk. Both were institutions founded to redress peculiarly Chinese problems through means devised by Chinese themselves. These problems came down to two unsavoury practices: the treatment of the dead and dying, and the sale of mui tsai for domestic servitude or worse.

The adoption of children—usually girls—from poor families by rich ones in exchange for a cash payment had long been embedded in Chinese custom. In practice, however, the custom was frequently manipulated by those who sold the mui tsai for immoral purposes, as Ho Tung's own mother had known only too well. In 1875 new legislation for the protection of women and girls threatened to make criminals of all those who had—in good faith—bought girls as concubines or servants. The outcry this raised provoked several Chinese community leaders to petition the government for leave to tackle the abuses in their own way. What they proposed was the founding of a society under the wing of the Tung Wah Hospital expressly to prevent kidnapping and to help the victims. By pledging to deliver kidnappers and pimps into the hands of the law they secured the continuation of the legal sale of human beings.

Once again, it was Governor Hennessy who came up with the necessary support to set this society, the Po Leung Kuk, on its feet. Through the early 1880s it settled into its role of upholding virtue, sometimes with difficulty, especially when it lost its patron in 1882, the year Hennessy departed for England. His successor, Sir William Marsh, was less amenable and promptly withdrew a site Hennessy had granted to the Po Leung Kuk for its headquarters. Petitions for a suitable piece of land were still being lodged in 1887–1888, when Ho Tung was deputy chairman of the board; the government's rejection of a site near Possession Point that year was a disappointing blow to the community and adversely affected fund-raising.[9]

Ho Tung's term of office as chairman of the Tung Wah Hospital was rather more rewarding, since it culminated in a successful fund-raising drive to build a new annexe as well as a hospital for plague and other infectious diseases.[10] By then (1898) the Tung Wah was becoming a modern medical institution.[11] It had come a long way from its death-house origins. Before it was founded, there was nowhere for the destitute sick to go except the *yici*, a common ancestral hall and death-house where the dying lay among corpses, uncared for, in dark and gruesome rooms. This scandalous state of affairs alerted the government to the need for a Chinese hospital. But patients would consign themselves to a clean and airy ward attended by doctors only if the medicine dispensed was familiarly Chinese. Thus when it opened in 1872 the Tung Wah offered herbal cures, with rare resort to surgery which, when performed, was done without an anaesthetic. It also found itself providing other charitable services, free burial among them; as philanthropy was ever a springboard for political and social advancement, it gathered to itself through its board of rich and eminent directors an unusual degree of power. Before long the views of its members came to be acknowledged as a touchstone for the opinion of the Chinese population as a whole.

But for all Tung Wah's dominating presence, Chinese acceptance of Western medicine was making *some* headway in Hong Kong. Not surprisingly the conversion had a Christian impetus. A Canadian physician, Dr William Young, had arrived in 1878 and soon began prescribing remedies to the poorer Chinese from a clinic he opened at the Taipingshan chapel of the London Missionary Society. This was the same William Young whose grave at Happy Valley would be, for a time, tended at Ho Tung's expense. His clinic metamorphosed into the Nethersole Hospital, which would, still later, become one with the Alice Memorial Hospital, a monument to the short life of Dr Ho Kai's English wife, opened in 1887.[12] Ho Kai was a near contemporary of Ho Tung, being three years older and also an alumnus of the Central School. He trained in medicine at Aberdeen University and in law at Lincoln's Inn, London. Returning to Hong Kong in 1882, he became a leading figure among the colony's Chinese elite and played a notable role in public service. Ho Kai often found himself at odds with the more conservative of his peers, especially those associated with the Tung Wah Hospital, on account of his scientific training and modern attitudes. An advocate of reform, he is thought to have exerted some influence on the development of Sun Yat-sen's revolutionary ideas, generally finding no conflict between his own commitment to the welfare of colonial Hong Kong and his concern for his motherland. Although criticised for collaborating with the colonial government at the expense of China, 'his Chinese nationalism was inseparable from the colonial situation in which he lived'.[13] Reputedly the first Chinese in Hong Kong to wear Western dress, he scored another first when he was knighted in 1912.

It was the Nethersole and Alice Memorial which supplied the doctors and nurses to work in the emergency Glass Works Hospital when the great bubonic plague struck Hong Kong in 1894. This calamity, which claimed close to 2,500 lives, polarised the Tung Wah and the government. As soon as the first cases of plague were diagnosed, the colonial medical authorities ordered precautions to be put in train. Sanitary officers were detailed to inspect and clean the streets of Taipingshan, the dirtiest and most affected area. House-to-house searches were instituted to flush out stricken cases and to carry out disinfection and whitewashing. Isolation hospitals were hurriedly made ready, including the one at the Glass Works and on board a quarantine ship, the *Hygeia*. Those who had died of the plague were covered in quicklime and given an unceremonious burial. With crass briskness on the part of the colonial authorities, and fear and superstition in the minds of the Chinese, the situation soon became explosive. Dreading forcible removal of victims to the emergency hospitals and to the *Hygeia*, Chinese families went to great lengths to hide their sick and thus fend off the evil designs of foreigners who were—so the rumour went—planning to ship the patients to Europe to be pulverised into medicine for the royal family.

Through that hot and steamy summer, casualties mounted and the hospitals became ever more overcrowded. At the Tung Wah, there were still those who distrusted Western medicine; others, like the chairman of the hospital committee, were more sympathetic to the government's sanitary controls, though this only had the effect of turning the Chinese population against him. The smouldering hostilities of the more ignorant and prejudiced among the Chinese population detonated one day when an angry mob of rioters toppled the chairman from his sedan chair and pelted him with stones as he came out of the hospital from a meeting. In this atmosphere of panic and hysteria, thousands of people abandoned their jobs and fled to the mainland.

By the time the epidemic was brought under control the vacillation and obstructiveness of the Tung Wah's riven committee had considerably tarnished the hospital's image. Now its medical conduct came under scrutiny, too. This 'hotbed of medical and sanitary vice', as the superintendent of the Government Civil Hospital called it, urgently needed to be reformed. And reformed it was, though only after more conflict and struggle between the hospital's diehards and the government. Finally the Tung Wah capitulated, in 1896 accepting Dr Chung, house surgeon at the Alice Memorial Hospital and trained in Western medicine, as its superintendent.

Had Ho Tung been elected to the chairmanship earlier his tenure would have posed a dilemma, since he was a most willing patient of Western doctors himself, having consulted several in Hong Kong and the United States. As it was, all he needed to do was to give his support to improvements that were already underway. The aftermath of the plague outbreak saw him being appointed to a committee to select for the honour roll those volunteers who had rendered service during the epidemic. There was something else that claimed his attention. As a preventive measure, an ordinance was passed condemning to demolition a large number of houses in the Taipingshan slums. Ho Tung, in company with the Hongkong Fire Insurance Co. and the Tung Wah Hospital, was one of several property owners to dispute the government's compensation offer. The wrangle with the arbitration board was long and tortuous. Although the outcome was hardly as satisfactory as the press had hoped—that 'phoenix-like, purified by fire if necessary, and certainly with carbolic acid, cement flooring, proper ventilations and drains, Taipingshan will rise redeemed from her ashes, and be hailed as a useful adjunct of a great city'[14]—at least the plagues that visited Hong Kong in subsequent years were less virulent.

In 1897 it was not plague but smallpox that afflicted the colony. Now there was a better understanding of infectious diseases; within two years the Tung Wah, with Ho Tung as chairman, became champion of the very thing that it had previously thwarted: isolation wards. The governor, Sir Henry Blake, readily assented, and the community, both Chinese and European, generously opened their wallets. In 1899, the year after Ho Tung's chairmanship of the Tung Wah, the foundation stone of a new wing to the hospital was laid. Then the happy moment arrived when the Tung Wah Infectious Disease Hospital building was inaugurated. 'Over 4,000

Ho Tung in Chinese jacket and robe, with Governor Blake and Lady Blake (carrying bouquet) to his left, and Margaret Ho Tung in formal Chinese tunic and skirt, beside Lady Blake; Tung Wah Hospital, 1898.

men, women and children have been buried in the Plague Cemetery during the past three years,' Sir Henry Blake said at the event, 'I want to stop this scourge, if it can be stopped by human agency . . . I think that the Chinese community will understand that nothing is being done or has been done, which is not in their interests.'[15]

Ho Tung would become a permanent adviser to the hospital; in 1933 he would be elected to a sub-committee convened to oversee a scheme to rebuild the hospital along more modern lines. In the intervening period, his benefactions to medicine continued. When the Hongkong College of Medicine for Chinese, established at the Alice Memorial Hospital in 1887, was subsumed into the new University of Hong Kong in 1911, various philanthropists came forward with donations to equip this new medical school. Ho Tung in 1915 gave $50,000 towards the cost of the teaching faculty on condition that a part of the interest would be used to fund a

Ho Tung Chair of Clinical Surgery, tenable at the Government Civil Hospital. The university awarded him an honorary doctor of laws degree for this magnanimous gesture. Ho Fook and Ho Kom-tong were also quick to respond, for the breadth of their acts of philanthropy and public service was no less wide-ranging. They contributed to the schools of physiology and tropical medicine at the new university; both served as advisers or directors of the Tung Wah Hospital and the Po Leung Kuk. Besides maintaining free schools and endowing prizes at the University of Hong Kong, Ho Fook served on the District Watch Committee, while Ho Kom-tong became a benefactor to both St John's Ambulance Brigade, which he founded, and the Helena May Institute for Women. Probably the most versatile of the brothers, Ho Kom-tong took pleasure in many activities. The Cantonese opera shows he mounted to raise money for charity clearly chimed with his own interest in the art form. An enthusiastic amateur, he was adept at singing a number of well-known roles in the repertoire, but his favourite was that of the warrior Cao Bawang in *Farewell My Concubine*, which he performed in his last appearance on the stage—at a charity event at the University of Hong Kong—in 1947, when he was eighty-one years old. He died three years later and was given a grand send-off, the funeral procession starting from his home in the Mid-Levels and proceeding along Seymour Road to the University of Hong Kong, where friends and relatives had gathered to pay their respects.

Education in general became a focus of Ho Tung's largesse. He would always remain grateful to Frederick Stewart and Alexander Falconer, and he had visions of opening up similar opportunities for a younger generation. There was no doubt in his mind that, with good education, Chinese in Hong Kong would achieve distinctions equal to his own. At the turn of the century, after stepping down from the Tung Wah, he informed the government that he would fund an English-medium school in Kowloon for children of all races. A site was soon found and approved, but the school proceeded in fits and starts, while the correspondence over its composition took up the best part of two years. The stumbling block, as the government's advisers had it, was Ho Tung's insistence on a 'mixed' intake, which ran counter to the latest educational theories. Far from being workable, they said, such a school was 'foredoomed to failure'.[16]

An advance in educational theories is a plausible enough explanation for second thoughts, yet a faint question mark hangs over the government's candour. The unstated reality was that English parents in Kowloon would never have countenanced a school in which their children would be mingling with Chinese boys and girls. Ho Tung was to have a taste of the same prejudice in 1914, when he tried to send his own children to the Peak School.

Ho Tung in Western dress, early twentieth century

The government had looked a gift horse in the mouth; now, with some embarrassment, it approached Ho Tung with an alternative proposal. What was urgently needed in Kowloon was a school for British children; since Chinese pupils were already catered for in an existing school which was by no means overcrowded, would Ho Tung allow his gift to be redirected? Ho Tung felt aggrieved, but the new school was ready and only waiting for his blessing. There was nothing else to do but submit with good grace:

> It is hardly within my competence, speaking from the point of view of the educationist, to enter into any discussion on this latest decision of the Government, but I cannot refrain from an expression of very sincere regret for so radical a change in policy and one that is so much opposed to the spirit which prompted my offer of the school to the Colony . . . It will be remembered that I attached the utmost importance to the stipulation that no distinction should be drawn as regards either the nationality or creed of any scholar applying for admission to the Kowloon school . . . On the other hand I have no desire that my gift should be hedged in by conditions not capable of reasonable modification. I am prepared therefore though with very much reluctance, to yield to the request of the Government to waive my original condition to the extent desired. I do so, however, on the definite understanding that the Government, on their part, undertake to appoint for the new Yaumati School for Chinese, at least one properly qualified English master and to maintain the standard of education there on the same level as that in the Kowloon School for European children.[17]

Nor should there be any disparity, in his view, between the choices available for girls and those for boys. Education was one leveller, but certain customs subordinated Chinese girls and hindered them from going to school at all—foot-binding, for one. Alicia Little was a fervent campaigner against this cruel practice. She had followed her businessman husband Archibald Little to China in 1887. In 1900 she visited Hong Kong from China to promote the message of her Natural Feet Society (Tianzuhui). Ho Tung, whom Little knew by reputation as the richest man in Hong Kong, lent his support and presided at one of her meetings. Held at the Chinese Club, it was attended by many leading Chinese men in Hong Kong. Members of the committee then entertained Little to tea and cakes in an upper room, where 'European comforts of curtains and cushioned armchairs were judiciously intermingled with Cantonese elegancies of black carved wood and landscape marble', Little reports in her book, *In the Land of the Blue Gown*. Then it was the women's turn to hear her lectures. For the occasion Lady Blake, the governor's wife, opened Government House to welcome a large number of hobbling ladies to its ballroom, including Mrs Ho Tung.

It comes as no surprise to find Ho Tung presiding over Alicia Little's speech to the Chinese Club, for he, along with his brother Ho Kom-tong and several other prominent business and professional leaders in Hong Kong, was one of its founders. Other distinguished members included the likes of Lau Chu-pak, compradore to A. S. Watson's, and the Eurasian businessman Sin Tak-fan, who was president from 1906 to 1908. The club was the local community's answer to the exclusive Hongkong Club—so much more socially impregnable than Government House, it seems, that a similar institution, organised on the lines of a British club, was brought into existence to affirm the status of the Chinese elite. The Chinese Recreation Club, founded by Ho Kai and Wei Yuk in 1912, was another club on the British model, in this case one devoted to sports, particularly cricket, the 'gentlemen's game'. As with the Chinese Club, membership conferred cachet and respectability. One of its most renowned members was the businessman and community leader Chow Shouson, who was fond of joking about the piratical origin of his family, one of the oldest in Hong Kong, but who just as frequently reminded his listeners that, unlike Ho Tung and Ho Fook, he was full-blooded Chinese.

The mixing of races caused far more anxiety among the colonists, as another episode shows. Though trivial in itself, the matter was pursued all the way to Whitehall with a thoroughness which demonstrates all too plainly how keenly colonial aloofness was defended. A house on the Peak, The Eyrie, was the battleground; its leaseholder, Sir Francis Piggott, Ho Tung, and the governor, Sir Frederick Lugard, were the protagonists. It happened that Piggott, the famously troublesome chief justice, having agreed to sublet his house to Ho Tung for three months while he went on leave, applied to Lugard, who had recently arrived in the summer of 1907, for exemption from the Peak District Reservation Ordinance. He applied for exemption on the grounds that his would-be tenant was not strictly Chinese. When his application was denied, he made an enormous fuss, even going so far as to take his grievance to the secretary of state for the colonies, Lord Crewe. The fact that The Eyrie stood above Mountain Lodge, the governor's summer residence, and commanded a lofty view of it, made a Chinese tenant particularly unpalatable to colonial sensibilities. In presenting his version of the case, Lugard made no secret of his opinion of Piggott, who he said 'is simply pursuing the course which he has consistently followed since he went to Hong Kong—of making himself as unpleasant to the Government as he possibly can'. Yet there crept into his report a tone of characteristically imperial condescension at the mention of Ho Tung. He referred to the proposed tenant as 'an illegitimate half-caste whose wives and concubines numbered four.' When canvassed for advice, some members of the Executive Council had taken the view that Ho Tung was definitely a 'real

Chinaman' in his habits, so it was perfectly legal to ban him from the Peak. In the finer details of this Chinaman's *ménage*, though, Lugard had clearly been misled:

> the woman Mr Ho Tung first took as wife is . . . the illegitimate daughter of the late Mr Hector MacLean, formerly a salesman in Messrs Jardine, Matheson and Company by a Chinese woman. She bore Mr Ho Tung no children.
>
> In accordance with Chinese custom Mr Ho Tung therefore took a secondary wife—a pure Chinese—by whom he had children. Later (I am informed) he took a concubine in the person of the daughter of a Eurasian pupil teacher in Victoria College. By her he also had children. This woman was elevated to the rank of First Wife passing her over the head of the secondary wife and ranking her equal with Mr MacLean's illegitimate daughter. In doing so he had broken Chinese Marriage Law and outraged Chinese etiquette. Not content with three wives and six children he has a second concubine—a pure Chinese—making a harem of four in all.[18]

Ironically, at that time Ho Tung already owned three houses on the Peak and had installed Clara and the children in two of them. More ironically, he had been considered an unacceptable candidate for the Legislative Council because he was not Chinese enough. As we saw, he had begun to raise his public profile before his retirement from Jardines; by the turn of the century he was being mooted for appointment to the Legislative Council. Since the selection of Ng Choy the government had continued to rely on a handful of Chinese councillors to ascertain general opinion on official policy and decisions. In 1902 one incumbent, Wei Yuk, was thought to be planning a prolonged stay in Shanghai; in anticipation of his resignation the *China Mail* and *Hongkong Telegraph* began putting forward Ho Tung as the fittest candidate to fill the vacant seat. But one Tse Tsan-tai challenged the choice, for a very simple reason: how could Ho Tung be a representative of the Chinese community when he was Eurasian? Tse was something of an iconoclast: opium smoking, foot-binding, geomancy, and the conservatives at the Tung Wah were all at one time or another the butt of his attacks. He was vociferous about the selection of Legislative Council members: 'It is a fact, and a glaring one,' he wrote in 1902, 'that the past and present representatives of the Chinese have been more or less Government automatons . . . How could it be otherwise, seeing that they were nominated and appointed by the Government?'[19] Born in Sydney and educated at the Central School, he was prone to firing off letters to Hong Kong's English press. One of these, opposing the selection of Ho Tung because he was not Chinese, provoked a flurry of letters from other readers.[20] Among the various correspondents who slugged it out with Tse in the columns of *Daily Press* and *Hongkong Telegraph* was one who signed himself 'A British Subject and a Eurasian':

If I have rightly seized the spirit of Mr Tse Tsan Tai's letter . . . he advocates—
I refrain from the word agitate, for he distinctly denies being an agitator—he
advocates, I repeat, the election by the Chinese Community of a representative
to the Legislative Council and impugns the hypothetical appointment by the
Government of Mr Ho Tung on the ground that he is a Eurasian . . .

I discern in his subtle letter, firstly, a direct attack against Mr Ho Tung; sec-
ondly, a not less direct attack against the Eurasians.[21]

Tse had characterised Eurasians as 'pushing yet law-abiding', but one corre-
spondent who signed himself 'John Chinaman', displaying all the xenophobia and
prejudice attached to the question of race, was more blatantly disparaging:

One of the principal reasons why the Chinese have allowed the Eurasians to come
into their society is that though they can distinguish them by their features to
be Eurasians, still they dare not say whether their fathers were Chinese or not,
for they have adopted as their surnames proper Chinese family names which
can be traced two or three thousand years back. You must remember, Mr Editor,
that there are two kinds of Eurasians, one who are born of Chinese fathers and
European or Eurasian mothers and the other who are born of European fathers
and Chinese or Eurasian mothers. For better reference I will classify the former
as A and the latter as B. According to Chinese social laws and customs Eurasians
of class A, if their fathers had their names entered in the ancestral register, have as
much right to be called Chinese as pure-born Chinese themselves; but those of
class B are no more Chinese than they are Europeans . . .

With regard to Eurasians of class B in this Colony, many of them have
adopted the dress and name of their fathers and it is a well-known fact that they
will resent, with the bitterest feelings, to be called Eurasians and much more so
if they are called Chinamen . . . at the present moment there is a number of these
men who were once in Chinese dress and professed to be Chinese, but who, being
now in European dress have simply refused to have any further social intercourse
with the Chinese . . . As there is absolutely no guarantee against any Eurasians of
this class from following the same example, is it not unnatural that the Chinese
should like to have a bona-fide Chinese gentleman to be their representative
rather than a Eurasian, however capable and good he may be?[22]

Ho Tung himself would later adopt Western dress—some time after cutting
off his pigtail (as he called it) or queue—only to discard it again for the elegant
ensemble of a Chinese gentleman in a deliberate reversal of the trend in Hong
Kong. The ensemble was not, of course, a tunic buttoned in the front paired with
loose trousers, but the long, flowing robe that dropped down to the ankles. Was
this assumption of Chinese dress some form of statement, making more visible
a commitment to the Chinese part of his identity? Or did he wear the outfit as a

sign that he was now above the daily grind of work and toil, the robe being more suited to a man of means and leisure than one still bound by the practical necessity of making a living? Perhaps both considerations were encompassed in his decision.

If he could not help being wounded by the sort of remarks made by John Chinaman and his like, at least he would never be accused of trying to conceal his Chinese blood. Nor did he, as far as we know, ever refer publicly to his conspicuous absence from the Legislative Council. His daughters Irene and Jean attributed the omission to his ill health and involvement in other spheres of public service. It would be strange, all the same, if the opposition of Tse Tsan-tai did not have some bearing on the issue. Ho Tung was later to champion the appointment of his brother Ho Fook to the Legislative Council, though being a representative did not turn out to be an entirely easy duty. Appointed in 1917, Ho Fook spoke against the government's attempt in 1919 to pass a bill reserving part of the offshore island of Cheung Chau for European missionaries, a bill which in his opinion was 'nothing more or less than racial legislation'.[23] The bill was, however, passed over the Chinese members' objections. Perhaps frustrated by this and other instances of official discrimination, he resigned before his term of office ran its course, an unprecedented step. For his part Ho Tung continued to cherish hopes of sitting on the Legislative Council—hopes that proved ultimately vain. He discovered soon enough, in any case, that he could serve as a bridge between the government and Chinese people more effectively by remaining on the sidelines; not being bound by an oath of office to the colonial government, he could be less inhibited from expanding his activities in China.

This bickering over how far he was or was not Chinese could be set aside when he was away from the pettiness and insularity of Hong Kong. He had in any case learnt to exploit his dual ancestry when it suited him: wearing his long silk robe, he was the quintessential Chinese gentleman; on other occasions, he was the urbane cosmopolitan, more 'Bosman' than 'Ho Tung'. As we have seen, when he visited the United States with Margaret in 1901, he identified himself as 'H. T. Bosman', although, as the *New York Times* explained, 'at home Mr Bosman is better known as Mr Ho Tung'. He did so again in 1908, this time taking both Margaret and Clara as well as three of his children. Arriving in San Francisco, the unwary travellers met a reception that was considerably less than welcoming: 'Robert Ho Tung Bosman, a Hongkong millionaire,' the *New York Times* reported, 'who with two wives and three children arrived from the Orient on the steamer *Korea* yesterday, will be deported. This decision was reached to-day by a special board of inquiry.'[24] In his own defence, Ho Tung said he saw no harm in polygamy, but it seems there were limits to what the American authorities could tolerate of cultural differences.

No self-made man has succeeded without hard work and a singular dedication to his chosen goal. It was the same for Ho Tung: behind his public persona he was unswerving in his pursuit of profit, never wasting a moment to put his money to the best use he could find. He had long outgrown the Hong Kong market; in 1902 there were only eighty-two listed companies, and he was a shareholder in the best of them. But since his first trips abroad he had been dealing in a range of international equities, commodities, currencies, and bonds through brokers in London and New York. After a dormant period from around 1910 to 1913, when he was bedridden, there set in a burst of energy and enterprise. In February 1913, the *Hongkong Telegraph* informs us, 'Mr Ho Tung, for several years an invalid but now taking an active interest in business affairs, was invited to join the Board of Directors of the Hongkong Land Investment and Agency Company'; in May 1923, at an extraordinary general meeting, he was voting alongside other major shareholders such as Sir Paul Chater for the acquisition by the Company of Hong Kong Central Estate Limited. With his brothers and three other local merchants (Lau Chu-pak, Chan Kai-ming, and Lo Cheung-shiu), he set up the Tai Yau Bank with a fully paid-up capital of $600,000. He also resumed his diversification into financial markets overseas. War barely interrupted the flow of telegrams to and fro, which show him buying British Glass Industries one moment, selling Ural Caspians the next, and tracking exchange rates at all times. His real estate interests spread further afield, all the way to mainland China. Three years after the first section of the Kowloon-Guangzhou railway opened in 1910, he built one of the first country houses in the New Territories, close to the Chinese border. In Tianjin the Hotung Baugesellschaft had been established as early as 1906 to hold and develop property in the Austro-Hungarian Concession, and we find him pondering the price of land in the British Concession, next to the Tianjin Club, in 1914.[25] Four years later, still trying to regulate his digestion and undergoing a 'milk cure' at the Battle Creek Sanitarium in Michigan, he was tirelessly writing to Wall Street brokers about American securities.[26]

Letters from this period tell us a great deal about the grand scale of Ho Tung's investments, so when we learn of his contributing to flood relief in central China, endowing a school, or buying an aeroplane for Britain, we are not surprised. We assume that his altruism was spurred by having money to spare. There is a tradition of philanthropy among Chinese, of course, but the truth is never that simple. Some donate money from benevolence, others to assuage a sense of guilt, still others to gain public recognition. It has even been said of Ho Tung that he did so out of superstition, a fortune-teller having apparently foretold a long life, provided he gave some of his wealth away to charitable causes. He did, as it happens, have a weakness for clairvoyants, but if that was one reason for his do-gooding he had another, no less compelling, one—he enjoyed being honoured for it. Human beings are all, to a greater or lesser extent, concerned with social status. Competition for status, as some sociologists claim, underpins our activities: we ally ourselves to those groups we consider worth belonging to, then strive for rank within them. Rank can be based on success—in achieving wealth, for instance—and on prestige, particularly through demonstrations of goodness and virtue, qualities reflected in philanthropy.

In 1914 China's president, Yuan Shikai, awarded Ho Tung a third-class Order of the Excellent Crop; a year later King George V bestowed a knighthood on him in the birthday honours. A telegram from the secretary of state for the colonies, reproduced in the *Hongkong Daily Press* on 4 June 1915, announced: 'It gives me much pleasure to inform you that His Majesty has been graciously pleased to approve of a Knight Bachelorship for Mr Ho Tung'. Britain had turned to her empire for contributions to the war effort; what with the Prince of Wales Relief Fund and other appeals, there were several channels for colonial subjects in Hong Kong to prove their patriotism. Ho Tung subscribed more than the rest. In May 1915 he and his fellow directors at the Tai Yau Bank presented an aeroplane to the War Office, and in December Ho Tung personally gave $50,000 to buy two aeroplanes for the Royal Flying Corps and motor ambulances for the Red Cross and St John of Jerusalem Societies. When an additional seven per cent on Hong Kong property rates was imposed as a special war tax, he undertook to relieve the burden on his tenants by paying the increase himself. It was a fine gesture by the new knight, who was now known as Sir Robert Ho Tung (his daughter Irene confessed that she never knew her father had an English name until she read the report in the newspapers);[27] at the suggestion of a journalist friend, J. P. Braga, the motto 'From Trial to Triumph' (later changed to 'Justice and Truth') was adopted for his coat of arms. Margaret was now Lady Ho Tung; informally, however, family and friends soon slipped into the habit of addressing Sir Robert's two wives as 'Lady Margaret' and 'Lady Clara'. It was a deft solution to what might appear as a slight to Clara, denied a title by protocol though she was an 'equal wife' in Chinese terms. As for the aeroplanes, they were to carry the inscriptions 'Sir Robert Ho Tung, Hongkong' and 'Lady Ho Tung, Hongkong'.[28]

Sir Robert was always tremendously proud of his decorations, which he accumulated apace as the years rolled by. Not to be outdone by King George V, two Chinese presidents upgraded his third-class Order of the Excellent Crop to second-class and finally to a first-class Order with Grand Sash. Other decorations were awarded by the governments or crowned heads of Portugal, France, Italy, Belgium, Annam, and Germany. He did not believe in hiding his light under a bushel either; much of the satisfaction from these honours lay in the wearing of his gleaming stars and ribbons. He was later to expend a great deal of energy trying to gain unrestricted permission from Buckingham Palace to don the insignia of the Order of the Brilliant Jade with Blue Sash, another of his awards from the Chinese government (permission was refused). After the Second World War, when his portrait was commissioned for the Jardines boardroom, and the artist and notable portraitist of British royalty, Sir Oswald Birley, did not fall in with his wish to be painted wearing his decorations, he had the satisfaction of having them depicted anyway, separately on a smaller canvas which still hangs beneath his likeness, showing all twenty-two medals in a row.

He was now a man of stature; if the great and powerful were not quite at his beck and call, at least the governor of Hong Kong usually made himself available for a private word if Sir Robert Ho Tung requested it. A chance to wield this authority came after the end of World War I. One of the provisions of the Treaty of Versailles hammered out at the Paris Peace Conference in 1919 was confirmation of Japan's claim to territories in Shandong Province which were formerly under Germany's sway. Seen as the Allies' betrayal of China, the treaty as formulated was a humiliating blow to Chinese national pride. It triggered a wave of protests, with students taking to the streets and workers laying down their tools in demonstrations, initially in Beijing and spreading to Tianjin, Shanghai, and other cities. These protests were soon conflated with a nationalistic crusade calling for political, cultural, and social reforms to strengthen China, a crusade that became known as the May Fourth Movement. Historians date the emergence of modern Chinese nationalism to this period. People in Hong Kong, though they were too far away to feel the most intense tremors of the movement, nevertheless showed solidarity by shouting anti-Japanese slogans outside a Japanese shop in Wanchai, a busy part of town on Hong Kong Island, and by sporadic boycotts of Japanese goods.[29] They had learnt to use strikes and boycotts to wage war on what they felt to be injustices, as well as to demonstrate their patriotic commitment to China, for all that they lived under British colonial rule. Their usual practice was to decamp to the Chinese mainland, and this is precisely what transpired in January 1922. Over the previous year, the Chinese Seamen's Union had appealed three times for an increase in their members' low rates of pay. At the shipping companies' third refusal, some 10,000 seamen struck and left for Guangzhou. During the next two months, 60,000 labourers, tram drivers, electricians, and other workers in foreign employ came out in sympathy. When the Servants Guild's demand for an eight-hour day and a thirty per cent wage hike was rejected, domestics joined the exodus and left their European employers high and dry. As one newspaper suggested, it was turning into 'a war against the European community'.[30] Approached for help by the colonial

Shipping in Hong Kong harbour, 1920s. Photography courtesy of gwulo.com.

government, the Chinese and Eurasian merchant elite, including Sir Robert Ho Tung, appeared less interested in mediating and more concerned about reining in the power of the labour unions.[31] Were they struggling with a conflict of interest? With shipping and trade at a standstill, the strike was devastating Hong Kong's economy, whose health was always a prime concern of the merchants.

Convoluted negotiations among the Chinese Seamen's Union, shipowners, delegates from the Office of Foreign Affairs in Guangzhou, and Hong Kong government officials eventually culminated in a settlement which more or less met the workers' demands. But then there was an impasse, for they were still unable to come to terms on strike pay. The seamen asked for up to five and a half months' half-pay from the end of the strike to the day they returned to work, but the shipowners were only prepared to cover one month. It was at this critical juncture that Sir Robert approached the governor. He would, he told Sir Reginald Stubbs in a private conversation, make up any difference himself. Sir Robert reiterated his offer to Luk King Fo, Chinese representative of the Guangzhou delegation to Hong Kong, as Luk's letter to the *Hongkong Daily Press* makes clear. He had learnt, Sir Robert said, that

> one of the outstanding points at issue was the half pay to be granted to the seamen before reinstatement pending the ships' return to port. While the shipowners were willing to concede one month's half pay, the delegates asked for 5½ months to provide against the contingency of these ships unable to return before that period, the half pay ceasing immediately upon reinstatement. Sir Robert

expressed to me also that he was very eager that this varying view between the delegates and the shipowners should not be allowed to remain as a stumbling block in the way of a satisfactory settlement . . . he gave the assurance of his personal assurance undertaking that he would himself make good the difference.[32]

Sir Robert's guarantee broke the deadlock and brought off a settlement that same day. Not everyone approved of his scheme, however. The *Daily Press*'s editorial considered the settlement 'humiliating to British pride and prestige', one which moreover was 'pregnant with possibilities of constantly-recurring trouble in the future'. To add insult to injury, the newspaper then accused Sir Robert of being soft on the seamen, implying that his intervention, though well meant, undermined the shipowners' resolve to stand firm against the strikers.[33]

At the conference to sign the final agreement, a fund under the control of an administrator was set up. The relevant clause in the agreement stated only that the fund would in time be responsible for dealing with claims for strike pay for the period of unemployment up to five and a half months. The shipowners' pledge to discharge one month's half-pay should any seaman have to wait for reinstatement by his ship was forgotten, as was Sir Robert's undertaking to bridge the difference between one month and five and a half months. By this stroke the shipowners made Sir Robert liable for the entire sum rather than for claims beyond the first month's half-pay that they had initially guaranteed. But Sir Robert had not actually been invited to the conference, which may account for his promise being misconstrued.

In the event Sir Robert did not dip into his pocket at all, for as soon as settlement was reached the seamen flocked back to their ships. Nor was a single case of difficulty with re-employment brought to the attention of the union; having lain idle in the harbour for so long, the ships were only too eager to be off, and crews were signed on with alacrity. Nevertheless, seven months later the seamen's union presented Sir Robert with a bill for strike pay of $340,000. Not unnaturally he questioned the legitimacy of this claim and asked for proper accounts to be certified by the shipping companies. Those accounts, he said to the union, should provide details of the names of the claimants, their ranks, amounts claimed, and the periods covered. Although no certified accounts were ever produced, it began to be whispered that Sir Robert had reneged on his promise. He was first accused of being a 'labour thief'; in 1926, at the Chinese Seamen's Conference, the communist labour leader Su Zhaozheng condemned Sir Robert as a 'running dog' of imperialism.[34] These criticisms and rumours caused Sir Robert great anguish; he continued to worry about the possible stain on his reputation, on several occasions appealing to the governor and the colonial secretary to put the record straight and make his version of the story more widely known.[35] For instance, he followed up an article in the *Daily Press* on 22 January 1926, which he thought 'capable of an entirely erroneous construction', by a long letter of explanation to the colonial secretary.[36]

At the end of 1922 he celebrated his sixtieth birthday. The anxieties of the past nine months must have left him feeling older, if no less interested in a public role. In fact he had already found another outlet for his still formidable energies. This time he would throw himself into the heat and dust of a much larger arena of action.

6

In Search of a Cause

An inside page of the *Hongkong Telegraph* of 4 September 1895 carries a drawing of a young Chinese dressed in what can only be described as an approximation of a mandarin's robe. A winter hat with its top knob just visible is perched above his high, clean-shaven forehead, and a string of court beads hangs from his neck. The embroidered rank badge on his flowing, loose-sleeved coat is partially hidden by his hand and by the beads, but then an insignia would have been imaginary, anyway, since he was not a Chinese official. Thus had Ho Tung originally appeared in the *San Francisco Chronicle*, from which the portrait in the *Telegraph* was taken. The *Telegraph* then reproduced the accompanying article in its entirety:

> A passenger by the *Peking* yesterday was Ho Tung, a wealthy merchant of Hongkong, who has some interesting things to say of the effects of the late war on the Chinese Government and on trade. Ho Tung speaks English almost fluently, he is a constant reader of English papers and is altogether an exceptionally well-informed man.

This well-informed man observed: 'The war is sure to be a good lesson to China, but it was rather too dear . . . I do not think that taxes will have to be increased to pay the indemnity.'[1]

He went on to explain that, thanks to Sir Robert Hart, the collection of customs duty, a large portion of which used to end up in officials' own pockets, was now competently administered. Higher returns together with improved trade from the opening of more Chinese ports were certain to result in enough income to meet the indemnity payments. Nevertheless there was no doubt, Ho Tung added, that China needed reforming,

> and the principal cause of the delay is that the people pay little attention to the government and are willing to allow the officials to do as they please. They are willing to put up with any sort of government. That feeling is largely the cause of

Ho Tung in the clothes of a Chinese official

the abuses. What they want is an emperor who will make himself seen and felt and let the people know that he is taking an interest in their affairs.[2]

This interview is illuminating in making clear Ho Tung's budding reputation as a commentator on Chinese politics. The war in question was of course the humiliating engagement with Japan which had resulted in a complete rout of the Chinese army and navy. Under the terms of the 1895 Treaty of Shimonoseki which ended it, Korea—a bone of contention and Japan's excuse for the war—emerged independent, Taiwan was ceded to Japan, more treaty ports were created, and a huge indemnity was to be paid. These humbling terms threw the Qing dynasty's decadence into stark relief and pushed nationalistic feelings in radical directions. But for Ho Tung, as for many overseas Chinese, the real political awakening happened as a result of meeting Kang Youwei. Born in Guangdong in 1858, Kang was a brilliant Confucian scholar who, as a young man on a first visit to the British colony of Hong Kong, saw with his own eyes the benefits of Western administration in 'the elegance of the buildings of the foreigners, the cleanliness of the streets, the efficiency of their police'.[3]

Profoundly disenchanted with China's backwardness, repeated military defeats, and humiliating loss of sovereignty, Kang vowed to dedicate his life to his country's salvation. From 1888 he began addressing memorials to the emperor advocating change, at the same time teaching and writing about his social and political theories. At first his memorials were ignored; it was not until the closing years of the nineteenth century, when foreign powers—led by Germany seizing Qingdao in 1897—stepped up their scramble for concessions in China that the sense of national crisis was felt forcibly enough by the throne to summon Kang to court.

At the historic audience in June 1898, the Guangxu emperor could not but be moved by the impassioned scholar, who likened China to

> a large building that, because its timbers have decayed, is about to fall down. If small patches are made to cover up the cracks, then as soon as there is a storm the building will collapse. It is therefore necessary to dismantle the building and build anew if we want something strong and dependable.[4]

Kang also cited the reforms of Peter the Great in Russia and of the Meiji emperor in Japan as templates for modernising China; notable among his suggestions for institutional change was the construction of a national railway network, an idea echoed by Ho Tung in 1901. Following his audience with Kang an excited Guangxu made haste to adopt the proposed reforms: over the summer of 1898 he issued a veritable barrage of edicts ordering changes in education, the civil service, and industry, and encouraged officials to make study tours abroad. Unfortunately these 'Hundred-Day Reforms' were to wither on the vine: not only were they not implemented, but the emperor himself would be punished for his pains. Alarmed by the reforms' radical nature, the deeply conservative officials at court urged the emperor's aunt, the empress dowager Cixi, to oppose them. Convinced that Guangxu was plotting against her, she moved swiftly to put him under house arrest at the Summer Palace outside Beijing and to take power into her own hands.

Before the empress dowager could round up Kang, he had fled to Tianjin and from there by an English steamer to Shanghai, where a warrant for his arrest had preceded him. Meanwhile, six of Kang's supporters, including his younger brother Guangren, were captured by the police in Beijing and summarily beheaded for treason. Kang was able to elude his pursuers, however, for the British consul at Shanghai offered protection and arranged for him to travel on to Hong Kong. It is at this point that Ho Tung enters the story:

> As I knew K'ang a little before, with the consent of the Hong Kong Government I went on board with Mr Dyer Ball, then Secretary for Chinese Affairs, to receive K'ang and he was temporarily lodged at the Central Police Station as a political refugee.[5]

Their slight acquaintance (which might have been made in Guangzhou) was now turned to good account by the fugitive, who asked Ho Tung for help. Clearly he could not stay indefinitely at the police station; on being appealed to by Henry May, captain superintendent of police, Ho Tung 'gladly acceded' to the request to provide Kang with shelter. Kang's two wives and daughters, as well as his mother, his brother's widow and daughter, had also managed to escape to Hong Kong; some of the family, if not all, were accommodated at Idlewild for about two months. Ho Tung left this account of his house guest:

> During his stay with us many visitors came to see him every day and we had to provide at short notice several lunches or dinners for his friends. Whilst he was staying in my house he confided to me his scheme for the capture of Canton with about 50 of his followers because although he was supporting the emperor in name, actually he and his Party were also revolutionaries if necessary. He pressed upon me to give my opinion and I told him at once that his scheme was entirely unpractical and would certainly lead to a complete failure with the loss of many lives.[6]

In fact, at that stage Kang was still fervently loyalist, and indeed showed by his next moves that he had no thought of overthrowing the Qing dynasty, for he bent his efforts towards raising international support for restoring Guangxu to power. To rally Chinese subjects around the world, he left Hong Kong, generously funded by Ho Tung, taking ship first for Japan, then travelling on to North America. Landing in Victoria, British Columbia, he was welcomed by the Canadian Chinese community very enthusiastically, even if he would depart empty-handed from the visit. His hopes of enlisting the British government to his aid were also dashed, for the simple reason that parliament could not quite decide where its best interests in China lay, and, being in doubt, voted to take no action.

Returning to British Columbia, Kang fell back on the rich overseas Chinese, always ready with donations to demonstrate their patriotism, a patriotism that was still, for some, a desire to see China regain her strength through the development of a modern constitutional monarchy. There, on the west coast of Canada, Kang founded the Protecting-Emperor Society (Baohuanghui). Through branches which soon proliferated in the Chinatowns of North America, funds were collected and remitted back to Hong Kong and China (occasionally through the intermediary services of Ho Tung). The society enjoyed widespread support until the more radical republican movement instigated by Dr Sun Yat-sen eclipsed its influence some seven or eight years on.

If Ho Tung had misgivings about Kang's 'revolutionary' ardour, he was nevertheless unstinting in his support. It was impossible not to be inspired by this

Sketch in Shanghai Daily *depicting Kang Youwei and his adherents preparing to address memorials to the emperor, advocating reforms and the modernisation of China*

dynamic and articulate reformer; nor did Margaret and Clara escape the influence of his ideas. Part of being modern was to believe in the equality of women and to work towards their emancipation; for years Kang had protested against the barbaric practice of foot-binding, emphatically forbidding it for his own daughters. In March 1900 we hear of 'Mrs Ho Tung' (presumably Margaret) being invited to a meeting of the Natural Feet Society (Tianzuhui) at Government House, where she pledged 'to do what I can to get rid of this cruel custom'.[7]

In early 1900 Kang revisited Hong Kong and again asked Ho Tung if he might put up at Idlewild. 'This time I politely declined to have the honour and a house in Hollywood Road near the Central Police Station was rented as his lodgings,' Ho Tung recalled. Perhaps it had become clear to him that frustration with the lack of progress in China had made Kang desperate: the empress dowager Cixi still held sway at court and Guangxu remained in confinement at the Summer Palace. Later events suggest that, by the time Kang returned to Hong Kong, he was already deeply involved in an armed offensive to be launched by his follower Tang Caichang. Planned to start in Hankou in August 1900, the uprising eventually ended in disaster, with the plot exposed before it could be implemented and Tang losing his life. We can be sure that Ho Tung recoiled from such acts of violence.

Nor was he ready to nail his colours to the Qing dynasty's mast. At the height of the Boxer Rebellion—in fact on the day that the allied foreign forces left Tianjin for Beijing to relieve the siege of the legations—he obeyed a summons to see the elder statesman Li Hongzhang, governor-general of Guangdong and Guangxi at the time. By the turn of the century Ho Tung had clearly been marked out by Chinese officialdom as someone who could be of infinite use. On 4 August 1900, while he and Margaret were en route to the United States, a meeting was arranged in Shanghai, where their steamer *Empress of China* briefly docked. He felt embroiled against his will, for the dilemma in prospect did not admit an easy resolution. Here was Li Hongzhang, a minister of the Qing and servant of the empress dowager, and there was Ho Tung, a manifest supporter of Kang Youwei, Cixi's enemy. Unlikely as it was that they would see eye to eye, Li nevertheless asked Ho Tung to drum up funds from the Protecting-Emperor Society in San Francisco for the purpose of expanding China's navy. Commenting on this four decades later, Ho Tung said that he would not have acted fairly by Kang if he had gone ahead. At the time the events were unfolding, however, his ambivalent position caused him great worry. Li terminated the interview by promising that an official dispatch to confirm his instructions would follow Ho Tung to San Francisco.

Shortly after arrival in San Francisco Ho Tung put himself into the care of the Waldeck Sanitarium. He had just resigned his compradoreship of Jardines and was looking forward to a rest cure. The delicate state of his health was an abiding preoc-cupation with him, as was the preservation of his good name. He could not bear his character to be impugned. It is anyone's guess whether his vulnerability to criti-cism had anything to do with his humble birth, or whether he was as often ill as he claimed, but he did expend an inordinate amount of energy on these sensitivities. In the course of his travels he received news of the aborted Hankou uprising. Funds raised in San Francisco and Honolulu before his arrival had already been remitted to Shanghai and Macau but had plainly failed to reach Tang Caichang in time. The atmosphere was hardly conducive to further fund-raising; nevertheless, on receipt of Li Hongzhang's dispatch in late September, Ho Tung duly called upon the Chinese consul-general, Ho Yow, with whom he was very likely acquainted, and asked whether he could count on Ho Yow's cooperation if fund-raising was to be undertaken.[8] Ho Yow advised Ho Tung first to seek approval from the minister for China in Washington, DC, who was none other than his old acquaintance Ng Choy, or Wu Tingfang. Later, in November, when Ho Tung felt more robust, he took soundings from several leading Chinese in San Francisco, even going so far as to show the dispatch to them all, over a dinner given in his honour at a Chinese restaurant in Dupont Street. Their discussions were inconclusive; at any rate, Ho Tung sensed that he had gone as far as his caution and his conscience could allow. Stress took its toll again; almost the day after the dinner, he suffered a relapse. He now had no better justification for bowing out of the whole affair, and as soon as he could he made his excuses to Li Hongzhang by letter.

There would be an unpleasant postscript to the proceedings, however, a reflection of the high emotions aroused in the breast of some overseas Chinese where the motherland was concerned. Some months later a Chinese consulate attaché Chan Pak-choi insinuated in a letter to the *China-Western Daily News* (*Zhongxi ribao*), a journal published in America, that Ho Tung's authority to raise donations was spurious. Outraged by this traducement, Ho Tung made an enormous effort to obtain a public apology and retraction. To be sure that all shadow of doubt was expunged, he explained the whole to Wu Tingfang. His sense of grievance was obvious:

> How and why Mr Chan Pak Choi should attack me in the name of the Consulate and publicly in such a manner without first obtaining your Excellency's authority or even that of Mr Ho Yow, is entirely incomprehensible to me. The original draft to the Chung Sai Yat Po [also *Zhongxi ribao*, or *China-Western Daily News*], which later, I had the opportunity of seeing, is even more abusive, insulting and intolerable than the letter as published, as the attacks therein were not only directed to myself but also to my parents. Fortunately, the editor refused to publish those most objectionable parts; otherwise, it would have made matters worse.

Was Chan's attack on Ho Tung's parents a crude reference to their irregular liaison? If so, it must have touched a very tender spot with Ho Tung. He had always been private about the details of his birth and would remain so to the end of his life. He continues in his letter to Wu:

> On Sunday afternoon the 6th inst., upon the invitation of Mr Ho Yow, I called at the Consulate and, after showing Mr. Chan Pak Choi the original despatch in the presence of the Consul General and others, I endeavoured by every honorable means to induce him to write me a letter of retraction or apology for publication, which he promised to do, but to my great surprise he sent me the inclosed note (copy only), which Your Excellency will readily perceive is no retraction or apology at all. In the contrary, it but adds insult to injury.
>
> Your Excellency having known for many years my personal character and standing, I have no doubt but that Your Excellency will see a way to do me justice before the public so as to remove the false opinion concerning me which may have been created by the unwarranted attacks of Mr Chan Pak Choi.[9]

It was not until the Ho Tungs reached New York some three months later, to a favourable reception by the *New York Times*, that the petty wrangles of west-coast Chinatowns could be forgotten. Ho Tung, or H.T. Bosman as he called himself on this visit, though he possessed the 'physical characteristics of the Oriental', struck the reporter as 'altogether Occidental' in manner, dress, and habits of thought. 'He discusses in perfect English enterprises of large scope, with a mental grasp which equals that of his distinguished countryman, Mr Wu T'ing-fang. But, although a fellow countryman, Mr Bosman is not a compatriot of Mr Wu, being a British subject himself and a Justice of the Peace in His Majesty's service,' the paper reported.[10]

The purpose of this interview was to solicit Ho Tung's views on solutions to the 'China problem' then preoccupying not only the United States but also Britain, Germany, Russia, France, and Japan, among several foreign powers. In the previous summer, the world had been gripped by news of the Boxers' siege of the legation quarter in Beijing. Made up of secret-society members and disaffected peasants who denounced the West's intrusion into China as the root of all their economic ills, the Boxers had begun by wreaking their vengeance on foreign missionaries and Chinese Christians in Shandong before proceeding to Beijing. There they shot dead the German minister and forced the foreign community to retreat behind a roughly assembled barricade around the legation quarter, in which, surrounded by Boxers and imperial troops and repeatedly fired upon, the diplomatic corps, missionaries, teachers, officials, and their families sweltered for fifty-five days. At last, on 14 August 1900, an allied force of European and Japanese troops arrived to raise the siege and compel the Qing court, which had backed the Boxers, to submit to stringent terms. These included a staggeringly large indemnity to compensate for the loss of lives and property in Beijing, which aroused much debate in early 1901.

Ho Tung's interest in the Boxer indemnity was sharpened by events only a month before his interview. In March, the American commissioner-plenipotentiary in China had proposed an indemnity of £40 million, a sum already considerable but deemed insufficient by the German delegate, who increased it to £63 million. Payable over thirty-nine years with interest, the indemnity would have a crippling effect on the Chinese economy. At the interview Ho Tung proposed a compromise:

> I believe that this is a golden opportunity for the introduction of Western ideas into the Middle Kingdom, and that the apparent disagreement of the powers on the amount of indemnity to be paid for the Boxer disturbances should lead to some sort of compromise having for its object the development of undeveloped Asia, rather than the levying of a mere monetary fine, which could be raised by additional taxation, and in the end perhaps leave the real status of the country

unchanged. I have a plan in my own mind which I think is worthy of the attention of the diplomats, because I believe it would be a civilizing influence. It is this:
Let the powers agree upon the amount of indemnity to be paid and then contract
among themselves and with the Peking Government that the entire sum, say $200
million, shall be used for building railroads and for other internal improvements
in China under the joint control of the powers, to be operated by them until the
full amount of the investment is returned, and until China is in a position to
become, by purchase, the sole owner of the improvements.[11]

In an editorial published the next day, the paper praised his proposal as 'so
attractive that we shall be disappointed if it does not meet with a wide suggestion
as the solution of the pending "China problem".' That foreign investors were in
favour of extending railway-building loans to China can be seen from the fact that
tracks laid between 1900 and 1905 were to increase nearly twelve-fold compared
to the previous five years. But railroad development proved yet another way for
Japan and the West to encroach upon Chinese sovereignty; as far as nationalistic
reformers were concerned, it was another nail in the coffin of the Qing government. A growing number of Chinese overseas had also begun to despair of the
progressive approach; that China would be saved only through revolution was
becoming more apparent as time went by. It was certainly a conviction held ever
more intensely by Sun Yat-sen.

In the spring of 1884, six years after Ho Tung left the Central School, an
eighteen-year-old from a village near Guangzhou enrolled for its classes as Sun
Tai-tseung. He would become renowned as Sun Yat-sen. Among his contemporar-
ies at the school were Ho Kai-gai or Walter Bosman (who won the Government
Scholarship that year) and Lau Chu-pak (later a partner of Sir Robert Ho Tung's
at the Tai Yau Bank). For a month before his entry Sun had been studying at the
Diocesan Home and Orphanage; before that he had attended Oahu College in
Honolulu. In 1887, after return visits to Honolulu and Guangzhou, he proceeded
to the College of Medicine at the Alice Memorial Hospital, where he was one of
the first students of its dean, Dr James Cantlie, and from which he graduated in
1892.

His medical career was brief; for a time he had a practice in the Portuguese
colony of Macau. Fifty years later Sir Robert recalled making his acquaintance
there, admitting that, although he had not at first thought Sun in any way remarkable, he would fall under the spell of the doctor's magnetic personality later. In
1894, gathering support among overseas Chinese to overthrow the Qing dynasty,
Sun had established the Revive China Society (Xingzhonghui) in Hawaii. Back
in Hong Kong a year later, he organised a base for the society there and laid his
plans for a coup in Guangzhou, but despite the ingenious ploy of concealing guns

in cement barrels, the scheme was discovered before a single shot was fired. His presence now became an embarrassment to the colonial government, which, under pressure from Guangzhou, banned Sun from Hong Kong for five years.

In the notes he kept for his memoirs, Sir Robert makes no mention of being involved in the republican movement. He recorded his encounters with Sun in a matter-of-fact way, merely casting himself in the role of an intercessor between the Guangzhou government and the colonial authorities in Hong Kong. If he ever assumed a more activist part, it was thought to have been in another abortive uprising in 1903, of which Sun, in Indochina at the time, was apparently unaware. For this attack an attempt was once more made to smuggle arms into Guangzhou, this time in coffins; again the conspiracy was detected before it could be launched. An agent of the Qing later alleged that Ho Tung was implicated; in a confidential dispatch from the Hong Kong governor, Sir Henry Blake, to the British Foreign Office, which contains a translation of 'what purports to be a report by a Chinese military officer . . . obtained from Canton by means of a bribe', Ho Tung and seventeen other Chinese residents were named as having been concerned in the rebellion.

A British subject Ho Tung, 'alias Ho Tu Shang Compradore in Jardine, Matheson and Company, a native of Heung Shan, tall, with false teeth and wearing European clothing', heads the list in the report, together with other prominent Hong Kong figures such as Tse Tsan-tai and Lau Chu-pak.[12] Whether this nomination was fact or conjecture, we know of no serious repercussions for Ho Tung or the others afterwards. The report contains some errors of detail, which cannot but cast doubt on the agent's sources of information. It is all the easier to distrust the agent's story when we learn that the leader of the failed revolt was Tse Tsan-tai, the polemical letter-writer who had opposed the appointment of Ho Tung to the Legislative Council the previous summer (see Chapter 5). It is questionable whether Ho Tung and Tse Tsan-tai would have made comradely co-conspirators.

Other attempts at revolution, orchestrated from Hong Kong or abroad, were made from time to time until the successful mutiny in Wuchang in 1911, which turned the tide in favour of the republicans. But the collapse of empire did not mean the end of Sun's struggles. Though elected provisional president of the new republic in Nanjing on the first day of 1912, he would yield the presidency to the army chief Yuan Shikai, who proceeded to establish a government in Beijing. The ambitious Yuan soon overreached himself, however, betraying Sun's revolution by proclaiming himself emperor in 1915. Only on his sudden death in 1916 were his monarchical designs halted, but the power vacuum that resulted simply unleashed civil strife, as military commanders started jostling for dominance. Thus began what historians call the warlord period. By 1917 many provinces had broken free of the control of the central government. Sun was driven back to his old base, Guangzhou, where he set up a government under his recently formed Nationalist Party or Kuomintang (Guomindang).

The early republican years also witnessed the rise of fierce nationalism among many Western-influenced intellectuals in China. Ho Tung, too, was thinking more deeply about Chinese politics around this time. Unlike the intellectuals he was not turning philosophical, ideological, or partisan, but like them he felt the tug of patriotism. Since before the First World War he had begun spending more time in China, initially passing summers in Shanhaiguan or Qingdao, and afterwards establishing a residence in Shanghai. He was all too aware of the chaos and flux of national life, of the dizzying changes of leadership and power which brought to the fore many men of rampant ambition but no heroes. Existing simultaneously were a government in Beijing under the sway of one warlord clique after another, autonomous warlord domains in the provinces, Marshal Zhang Zuolin's sphere of influence in the strategically important region of Manchuria, and Sun's Nationalist regime in Guangzhou. (In 1926 Zhang Zuolin had a fleeting moment of glory when he gained control of Beijing, the seat of the internationally recognised Beiyang government. He was killed in 1928 by a bomb planted by an officer of the Japanese Kwantung Army, which controlled the South Manchurian Railway.)

Sir Robert was clearly of interest to more than one faction, for in May 1921 we hear of him being invited to a special audience and banquet with President Xu Shichang in Beijing.[13] Xu Shichang, a Qing official before the empire was toppled in 1911, was elected president of the Republic of China in 1918 and served until 1922, staying in power by keeping his distance from the various militarist warlord cliques. He was succeeded briefly by Li Yuanhong. That Sir Robert's visit coincided with the arrival of Hong Kong's governor, Sir Reginald Stubbs, on a separate errand to negotiate coal-mining rights on behalf of British investors, was too surprising for rumour mongers to ignore. Feelings in Guangzhou were already running high over the foreign acquisition of mining concessions, regarded by many as the thin end of the wedge where China's sovereignty over Guangdong Province was concerned. Reports were then published in the Chinese newspapers implying that Sir Robert was in Beijing not only in connection with the coal agreement but also to assist the government with money to finance a military expedition against Guangdong. Determined to scotch these rumours, he thought he should appeal to the foreign minister, his old friend Wu Tingfang. There was absolutely no truth, he stressed, in any of the rumours; he had

> come up on a pleasure trip which may combine with certain business proposi-
> tions that have been submitted to me since my arrival. These propositions have

all to do with commercial and industrial enterprises and have no relation to politics. It obviously is . . . absurd to connect me with hostility towards Kwangtung [Guangdong] . . . You know very well the extent of my interests in Hong Kong. You know also that I have always held that what is good for the trade and commerce of Canton is also good for Hong Kong and vice versa . . . At the same time I hold as you yourself have more than once particularly expressed to me, that a unified country is the greatest blessing we can hope to secure for the wonderful country of China and her people. I have, therefore, a great wish to be of service towards its unification. If, therefore, at any time you think my humble efforts might be utilised in the service of China in the direction of securing the end in view, I hope you will not hesitate to indicate to me the manner how best I may be useful to you and to the country . . .

I am having a very enjoyable time in Peking using a very fine furnished house kindly placed at my disposal by a friend in the West City. If there is anything I can do for you here please command me.[14]

To Sir Robert's consternation the foreign minister showed himself sceptical. Wu's reply began politely enough—he expressed his pleasure at learning that the rumours were unfounded—but his words soon took on a more challenging tone.[15] Having expected Sir Robert to be heading north to Shanhaiguan, 'where you had spent several summers before and where you still have a quantity of furniture stored', he was astonished to find that Sir Robert was staying put at a friend's 'fine furnished house'. Beijing, well known to be a dusty and very hot city in summer, he continued,

is not the place for a wealthy man seeking rest and health as all foreign diplomats and others, unless detained by necessity, generally flee from Peking and go to the Western Hills or to Peiteiho [Beidaihe]. You say that certain business propositions have been submitted to you since your arrival, that these propositions have no connection to politics and are industrial and commercial enterprises. Let me as on old friend give you honest and disinterested advice. Don't fall into the trap of these schemers who in order to lure you will not scruple to hold out fine and bright prospects for their propositions.

Now Sir Robert, you are reputed to be the richest man in Hong Kong, and as you are not young you should no longer embark on new schemes. I would strongly advise you to be content with what you have but do not worry yourself with schemes for adding more wealth which cannot possibly make you more happy but may cause you anxiety and trouble. I appreciate your good wish to see China reunited and your loyal offer of service to that end. This is what I have been endeavouring to accomplish during the last several years but I find all my efforts have been thwarted by the militarists, bigoted officials and wily politicians. As you are in Peking you must be aware that Hsu Shih-ch'ang [Xu Shichang] and his Cabinet are under the domination of the warlords and have to obey their sweet wills. Hsu Shih-ch'ang and his party are, as is well known, utterly unfit to run the government on modern lines or honestly without corruption. China has become insolvent through their maladministration . . . Reunification is a grand idea but can it be accomplished with such incompetent and corrupt officials for the benefit of the nation?

. . . What is urgently needed is an honest, clean and competent government conducted on modern lines. This is being done in Canton by the provisional authorities and by the members of the federal administration.

He added in a postscript,

Since you are anxious to see China reunited it occurs to me that the best thing you can do under the present circumstances is to advocate the withdrawal of the recognition of the Peking government by Foreign Powers, because as long as the Foreign Powers continue their recognition of Hsu Shih-ch'ang and his government relying on the goodwill of the foreign nations will make no efforts to introduce real reforms and China will become worse and worse every day . . . You will be doing a good thing for China if you carry out what I suggest by constantly speaking to the British officials and merchants at Peking and elsewhere.

As we saw in the previous chapter, Wu Tingfang—or Ng Choy in Hong Kong—comfortably straddled allegiances to both colonial Hong Kong and to China. Following a financial setback in Hong Kong, he accepted an offer from Li Hongzhang in 1877 to work in China. He was all too aware of China's weakness

Wu Tingfang, foreign minister under Sun Yat-sen, early twentieth century

and, given his upbringing and career in the colony, he was predisposed to put his trust in Western, British-style liberalism for saving the country.[16] He believed in negotiation rather than confrontation; the stance of reformers like Kang Youwei struck him as too radical. On the other hand, he had no illusions about the foreign powers' inclination invariably to keep the peace and protect their financial and commercial interests. He had little time left, however, to provide further support to the provisional government in Guangzhou, for he would die there the year after his correspondence with Sir Robert.

Wu Tingfang's advice—'as you are not young you should no longer embark on new schemes'—was too much for Sir Robert, and one detects an uncharacteristically waspish note in his answer.[17] He was the last man to tolerate aspersions on his old age. Wu was mistaken if he thought 'that in taking up new schemes in commercial and industrial enterprises I am actuated solely with the object of acquiring more wealth'; after all, he said, it was precisely those who had attained a certain age and accumulated a certain amount of wealth who could afford to be altruistic, to foster new enterprises for the benefit of their country and its people. And far from taking up cudgels for the Guangzhou government, he had no intention of persuading foreign powers to transfer recognition from Beijing to Guangzhou. 'That is a matter not within my province. Speaking as a layman and not a professional politician, which I am not, I think your government and the Peking government should adopt a give-and-take method and endeavour to reach a modus vivendi satisfactory to all parties concerned. A little good will, and a little conciliation may effect incalculable good,' he suggested.

His own good will was to the fore when he accepted an invitation to a lunch given by Xu Shichang for Governor Sir Reginald Stubbs; the day before he returned to Hong Kong, he had another audience with the president. He emerged from this meeting with the second-class Order of the Excellent Crop with Brilliancy, an appointment as honorary adviser to the president of the Chinese Republic, and another as honorary adviser to the Chinese delegation to the Washington Conference.[18] Convened by US president Warren Harding, the Washington Conference (November 1921–February 1922) sought ways to limit the build-up of naval power of the main signatories (USA, Britain, and Japan), in the process helping China towards a stable and sovereign government. The conference discussions centred on disarmament and maintaining peace in East Asia and the Pacific, and provided for the abolition of extraterritoriality in China. In one of the agreements resulting from the conference Japan agreed to return the formerly German-controlled territory in Shandong, including Qingdao—a bone of contention at the Paris Peace Conference in 1919. Sir Robert's participation in the conference amounted to no more, however, than lending his name.

Sir Robert had ignored Wu Tingfang's advice to have nothing to do with the Beijing government; on the other hand, he was not going to rebuff overtures from the Guangzhou regime either. He seemed not in the least troubled about where his political loyalties should lie. Sun Yat-sen remained interested in Sir Robert, constantly in need of financial backing as he was for his administration in the south. When Sun made a visit to Hong Kong in 1923, we have Sir Robert's word that he urged the governor to agree to a private meeting.[19] Sir Reginald Stubbs, it transpired, was more than happy to welcome the revolutionary and gave a lunch at Government House for him. It must have given Sir Robert immense satisfaction to be one of such an exclusive party. Sun, his fellow revolutionary Eugene Chen, and Sir Robert were the only guests, and we can be sure that Morris 'Two-gun' Cohen, Sun's bodyguard, was not far away. In the afternoon Sun was entertained to tea at Idlewild—still with Cohen close at his heels—and confided to Sir Robert his hopes of raising funds to demobilise half his troops and of creating a stable government in Guangzhou.[20] He may very well also have alluded to his frustration with the state of the republic, now fast unravelling as one warlord clique fought another.

A day or so later Sun was invited to deliver an address at the University of Hong Kong. When his car pulled up at the gate, four eager students carried him into the hall on their shoulders. Sir Robert's undergraduate son Eddie, chairman of the students' union that year, made the introductory speech. Dr Sun then spoke for an hour, remembering his school days and touching on the seminal role Hong Kong had played in his revolutionary and modern thinking. Years later Sir Robert recalled that he was present when Sun spoke.[21] Why was Hong Kong, Sun had asked himself, with its clean streets and beautiful parks, so different from the disorderly and backward village in his native Guangdong, when they were only fifty miles apart? 'Afterwards I saw the outside world, and I began to wonder how it was that foreigners, that Englishmen could do such things as they had done, for example with the barren rock of Hong Kong.'[22] As a medical man his object was to treat physical ills, but he had soon been driven to the conclusion that it was better to cure his country than his patients. His praise of the British parliamentary system as an example of good government drew deafening cheers from the audience.

Within two years of this visit Sun would travel north to Beijing for a conference on national unification; by the following spring he would die there, a profoundly disappointed man, his vision shattered. He had nevertheless lit the torch of reunification, and the flame continued to burn, if fitfully. Kang Youwei felt no less agonised about a fragmented China; from Shanghai, where he had more or less settled after the revolution, he regularly bombarded the warlords with telegrams and memorials on the subject of reunification.

Sir Robert, too, had been touched by the reformers' patriotic fervour. After his sojourn in Beijing in the summer of 1921 he must often have mulled over Wu Tingfang's words; he was certainly preoccupied by his own wish, as he had said, to be of service towards the unification of China. Increasingly he found himself wondering what could be done to save the country. He looked about for a cause to take himself onto the national stage. It was true that China had disintegrated and coalesced many times in its history, but never had it seemed so divided and chaotic as in the warlord era. The answer that came to him, like all great ideas, seemed stunningly simple. Surely the warlords should be brought together, face to face, to settle their differences and work towards a peaceful resolution? Was he not exalted enough to win their confidence? As the notion took hold, he became convinced that, once the warlords could be persuaded to meet around a conference table, half the battle would be won. And how appropriate it would be to hold the conference in Hong Kong, a neutral territory, and to invite members of the diplomatic corps to participate as observers—here at last was a cause worthy of him.

And so in 1922 he set himself to the task. First he founded an Association for the Promotion of Internal Peace, to whose executive committee of twelve he invited the chairman of the Shanghai General Chamber of Commerce, the chief editor of the publishing corporation Commercial Press, and other luminaries. Then followed for him nearly two years of toil, excitement, even glory. To rally public opinion the committee, with Sir Robert in the chair, began by seeking pledges of support from the principal military and political figures in the land. Once those leaders had consented in principle, he felt, assembling them in one place would be only a matter of time. An editorial in the *China Mail* applauded his initiative. There were indeed many Chinese who might help, it suggested, omitting

> the rival warlords, who are too busy scheming their own ends; who are too confident that they can solve the problem by conquest . . . who are anyway too deeply involved in ancient feuds for their action to be above suspicion now . . . But [those] patriots who would openly champion the unity cause . . . lack either the energy or the courage. These men, be their homes in the North or the South, can alone save China. But they must be led. Only one real leader has yet arisen to guide them, to weld their views into that potent weapon which even the greatest warlord cannot ignore—public opinion. This leader, as all the world now knows, is Sir Robert Ho Tung. Hongkong may be rightly proud that one of its citizens should have been found to accept this onerous role.[23]

His project threatened to founder, however, almost as soon as it commenced, for in early 1922 fighting broke out between the so-called Zhili Clique of warlords, whose authority encompassed seven provinces in north and central China, and the Fengtian Army, led by Zhang Zuolin, which controlled Manchuria. When the Zhili Clique emerged victorious, a short-lived possibility of peaceful reunification did materialise, only to be crushed by the more pugnacious stance of the Luoyang faction under Wu Peifu, who favoured a military takeover. Nevertheless Sir Robert lost no time in approaching the Zhili Clique's presidential candidate, Li Yuanhong, and it was no doubt with a sense of accomplishment that he was able to send a press release to the Hong Kong papers announcing President Li's support a year later.[24] The picture Sir Robert leaves of Li in his recollections, though, is not as a statesman but as a private citizen out of office, living in Tianjin in a beautiful house with a theatre graced on several occasions by the famous opera singer Mei Lanfang.[25] From President Li he received the first-class Order of the Excellent Crop with Grand Sash.

Through the summer and autumn of 1923 Sir Robert was unremitting in his drive to secure pledges from Chinese leaders. General Lu Yongxiang, *dujun* (military commander or 'big warlord') of Zhejiang, promised to co-operate 'with his handful of earth to shake the course of the stream';[26] Zhang Zuolin sent a letter through his Chief of Staff expressing himself entirely in favour of the proposal; Tang Jiyao, *dujun* of Yunnan, replied in similar vein; and even Wellington Koo, the foreign minister at Beijing, wrote to wish him success. He was particularly flattered to be asked to present his plan at a dinner given by Qi Xieyuan, the warlord of Jiangsu, in the former Nanjing palace of Taiping Heavenly King Hong Xiuquan.

He also solicited the approval of Sun Yat-sen and Wu Peifu, arguably the most powerful *dujun* in China at the time. While the former reiterated his promise to attend the conference 'if other principal leaders will meet me',[27] the latter loftily issued an invitation.

Sir Robert needed no persuasion, and the visit made in the winter of 1923 turned out to be the experience of a lifetime. 'Mrs Ho Tung' accompanied him, though it was actually Clara, not Margaret. Luoyang, once a capital city, lies east of the middle stretch of the Yellow River, high up in the hilly loessland of northwest Henan, about a day and a half's train ride from Shanghai. At every station, goes an account written by an English secretary of Sir Robert's entourage, a guard of honour was drawn up on the platform, and as bugles sounded and bands played, Sir Robert would alight to make an inspection.[28] By nightfall this routine had become so tiresome that Sir Robert could bear it no longer, finally resorting to making his excuses and sending an aide to distribute his name card to the honour guards instead.

At Luoyang, where their coach was shunted off to Marshal Wu's headquarters, the party was met by two cars, one of which immediately whisked Sir Robert off to see his host. Wu was writing telegrams in his office. Sir Robert's instant impression was of an 'extraordinary man, with sparkling eyes, a high nose and a moustache which was rather reddish in colour.'[29] The warlord's brilliant and highly unusual amber eyes were indeed remembered by all who met him.[30] We have another image of him

> in a cotton gown in a rough office with ordinary wooden chairs, a cheap wooden table and bare, unplastered walls, and privates came and went without ceremony. Between his quarters and those of his lieutenants there was no mark of distinction. Between his clothes and those of a moderately successful lantern-shop proprietor the distinction would be all in the shopkeeper's favour. Tall, thin and somewhat bowed, with the face and manner of a student, he, like Chang Tso-lin [Zhang Zuolin], looks more the esthete than the warrior. But unlike Chang Tso-lin, he really is a scholar, if not an esthete.[31]

Earlier that year, this scholar-warrior had put down a workers' strike on the Hankou–Beijing railway line with callous and bloody dispatch. He was nevertheless still regarded as an honourable man, a leader with enough prestige and muscle to stop the civil war and help mould a national government. His imprimatur was crucial to Sir Robert's round-table conference. On the first evening the guests were of course wined and dined. The next day the two men got down to business. Wu agreed that Sir Robert should try to see the new president in Beijing: just two months previously the warlord Cao Kun had ousted Li Yuanhong and greased his way to the presidency by bribery. On the important question of whether Wu would himself consent to attend a peace conference, however, the Luoyang *dujun* 'expressed the opinion that the present time was premature for such a move.'[32]

The warlord Wu Peifu, about eight years before Sir Robert visited him in Luoyang

Without Wu's endorsement the proposed conference was all but scuppered, although Sir Robert kept his hopes alive for several more years. In 1928 he found himself drawn into warlord politics once again, but in a field closer to home. The flotation of a massive loan to the Guangzhou government, in which he was asked to participate, was played out against a China that was still politically riven. As recounted earlier, Sun Yat-sen's party, the Kuomintang, managed to organise a government in Guangzhou in 1917. Co-existing simultaneously with a warlord government in Beijing, this national government planned to embark on recon-struction and transform Guangzhou into a modern city. To implement such a plan, it hoped to garner contributions from its prosperous merchant community, a community which already had strong social and economic ties to Chinese entre-preneurs in Hong Kong. Sir Robert was, of course, a leader among those entrepre-neurs. In the spring of 1928, when the Guangzhou authorities tried to raise a loan in Hong Kong, Sir Robert was invited to visit by the military leader Li Jishen. Sir Miles Lampson, the British minister to China (1926–1933), took a marked inter-est in the negotiations:

> The credit of the present Canton government is practically nil. This question of financial aid to General Li Chai-sum [Li Jishen] is a most important one and my feeling is that, as it is to our interest that he should remain in power and con-solidate his position, we should certainly not discourage any attempt that may be made in Hong Kong, or elsewhere, to help him meet his financial difficulties, provided he can establish the necessary credit.[33]

Sir Miles Lampson's attitude exactly reflected the ambivalence of the Foreign Office towards the various regimes in China: on the one hand, it preferred to recognise Beijing as the legitimate government; on the other, it would attempt to navigate the confused political situation in China for its own economic benefit if it could. In this case, Sir Miles considered it to be in Britain's interest that Li Jishen should remain in power and for a loan to be floated to keep him there. But such a loan, he observed, could not come from His Majesty's Government or the Government of Hong Kong. It was instead up to the Chinese merchants in Guangzhou and Hong Kong to decide whether to back the new regime with something more tangible than mere good wishes. Sir Robert Ho Tung, 'the head of a well-known family, which comprises many of the leading compradores of foreign firms and controls a good deal of the native wealth of the Colony', might just be the man to head a loan syndicate. It seems that the overtures of Xu Shichang, Li Yuanhong, and the Beijing government were forgotten. It was now the Guangzhou government's turn to woo the southern capitalists. Sir Robert duly arrived in Guangzhou, no doubt bearing good wishes, but his undertaking to anchor a loan for five million dollars on the security of 'the Washington surtaxes' was what Li Jishen really wanted. Astute businessman that he was, though, Sir Robert doubted whether, in the absence of tax collection by the Chinese Maritime Customs (formerly the Imperial Maritime Customs), he could induce his friends to lend their money on such security. Negotiations nevertheless continued: we hear of a syndicate consisting principally of Sir Robert Ho Tung and E. D. Sassoon and Company proposing to underwrite an issue of bonds for three million dollars by the Guangzhou government, with the Hong Kong merchants raising the balance.[34] In the event the loan fell through, the face-saving reason given being the excessive terms demanded. Actually, it was the Foreign Office that withdrew its support: besides uncertainty about the Chinese authorities' ability to honour the loan, political concerns had also become pressing. The loan negotiations took place in a tumultuous period during which the Kuomintang armies were steadily regaining control of the country from the warlords. Sun Yat-sen had died in the spring of 1925; his successor in the party was the young officer Chiang Kai-shek (Jiang Jieshi), who moved the party's centre of power to Nanjing in 1928. Britain had to come to terms with a China reunified under his leadership. It was not the right moment for the Foreign Office to take sides or to antagonise the Nanjing government. Li Jishen himself fell in and out of favour with Chiang Kai-shek: in 1934, his opposition to Chiang crushed, he sought refuge in Hong Kong for a time. Was Sir Robert relieved that the Foreign Office pulled the plug on the deal? We will never know, but it is highly likely that in the end his own well-honed financial sense operated more on his judgement than any arguments by the Guangzhou authorities or the British government.

How he finally viewed the failure of his round-table conference is also shrouded in obscurity. He recorded no reflections on the subject other than fairly bland observations on the support and hospitality he received wherever he went. All the same, the mission must have given him an absorbing and stimulating two years at a time of life when most ambitions and cravings, being already fulfilled, no longer challenged him. As he himself explained,

> I was born and brought up in Hongkong and so come under British laws, but I have never lost my love for the land of my fathers. I am still a Chinese and am not ashamed of it. Others thought I was using this scheme of unification to feather my own nest . . . It is of no use to simply assert that my motives are all right. If I say anything at all, it is that being free from business cares and having enough money to live on, I find it a pleasure to put forth my energy to help my country to become strong and be at peace. I also have the natural desire to succeed in this new kind of work. Is there anything wrong about this?[35]

That his fidelity to the cause remained unshaken for so long was perhaps proof of his political *naïveté*. He vastly underestimated the complexity of his task. Like all well-meaning men, he sometimes suffered the failings of his best qualities: his public spirit and simple faith would always be baffled by cynicism and duplicity; he was less fit to deal with the warlords' convoluted loyalties and venal opportunism than his brave attempt to bring them together would have us believe. Few countries have been saved by good men, after all, for good men lack the ruthlessness to go the distance.

7

Sons and Heirs

However incompatible it may be with the demands of modern life, the ritual of paying respects to ancestors continues to be observed by many Chinese today. For Eric Hotung, Sir Robert's grandson, the anniversary of his father's death was marked every year by offerings of meats and incense.

Two people were honoured on these occasions, and the photographs set behind the altar told us who they were—Mordia, blonde of hair and delicate of features, was in one frame, while Eddie, his dark eyes peering from thick spectacles, an air of vulnerability belying the vigour suggested by his heavy shoulders, was in another.

The marriage of Eddie and Mordia in 1925 was a grievous disappointment to Sir Robert, causing a breach which lasted long enough for Robbie to step into the position of favourite son and acknowledged heir. We left Sir Robert at the end of

Mordia O'Shea, wife of Edward Ho Tung

1923 still optimistic about his round-table conference but committed elsewhere to another assignment requiring his presence. Accordingly, after a brief respite in Hong Kong he was off again, to London. It was in London that Eddie met Mordia O'Shea.

Eddie, last seen in these pages greeting Sun Yat-sen at the University of Hong Kong, graduated in the summer of 1924, justifying his parents' fondest hopes for him. That he had reached adulthood at all was a miracle for which Clara, by then a devout Buddhist, must have offered daily thanks at her shrine. In 1919 Sir Robert himself remembered with gratitude that nerve-wracking time when Eddie's life hung in the balance. It is not clear what prompted him to write to Dr George Harston, the medical practitioner and surgeon he consulted, but there is no doubting Sir Robert's heartfelt appreciation:

> It is just possible you might think I minimised your unremitting care and professional attention to my eldest surviving son Eddie when he was so seriously ill seventeen years ago.
>
> Those were anxious days, when my son lay between life and death at my brother Ho Fook's house. I will never forget the cheering words of comfort you gave me which then encouraged me to hope for the best.
>
> I cannot say how happy I feel today that Eddie survived his serious illness and gives promise of developing into a strong and robust young man. I owe you much for restoring my son in health and strength to me. I wish to renew my expressions of deep thankfulness for Eddie's complete recovery and to mark that appreciation I would beg you the favour to accept the enclosed cheque with which I would ask you to obtain some souvenir acceptable to yourself and which please keep as a mark of my gratitude.[1]

The younger son, Robbie Shai-lai, was a far lustier baby. Born four years after Eddie, he bounced into the world with a quite different temperament, being mischievous and impetuous where Eddie was serious and collected. At Queen's College Robbie 'used to keep the class merry'[2] (presumably with jokes and pranks), and though he was once rude to the Peak tram inspector, for which he was caned on the hand by his father,[3] he was more often on easy terms with the people around him, keeping company with the sedan chair and rickshaw coolies when he had nothing better to do.[4] When he was on his best behaviour he could be charming. Miss Catharine Hartshorn, Lady Margaret's English companion who lived with the family before the First World War, obviously preferred him to Eddie, asking in a letter to be remembered to her 'sweetheart Robbie—he will be a big boy now,' enjoining him to work hard like his father and 'make a name for himself'.[5] He would indeed become successful, though in a different sphere from that of his father and brother. Yet he was not so much younger than Eddie as to escape totally the painful sense of needing to compete.

In both boys there may have been a feeling of being smothered and over-protected in a world occupied almost wholly by women, from their two mothers and eight sisters to a parade of nannies and maidservants. Robbie, conscious of Clara's preference for Eddie, felt especially close to Lady Margaret. Their father was, as Irene and Jean inform us, a distant figure who came into sharper focus only when they reached manhood. All too often the sons of very successful men find it hard to extricate themselves from the long shadow cast by their fathers; neither Eddie nor Robbie managed to break free of Sir Robert—financially at least—until after his death. Though temperamentally incapable of showing affection to his sons (after all, he had never experienced any sort of bond with his own father), Sir Robert had a highly developed sense of duty, which meant being conscientious about his family responsibilities. He tried to instil in his children diligence, abstemiousness, and prudence—the qualities to which he frequently attributed his own prosperity. (In his will, he specifically adjured them to refrain from extravagance, drinking, and gambling, and, as we noted earlier, to exhibit 'modesty and public spiritedness . . . and thereby following in the ways that have enabled me to establish my reputation and to build up my financial position from nothing'.) He succeeded to a large extent, for none of his daughters, nor his sons Ho Wing, Eddie, and Robbie could be described as remotely dissolute or profligate. Nevertheless, the prospect of one day coming into a stupendous inheritance could not have failed to sink in very early; that knowledge must have coloured their perceptions and ambitions more than any other formative influence in their adolescence. In fact, the terms of the brothers' relationship, instead of improving with age, actually deteriorated as the question of birthright and patrimony loomed larger with the passage of years.

Clara saw to it that the daughters, instead of living on their expectations, learnt the discipline of self-reliance very early on. In traditional Chinese families daughters hardly ever inherited equally to the sons; as Clara constantly reminded them, they could not rely on marrying rich men either. She tried to do the best for them all the same, arranging the marriage of Vic, the eldest, to Lo Man-kam (or M. K. Lo), a bright lawyer and son of Lo Cheung-shiu, and that of Daisy to Au-Yeung Pak-cheong. Vic's wedding in 1918 was the talk of the season, the reception at Idlewild being attended by no less a personage than the governor, Sir Henry May, who proposed the toast to the bride and groom. The bride was certainly 'good to look upon', as he declared; she was dressed in a gown of white charmeuse and georgette crêpe richly trimmed with lace, and falling from her head in soft folds was a veil of white silk net.[6] The groom, M. K., as he was generally known to his family and friends, had been educated in England, where he distinguished himself both in the field of sport and in his profession.

Daisy's in-laws, a Cantonese family living in Hankou, were a connection of Clara's father, who had been old Mr Au-Yeung's teacher. Although poor Daisy had been slower in mental development than was usual for her age, the ties of obligation between student and mentor are felt very strongly among traditionally minded Chinese. What other incentives were brought to bear on young Mr Au-Yeung to ally himself to a wife who was so handicapped, and who could never be a true companion, were tactfully not mentioned by either family, but some kind of agreement must have been reached between the parents. As befitting a daughter of Sir Robert Ho Tung, Daisy was given a fine wedding, celebrated with a reception in the Great Eastern Hotel, Shanghai, at the end of 1924. Sadly, she was widowed within a few years of the marriage and eventually went back to her parents. For a time she was placed in St Francis' Convent and Hospital in Wanchai on Hong Kong Island, but her behaviour became intolerable to the Canossian nuns; in 1939 Mother Eliza Superioress asked Sir Robert to remove her.[7] Daisy continued to cause great anxiety after she was lodged in a Buddhist temple below the Jockey Club stables in Happy Valley, where the racecourse was located, as she was in turn petulant and complaining, and habitually screamed and wailed at all hours of the night. She was, according to doctors who examined her, 'suffering from mental deficiency, together with some endocrine disorder'. Sir Robert confessed to a complainer in the Jockey Club stables neighbourhood that 'I myself did not really know what to do in the matter'. His daughters Vic and Irene, as well as George She, who was his private secretary at the time, took the brunt of consulting doctors and reporting to Sir Robert. In the early summer of 1940, after soliciting medical opinion, including that of Dr Selwyn-Clarke, director of medical services, Daisy was certified and committed to a mental hospital.[8] She lived on into her seventies.

The year 1924, culminating in the marriage of Daisy, was eventful for the Ho Tung family in more ways than one. Sir Robert, freshly returned to Hong Kong from Luoyang and Shanghai, went onwards to London. He had been appointed honorary commissioner to the British Empire Exhibition at Wembley; in February he duly embarked with Lady Margaret, whose own contribution to the Hong Kong section of the exhibition was a working demonstration of silk production, complete with a supply of silkworms and cocoons. With them went a team of women from Shunde in south China, all adepts at sericulture, and their third daughter, Mary, recently engaged to her cousin Wong Sik-lam, a student of architecture and engineering at London University. On arrival they settled into a rented house in Northwood, Middlesex, a suburb of northwest London, for the exhibition would go on for five months and they were there for the duration.

*Sir Robert with his daughter Mary; the identity of the English lady to
Mary's left is not known; 1924.*

Wembley, in northwest London, had been decked out like a gigantic fair, with
a stadium and a 'Never-Stop Railway' which took you round and round the 200-
acre ground on elevated tracks. You could catch a glimpse of modern technology
at the Palace of Industry or the Palace of Engineering, and have some fun at the
Queen's Doll House or a replica of the tomb of Tutankhamun. In between were
the pavilions of all the countries of the empire, from Canada to New Zealand. The
most prominent showcases of the Hong Kong Pavilion were two gate towers and
a 'Chinese Restaurant' serving such traditional dishes as birds' nest soup and fried
rice. Sir Robert, through the kindness of the superintendent, was allowed to be
driven in his motor car (a 1913 Rolls Royce) right into the Hong Kong section.
King George V himself opened the exhibition; touring the stands with Queen
Mary afterwards, he graciously accepted from the Ho Tungs some dried lychees
and a few pairs of silk stockings. On midsummer's eve, the most illustrious of the

Sir Robert Ho Tung and Queen Mary at the Wembley Exhibition, 1924

Wembley representatives attended a garden party at Buckingham Palace, in the course of which Sir Robert, Lady Margaret, and Mary—invited to assemble opposite the royal tea tent beforehand—were presented to the king and queen.

Being in the thick of the social season—for besides the garden party there was Ascot week—Sir Robert had the time of his life. In 1922 the Prince of Wales, on a visit to Hong Kong, had been invited by the Chinese community to a dinner in the Taiping Theatre at which Sir Robert had been present. Now it was His Royal Highness's turn to return the compliment, receiving the visitor from Hong Kong at St James's Palace for an informal audience. The Honourable Stanley Baldwin, who had just stepped down as prime minister, granted Sir Robert an interview, and Lucy Baldwin entertained him to tea. Other invitations poured in from a veritable who's who of British politics: there was lunch at Chartwell with Winston Churchill and tea on the House of Commons terrace with David Lloyd George; there were meetings with Ramsay MacDonald and Neville Chamberlain. These encounters furnished Sir Robert with many agreeable memories.

In July Sir Robert and Lady Ho Tung were joined by Eddie and Jean. Brother and sister had travelled at a leisurely pace to London. Their ship, sailing down the South China Sea, called first at Singapore, where Eddie disembarked so he could visit friends in Kuala Lumpur. He rejoined the ship at Penang; from there they crossed the Bay of Bengal to Colombo and onwards to Suez, which provided an exciting opportunity to make an excursion to Cairo for a sight of its archaeological wonders.[9] They met the ship again at Port Said for the final stretch through the Mediterranean to Marseilles. Here they boarded the train for Paris. The rest of the journey passed in a whirl of treats, from sightseeing at Versailles and Fontainebleau to nights at the opera and the Casino de Paris.

Jean had come to London for an operation to remove a benign tumour from the back of her head, but for Eddie the trip was the climax to something very akin to the eighteenth-century Grand Tour, an essential part of a young gentleman's education. Indeed, he found this chance to broaden his horizons highly congenial, and when the moment arrived for them all to go home, he began to feel rather anxious to stay. His enrolment in a course at the London School of Economics struck Sir Robert as a good enough reason to allow him to remain. He would later acquire a job in finance, which boded well for his future independence. Just how decisively he was to sever the apron strings would not become apparent until the following year.

In 1925, when the decision was made to reopen the Wembley Empire Exhibition for a second season, Sir Robert volunteered his services once more. Eddie was still in London furthering his studies and working part-time. For Sir Robert the quiet suburb of Northwood now held no allure, and he took a house in fashionable Cadogan Gardens, Belgravia. This time all roads did not lead to Wembley, for the empire's great propaganda effort attracted considerably less public enthusiasm than the year before. India, Burma, and several other colonies had dropped out of exhibiting altogether. While people were still coming on excursions by train, bus, and charabanc, the numbers fell far short of the twenty-seven million who had thronged the exhibition in 1924. The Palace of Engineering was empty except for a railway display in one small corner and a few aeroplanes in another; and although the Palace of Industry was better attended, the standard of exhibits was lower than in the previous year. This did not detract from Sir Robert's enjoyment of the visit, however, since the London season was in full swing and he was once again hobnobbing with royalty and statesmen. There was time, too, to make an excursion to take the waters at an Austrian spa, on which Katie accompanied him.

That summer, Ho Fook's sixth son, Ho Cheuk, who had been working under Ho Wing at the Hongkong and Shanghai Bank, died of blackwater fever, a severe complication of malaria in which blood cells are rapidly destroyed in the bloodstream.[10] News of this sad event was followed quickly by a cable from Clara asking Sir Robert, guarantor of Ho Wing's compradoreship, to recommend someone for the vacancy. Clara's unspoken message was not lost on him: she clearly felt it was time Eddie returned to the family fold, and here was a suitable opening. This turn of affairs now forced Eddie to confess his secret.

It seemed he had fallen in love with one of the maids at Cadogan Gardens, an Irish girl called Mordia O'Shea, and had recently married her without telling anyone. Probably to avoid publicity, he had signed the marriage register on 7 May 1925 as Edward Samuel Bosman.

Eddie's revelation sent Sir Robert and Lady Margaret into shock. They thought it an ignominious match. Eddie could have had his pick of the eligible girls in Hong Kong; Hesta Hung, the lovely daughter of a family friend, for one, would have made an entirely suitable wife, and who could say whether he might not have looked higher? A Manchu prince had after all sought the hand of their young daughter Eva in marriage. When Sir Robert was in Beijing in the summer of 1921, he had been introduced to two princes of the blood by Reginald Johnston, English tutor to the deposed emperor Puyi. At a dinner Sir Robert then gave for them at his borrowed 'fine furnished house', Eva, then eighteen, had been present. One of the princes, Yu Lang, later asked Johnston to sound out Sir Robert on 'the desirability of arranging a marriage between your [Sir Robert's] family and his. His proposal is that one of his sons should be betrothed to your daughter.'[11] This great honour was, however, gently but firmly declined: his children, explained Sir Robert, not having been brought up strictly according to Chinese customs,

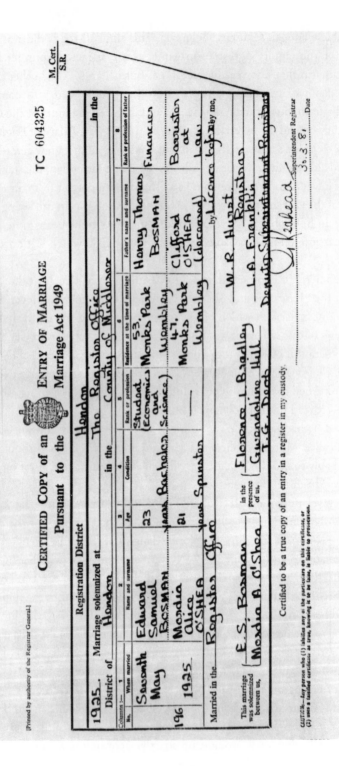

Eddie's marriage certificate, with his name given as 'Edward Samuel Bosman' and his father's as 'Henry Thomas Bosman'.

expected 'some sort of personal selection' in the matter of their future mates.[12] All the same, having received such an offer, Sir Robert could be excused if he hoped for a similarly exalted alliance for his eldest son; his professed aversion to arranged marriages certainly seemed to vanish in the face of Eddie's disastrous choice. Neither he nor Margaret—who felt the betrayal as keenly as if Eddie were her own son—could bear to recognise such a common daughter-in-law.

Their horror at the match also had racial elements which were, if anything, protective. This was evident later in the case of Jean, whose choice of a husband also failed to meet with unanimous approval. She said her father would not have opposed her engagement to Billy Gittins, a Eurasian, if Billy had had a Chinese name: 'I should have known that he would have been against any daughter of his marrying into an Eurasian family which did not subscribe to his view and adopt Chinese nationality, because he felt that they would not be accepted into any community.'[13] Sir Robert had lived with the problems created by his mixed pedigree by denying it, at least publicly. He thought his children all too likely to expose

Sir Robert Ho Tung's dinner for Manchu princes in Beijing, 1921. Eva, wearing spectacles, is at the centre of the front row, sitting on the floor. Clara, seated, is behind her.

themselves to racial discrimination unless they, too, chose to be Chinese. By marrying a European Eddie would suffer all the misery of being a perennial outsider, cast
adrift in a social no-man's-land. Having long felt an outsider himself, Sir Robert's
feelings were intensely against this fate, yet he could vent them in no other way
than by a violent repudiation of Eddie himself.

The prodigal son returned to Hong Kong to face the tears and pleas of his
distraught mother, but her favourite child remained unrepentant. Eddie knew
only that he loved Mordia; nothing mattered to him beyond this fact. With some
trepidation, he announced to his family that his bride was in fact expected at any
moment, for while he was making his way home by train through Siberia, Mordia
was travelling to Hong Kong by ship.[14]

Buffeted by disapproval, Mordia and Eddie became accomplices against the
world, and the strain would eventually take its toll on their marriage. They were
very young at the time, and neither of them possessed the aplomb to brazen it
out. It was worse for Mordia, catapulted as she was into an alien society and often
finding herself the only non-Chinese at a gathering or party. Her extremely modest
circumstances before meeting Eddie could hardly have endowed her with much
self-confidence. It did not help that she was evasive about her past; indeed she
resisted the searchlight of curiosity so well that uncertainty still hangs over her
parentage, for various discrepancies which emerged later were never satisfacto-
rily resolved. She had called herself Alice and Maude in addition to Mordia, and
had been known for a time by the surname Newman. Even if her story is a simple
one of abandonment by her father O'Shea when very young and fostering by a
family called Newman, it remains an open question whether she was in fact, as she
claimed, a Catholic.

At first, none of this was known to Eddie's parents, who condemned Mordia
simply for her class and for being of the wrong race. They refused to receive her
into the family. It is said that she was never allowed to set foot in Idlewild through
its front door; even Clara, who doted on Eddie, could not find it in her Buddhist
heart to champion them. Irene tells us that once or twice, when Eddie went home,
Clara became so hysterical that she actually fainted from the emotional strain. In
this overwrought atmosphere, Eddie took up his appointment at the Hongkong
and Shanghai Bank, and shortly afterwards started his own family with the birth of
Eric in June 1926. Clara, meanwhile, sought relief in prayer and became ever more
rapt in her devotions. Indeed, her children became so alarmed by her zealousness
that they implored her to make a trip abroad, which would at least, they thought,
get her away from the monks. Robbie felt particularly exasperated by his mother,
what with the favouritism she had always shown Eddie and the constant presence
of monks in the house. Her departure for Europe with Irene and Eva at the end of

1926 was greeted with a sigh of relief. Travel did bring many distractions to Clara, not least the chance to buy chandeliers in London for a new house, The Falls, being built for her on the Peak.

The fact that he had to earn his own living did not bother Eddie unduly. He joined the Hongkong and Shanghai Bank as an assistant compradore on a monthly salary of $200, fully intending to augment his income by dealing on the side, as Sir Robert had done when he was at Jardines. But he could not emulate his father's Midas touch. Instead, his speculations on the stock market and gold exchange went badly awry, plunging him into debt which ballooned to US$60,000, a reverse which alienated him from his father even more. Obviously his huge losses were soon the talk of the town; although Sir Robert came to the rescue with a timely loan, Eddie was no less ruined than if he had actually declared himself a bankrupt. The bank offered to keep him on the staff, but his father's displeasure made it imperative for him to disappear from the scene of the scandal. Bitter about the blemish to his family name and implacable in his disappointment, Sir Robert laid down his ultimatum. In exchange for the loan to discharge his debts, Eddie was to go into exile in Shanghai, where Sir Robert had extensive property holdings. In 1922 Sir Robert had bought from the executors of Edward Isaac Ezra (1883–1921) property in Hongkou for 1,050,000 taels. The property encompassed twenty-one *mu* (about three and a half acres) with 173 Chinese houses and nine foreign tenements. Born in Shanghai, the Jewish tycoon Edward Ezra had made an immense fortune through dealing in opium and real estate.[15] Managing the large property portfolio would at least provide Eddie with something to do.

Thus it was that in 1929 the eldest son of the richest man in Hong Kong began a new and rather humble career as a rent collector in Shanghai. He would live through a tumultuous time in that 'bawdy and gaudy' city, watching his family grow amid the chaos of the 'undeclared' Sino-Japanese War, World War II, and the pre-Liberation period up to 1947. After Eric, more children were born—Patrick (who died young of meningitis), Joseph, Antonia, and Mary. And the family's long association with Shanghai would be remembered sixty years later, when a gallery in the Shanghai Museum—rebuilt and inaugurated in 1996—was dedicated to the memory of Eddie and Mordia by their eldest son. The Hotung Pavilion, as it was named, was a stylish and finely wrought reproduction of a part of a Ming courtyard house.[16]

Eddie's disgrace not unnaturally precipitated the ascendancy of Robbie in their father's affections. Robbie once reminded his father: 'I have never for one moment forgotten what you wrote to me in 1927, saying that you depended on me more than anyone else in this world.'[17] This new-found closeness was enhanced when Robbie's choice of a military career threw him into the China arena, where

Sir Robert was himself still striving to play a role. 'I may be hot-tempered and prejudiced,' Robbie was to write in self-justification to his father some years later,

> but all the advice I have given you and all the services I have rendered were done
> with the one and only intention, i.e. making you a great personality in China . . .
> There are very few men in our country who could be more patriotic than we are
> . . . Every one of us knows that if we either let China or you down, he is through.
> You have confidence in us and we love China.[18]

Robbie's love for China would remain constant, but his attribution of the same love and patriotism to his father was perhaps somewhat ingenuous. Sir Robert, as we have seen, was more of an opportunist where political allegiance was concerned. He would declare his loyalty to Britain and British interests at the same time as he professed to be a Chinese patriot who wished China to be at peace and for his compatriots to live harmoniously and prosperously. He felt no conflict in espousing both claims.

Less academically inclined than Eddie, Robbie had early on decided that the army was his *métier*. At first Sir Robert considered sending his eighteen-year-old son to the military college in China, but he found that as a result of the disturbed state of the country the college was practically closed down. He thought of the Royal Military College at Sandhurst instead. Since that is an academy for training officers of the British and Indian armies, Sir Robert directed his enquiries to the War Office in London. In due course a vacancy was made available at the Royal Military College at Woolwich, where cadets for the Royal Artillery and Royal Engineers were trained, and to Woolwich Robbie proceeded in 1925. It proved a baptism of fire. The college was a hard, athletics-dominated institution: while there was no violent bullying, new cadets were still routinely humiliated by the senior boys, particularly during what they called the 'snooker dance', when

> we were stripped naked, i.e. with only a pair of shorts on, and we had to push a
> match box with our nose across the floor from one end of the gym to the other . . .
> [then] we had to pass another dark barricade . . . Naturally seniors were waiting
> with bucketfuls of cold water at the exit but . . . after we were drenched we still
> had to go to the taps and fill the buckets for them to pour on us . . . I thought I
> was going to die.[19]

Brought up in an almost entirely feminine household, Robbie no doubt seemed a rather spoilt wimp to the roughest boys at the college. Their rowdy ways made him desperately unhappy and his letters to Sir Robert were full of complaints and anti-British sentiments. In one he said: 'I arrived in England with the hope of extending mutual feelings between China and England one day, but before long I shall leave this country with the hope of revenge.' In another he asserted that 'though China was weak England was a bully.' He grumbled that for eighteen months the college authorities and cadets had treated him 'like a pig'. Foreigners, he informed his father, 'are called wogs, meaning pigs.' He strived to keep up in his training, as his instructors and professors were aware, but if he gained their sympathy, he could not entirely meet their expectations. In the second-term report his instructor in artillery said that the 'gentleman cadet Ho Tung, R.' worked hard but was handicapped by 'the language difficulty'.[20] The cadet showed 'little ability' in either mathematics or science, although his 'workshop work' was very good. Robbie was clearly adept with his hands, because by the third term the instructor was praising him for working well and being 'very attentive and diligent'. The soldiering part, on the other hand, did not show much improvement in the following term. Robbie continued to find the subjects of artillery, engineering, and tactics difficult; even though he was keen he was 'very slow'.

Those were miserable months, but more humiliation was to follow. After leaving Woolwich he was accepted for a short young officers' course at the School of Artillery at Larkhill; he hoped this would lead to Staff College and a stint with the Royal Tank Corps. In the summer word reached Sir Robert from the War Office that Robbie did not qualify, as Staff College catered only for experienced officers who already had ten to fifteen years' service. This was a blow, but in the holidays Robbie discovered rather more flexible entry requirements at the French Military Staff College, which would accept him if he held a commission in the Chinese army. As he explained to his father, he could take 'a gunnery course at Fontainebleau, which is certain if you can get the Chinese Government to apply ... If you cannot get a place for me, even the lowest rank of officer from your friend Wu [Peifu] and Chang [Zhang Zuolin], then it is not likely I shall ever get one at all.'[21]

Sir Robert did not personally know the Manchurian warlord Zhang Zuolin, who practically dominated the Beijing government of the day. Yet, on being solicited by the Hong Kong tycoon, Marshal Zhang obliged immediately, sending Sir Robert a dispatch appointing his son a lieutenant in the army. In fact, Marshal Zhang was so interested in Sir Robert, whom he had heard 'was the most successful and trustworthy man in Hongkong, perhaps also in the whole of China', that he invited Sir Robert to Mukden (present-day Shenyang) to manage his commercial affairs.[22] Sir Robert pleaded too much other pressing business to accept.

The trouble was, Robbie received his commission from Zhang Zuolin while still at Larkhill. When the War Office discovered it was nurturing in its midst not a British colonial cadet but an alien officer, all hell broke loose. Tagged as a security risk, Robbie was ordered to pack his bags and leave the School of Artillery within twenty-four hours. To an angry young man breathing fire and vengeance this was the last straw, so in a fit of pique he took himself off to the Chinese embassy in London and renounced his British nationality. When the news reached Hong Kong, Sir Robert was appalled, but despite his attempts to annul the result of this melodramatic gesture, things had gone too far. The only option open to him (or, rather, to his daughter Irene Ho Tung, who was in London at the time) was to put the matter on a formal footing. Irene wrote to the Home Office on behalf of her brother:

> My brother, Ho Shai Lai, alias Robert Ho Tung, was born in Hongkong in 1906, thus being a British subject until now. He wishes to become re-nationalised as a Chinese subject, and as this has to be done during his twenty-first year, he would be very much obliged if you could provide him with the necessary form for de-nationalisation.[23]

The Home Office informed her that, provided Robbie could prove he was born in British territory and that he acquired by birth or during his minority the nationality of a foreign state, it was open to him to make a declaration of alienage under the relevant British Nationality Act. Privately, the War Office thought it all an unsatisfactory business though there was nothing to be done about it. And if some bemused Whitehall officials doubted the wisdom of training up 'these warlords'— it seemed Robbie was suspected of desiring to become a 'Tuchun' (*dujun*)—nevertheless, as they confided to each other, 'Warlords had better get their military training here than at Moscow.'[24] Robbie duly renounced his British nationality. From that moment on he never wavered in his allegiance to the Chinese government, eventually serving and reaching the rank of general in the Nationalist Army.

At the end of 1927 we find Robbie in France and Sir Robert rather anxious for his return to Hong Kong. The idea that Robbie might convert his 'honorary' lieutenancy in Zhang Zuolin's army into active service had taken root. It would be a good plan, urged the father, for Robbie to accompany Clara home; 'I will certainly not go to Europe,' Sir Robert affirmed, 'until I have seen you and seen you fixed up in Manchuria. I can assure you that all my interests are centred in you and no matter what sacrifice I may have to make, I am prepared to stand it as long as I am convinced that it is in your interests.'[25] Few men of wealth and substance can avoid harbouring dynastic ambitions or at least making plans for their sons to step into their shoes. Sir Robert, on the other hand, though he had lost one successor, had apparently not only come to terms with Robbie's disinclination for business, but had become immensely proud of his soldier son and committed to advancing Robbie in his chosen career.

The marriage of Robbie Ho Shai-lai and Hesta Hung, 1928

Robbie was all too conscious that his own marriage was now an issue of intense concern to his parents. The year after Eddie's secret wedding, he was assuring his father that he would marry neither an English girl nor one of whom Sir Robert disapproved. Since he was destined for the Chinese army, he thought a Chinese girl might be the ideal partner. As it happened, his choice fell on someone very close to home: Hesta Hung, a beautiful Eurasian, a former classmate of Jean's at the Diocesan Girls' School and the girl his parents had hoped Eddie might marry. Their wedding in June 1928 was a brilliant occasion, quite literally, since Idlewild was illuminated for the reception and the grand dinner which followed. After spending their wedding night at Repulse Bay on the south side of the island, Hesta and Robbie boarded the *President Madison* for France.

Two days before the wedding, Zhang Zuolin was fatally wounded when the armoured compartment of a Beijing–Mukden train in which he was travelling was blown up by Japanese officers. Like other warlords, Zhang had intrigued to wrest control of the shadowy government in Beijing and by 1926 was established in the capital, comporting himself as a dictator and playing endless games of mah-jong. Supported by the Japanese, who controlled the South Manchurian Railway and valuable concessions in the northeast, he still held Manchuria. But in June 1928 he ran afoul of the more aggressive Japanese militarists when, in the face of advancing Nationalist troops under Chiang Kai-shek, he abandoned Beijing to retreat to Mukden. With Chiang's Northern Expedition now reclaiming much of the country from the warlords, China seemed on the verge of reunification at last. It was a prospect the Japanese viewed with alarm. Possibly suspecting Zhang Zuolin of Nationalist sympathies, the militarists decided that by killing him they would not only remove a potential foe but provoke a crisis in Manchuria and keep China divided. The assassination, however, did not plunge Manchuria into disorder. In fact, the warlord's mantle passed smoothly to his son Zhang Xueliang, the 'Young Marshal', who decided to give his support to the Nationalists shortly afterwards. With other warlords falling in line, Chiang successfully brought a large part of China back into the Nationalist fold. On 10 October a reorganised national government was established in Nanjing.

It was to Nanjing that Sir Robert and Clara journeyed in the summer of 1929, for they had been invited to the unveiling of the new Sun Yat-sen mausoleum built among the wooded Purple Hills. Dr Sun had died in Beijing, but it had taken four years to prepare for the burial in his capital. From Nanjing Sir Robert travelled on to the Japanese-controlled port of Dairen (present-day Luda) in southern Manchuria, where he and Clara spent a couple of months enjoying the cool weather in a bungalow outside the city centre. Whether it was then or earlier is not known, but Sir Robert did acquire extensive land in Manchuria; like the Japanese, he no doubt had his eye on the wealth of timber, minerals, and other resources there. In a radio broadcast recording his impressions of developments since his last visit to Manchuria fifteen years previously, he expressed full confidence that, with an 'influx of capital and enterprise, the future prosperity of this rich and vast country will increase by leaps and bounds.'[26]

He certainly had hopes of Zhang Xueliang, who was, he said in the broadcast, 'sparing no effort in trying to fulfil the great responsibilities that have been laid upon his young shoulders.' Perhaps Sir Robert still hung on to his dream of bringing warlords to a round-table conference. Despite the success of Chiang Kai-shek's northern campaign and the formation of a national government in Nanjing, real unification still proved elusive; apart from Zhang Xueliang, warlords such as Feng Yuxiang and Yan Xishan continued to dominate some of the provinces. When an invitation came from the Young Marshal to visit him in Mukden, therefore, Sir Robert was only too glad to accept.

As was his wont, he chose to stay at a hotel, on this occasion the Yamato. Zhang was then about thirty-one years old and, though a morphine and opium addict, had already shown firm resolution when it came to dispatching his rivals, two of whom he had ordered to be shot while they were dining with him earlier that year. Warlords generally managed to amass great wealth; to Zhang, investment advice from someone like Sir Robert would always be worth heeding. Some years later he would ask Sir Robert to manage his commercial and financial interests, as his father had done; however, the request was made just before the Mukden Incident, in September 1931, and was never raised again.

Sir Robert was given a warm welcome and even taken round the arsenal, which was clearly Zhang's pride and joy. The Mukden arsenal, considerably improved in Zhang Zuolin's day by an English engineer, was capable of turning out good-quality rifles, machine guns, hand grenades, and ammunition.[27] Sir Robert noted that it employed about 15,000 to 20,000 workmen. Threading his way around the production lines, Sir Robert no doubt brought up his younger son's artillery training. It would have been entirely natural then for Zhang to express an interest in Robbie, whom he appointed as his aide-de-camp not long afterwards.

Before going south again, Sir Robert would make one last attempt to put his views to the independent warlords. Clara was eager to make a pilgrimage to Wutai Shan, a mountain considered sacred by Chinese Buddhists. They accordingly bent their steps towards Taiyuan, the stronghold of Shanxi warlord Yan Xishan. At one time Yan had been part of the alliance (with Feng Yuxiang and Zhang Zuolin) that fought against Wu Peifu, but on the whole he stayed aloof from the civil war and preoccupied himself mainly with keeping power in Shanxi. In some ways he was more modern than his peers: his socialist schemes for the people he ruled earned him praise as 'the model governor'. It is doubtful though if he had much time for the peace plans of Sir Robert, who must by now have begun to resign himself to his round-table conference slipping into oblivion. In any case, the military, nationalist, and communist cross-currents then shaping China would soon be overwhelmed by yet another crisis—the Japanese seizure of Manchuria in September 1931, precipitated by what came to be described as the Mukden Incident. Using a bomb explosion which destroyed a section of the Japanese-owned railway near Mukden as pretext, the Japanese launched an attack on Chinese nationalists and rapidly overran the region, forcing Sir Robert to beat a hasty retreat.

Climbing up to some of the temples on Wutai Shan proved quite testing for Sir Robert and Clara, even with the help of mules and sedan chairs, though the picturesque views more than made up for the hardship. Soon after the excursion, as it had become very cold, they began their journey home, making first for Hankou and then taking a steamer to Shanghai. There they opened up the gracious house Sir Robert owned in the International Settlement.[28] Calm seemed to have been restored to the city since the violent suppression of trade union activists and communists in 1927. But it was the lull before a storm. Little did the residents—or Eddie—know what was in store.

Many of Sir Robert's properties in Shanghai were located in Zhabei and Hongkou, suburbs with a high concentration of Japanese residents. There was never much love lost between Chinese and Japanese. Ever since the occupation of Manchuria, anti-Japanese feelings had been running high, so much so that in January 1932 Japanese militarists had a perfect excuse for sending their warships to begin an attack on Shanghai. Since the naval units had been landed ostensibly to protect Japanese nationals against Chinese hostility, much of the fighting took place in Zhabei, where, as it happened, a large Cantonese force was temporarily quartered. It was this force which defended the city, and for a month 'Shanghai residents had their nightly thrill from the roar of heavy gunfire'.[29] No clear victor emerged from this battle—the truce merely established a 'demilitarised zone'—though a colossal price was paid in lives and much of Zhabei was bombed to smithereens. Eddie, acting for one of the suburbs' largest landlords, must have been in a constant state of tension. He sent his children briefly to Hong Kong, away from the scene of carnage (though Eric would remember for years afterwards the blown-off arms and legs and ripped entrails he saw as a boy of six). Fortunately, both his family and his father's properties came through unscathed. Two months after the fighting, Sir Robert was assuring Hesta that

> things in Shanghai are settling down a bit, but it will take some time to recover its past glory and prosperity. Apart from the loss of rentals, my properties in

Shanghai have luckily escaped any war damage. As such misfortunes are beyond one's control, I am taking my losses quite philosophically.[30]

Hesta and Robbie were still very much in favour and the recipients of a generous allowance. Despite the fact that Robbie had been gainfully employed since leaving Fontainebleau, his father was clearly not expecting him to keep Hesta merely on his soldier's pay. He was not seeing any action either: in Mukden one of his duties as the Young Marshal's aide-de-camp appeared to be playing golf with his superior. It was on a golf course that Zhang once asked him if Hongkong and Shanghai Bank shares were worth buying; Robbie quite rightly conjectured that this question was meant for Sir Robert, and duly passed it on.[31] In November 1932 Robbie resigned from Zhang's staff; by the following year he was in Beijing (renamed Beiping) and telling his father that, though wounded soldiers were seen everywhere, morale among the troops was high. If he had hopes of engaging in any fighting, however, he would be disappointed. His father supported his military aspirations, but now a feeling was growing that perhaps he had played soldier long enough; it was time the heir-apparent assumed some business responsibilities. Sir Robert owned a newspaper, the *Kung Sheung Yat Po* ('Industrial and Commercial Daily Press'), for long a losing concern which he hoped Robbie would salvage.[32] Contemplating this offer on his return from France in 1930, Robbie had rather

(Standing, at the entrance to Idlewild) Robbie and Hesta; (seated, from left) Clara, cradling their newborn son; Sir Robert; Lady Margaret.

liked the idea of earning his living through the *Kung Sheung*. Now, a couple of years later, the time had come for him to take over the management of the paper.

Robbie was not ready, however. In the autumn of 1933, accompanied by Hesta and their newborn son (also named Robert), he took himself off for further military training at the US Army Staff School at Fort Leavenworth in Kansas, where he learned, among other skills, to fly fighter planes. For a while the news from China was of continuing political instability and military separatism, although Chiang Kai-shek was making some headway in regaining control over a large part of the country. But soon more disturbing reports filtered through: Japan, having already seized Manchuria in the northeast, was now more blatantly aggressive. With two more years of study under his belt, Robbie decided it was time to return to China; by late 1935 he had assumed a position in the Nationalist Army.

Meanwhile, relations between Sir Robert and Eddie were on the mend. While he was not reinstated as his father's heir—his conspicuous absence from the list of executors in Sir Robert's 1932 will made that all too plain—he was being treated less like the black sheep.[33] Sir Robert could not, after all, remain unmoved by his deference—always so eager to please, so anxious to atone for the hurt he had caused. He was trying his utmost to be a conscientious agent, keeping under his eye not only Sir Robert's properties but a portfolio of China shares as well. With a further loan from his father, he had bought a seat on the Shanghai Stock Exchange and set up as a stockbroker.

The different paths his sons chose to tread probably left Sir Robert with a deeper understanding of the reasons behind his own success in business and politics. His adroitness in crossing cultural boundaries was one important factor: as compradore he had a foot in two camps—of Chinese merchants and of British traders—and this was an advantage he put to profitable use, as we have seen. He had no difficulty reconciling his acceptance of a British knighthood with patriotism towards China: he even applied to the British government to wear medals from both countries at the same time (permission was refused). Like most Eurasians at the time, he was all too aware of the delicacy of his social position and surmounted the prevailing racism by identifying himself as Chinese; in old age, on the other hand, he became more confidently unreserved about his European heritage, making arrangements for a Christian burial, for example. His sons also exemplified the two cultures, but, in contrast, Eddie displayed a leaning to the West, while Robbie showed a preference for the East. Robbie liked to give Bao'an, Guangdong, rather than colonial Hong Kong, as his provenance—an attribution avidly replicated in obituaries published in the Chinese press when he died in 1998. That their father recognised this difference is implicit in one of the bequests under his last will (4 July 1955), in which he gave his medals, stars, and other decorations conferred on him by the Chinese government to 'my son Ho Shai Lai' and the medals, stars, and other decorations conferred by the British government and by other governments to 'my son Ho Sai Kim'.

Robbie had an exemplary military career, distinguishing himself particularly in the Sino-Japanese War. When the United States entered the war after Pearl Harbor in December 1941, Robbie the Fort Leavenworth alumnus caught the attention of Generalissimo Chiang Kai-shek, who saw to it that Robbie was sent to liaise with the Allies in the Nationalists' temporary capital, Chongqing. To Chongqing, the generalissimo's last stand against the Japanese, Washington proceeded to send such high-ranking American officers as General Stilwell and General Wedemeyer, as well as thousands of servicemen. Robbie was clearly thought to have a part to play there.

Japanese surrender in 1945 did not lead to peace in China, for it removed the need for a united front of Nationalists and Communists and cleared the way for civil war. Following the Communist victory Robbie was appointed to a defence ministry position in Taiwan and later as head of the Nationalist Chinese Military Mission to the United Nations. Eventually rising to the rank of general, he retired in 1962 to Hong Kong, where he resumed his involvement in the *Kung Sheung Yat Po*, and where he died on 26 July 1998, aged ninety-two years.

8

Riding the Storm

One of the most frequently published photographs (see next chapter) of Sir Robert shows him posing with George Bernard Shaw in July 1949 at Ayot St Lawrence in Hertfordshire, both of them dressed in what the playwright called 'celestial garments'.[1] With their full white beards and exceptionally thin figures, they looked remarkably alike and quite the 'sages' of Shaw's characterisation.[2]

Their acquaintance was made sixteen years earlier, in 1933, when the Shaws, calling at Hong Kong on their world tour, had asked if Sir Robert might receive them. Sir Robert was only too delighted; not only did he invite them to Idlewild but he also took them up the Peak to The Falls.

No expense had been spared in fitting out The Falls, with its nine bedrooms and half a dozen bathrooms, when it was built for Clara in the late 1920s. Teak panelled the walls, and the brilliance of chandeliers (which Clara had bought in London) was nightly reflected in the polished parquetry of the floors. A wide staircase wound from the porticoed entrance to Clara's own private shrine for worship and meditation on an upper floor. A Buddhist since childhood, Clara was perhaps not the only woman facing an empty nest to be consumed by religion in middle age. She would recount her religious journey in an autobiographical publication, *Mingshan youji* ('Travelogue on Famous Mountains'), in 1934, and found a temple and school, the Tung Lin Kok Yuen, the following year. Shaw later described Clara's shrine in The Falls in an essay:

> a radiant miniature temple with an altar of Chinese vermilion and gold, and cushioned divan seats round the walls for the worshippers. Everything was in such perfect Chinese taste that to sit there and look was a quiet delight. A robed priest and his acolyte stole in and went through a service. When it was over I told Sir Robert that I had found it extraordinarily soothing and happy though I had not understood a word of it. 'Neither have I,' he said, 'but it soothes me too.' It was part of the art of life for Chinaman and Irishman alike, and was purely esthetic.[3]

Sir Robert Ho Tung and Bernard Shaw at Idlewild, 1933

Clara's shrine also inspired a scene in *Buoyant Billions: A Comedy of No Manners*, a play Shaw completed in 1948. Its plot hinges on how the elderly Mr Buoyant (said to be based on Sir Robert) plans to dispose of his wealth after his death. In Act III the billionaire finds serenity in observing the ritual conducted by a robed Chinese priest:

> His soul needs refreshment. He is a mighty man of business: in his hands all things turn into money. Souls perish under such burdens. He comes here and sits for half an hour while I go through my act of worship, of which he does not understand a single word. But he goes out a new man, soothed and serene.[4]

Whatever impression Sir Robert created that day in 1933, he cannot have been feeling his best, for shortly after the encounter we find him undergoing treatment at a London hospital.

Generally he never found illness a bore, often imagining himself indisposed when he was perfectly fit. He made a habit of consulting one doctor after another about trifling symptoms, and occasionally—somewhat perversely—disparaging their treatment or prescriptions. Once, after seeing a Japanese doctor in Mukden, he confided to his daughter Eva, 'To tell you the truth I have not much faith in doctors, not because I do not believe in their skilfulness, but my case is so exceptional it requires most careful handling'[5]—this to a daughter whose profession was medicine! However, in the spring of 1933, within a month or so of entertaining Bernard Shaw, he was genuinely laid low by a severe bladder infection. After being treated in London, he was found to have a prostatic obstruction; an operation to remove the tumour was performed in a private clinic in Berne, Switzerland. For much of that year, he really did become an invalid. Not that his life was ever in any danger, but his brother Ho Fook, dead of cancer seven years before, must still have been frequently in his thoughts.

The best of doctors attended him in London and Berne. He was now over seventy, and though the tumour proved benign, he did not recover as quickly as expected from his operation. It was when he was still recuperating in Europe and at his lowest ebb that the news of his nephew's suicide reached him.

Sir Robert and his nephew Ho Leung were related by a web of kinship that covered nearly the entire Eurasian community in Hong Kong. Ho Leung was Ho Fook's fourth son and, as the husband of Lo Cheung-shiu's daughter Edna, brother-in-law to M. K. and Vic. Well connected and a Jardines compradore backed by Sir Robert, he found trading without security all too easy. This proved the ruin of him, for it encouraged him to over-extend himself in a number of highly speculative ventures. He was especially reckless in the conduct of his import business at Jardines, leaving a trail of defaults and losses. One venture which unravelled involved dealing

Ho Leung

in luxury goods; when economic conditions declined they became a drug on the market, leading to more grievous losses.[6] Actually the warning signs were there if anybody had paid attention: writing to Jardines in the previous summer he had referred to his 'abnormal losses... in respect of your Import business.'[7] But Jardines, though sympathetic, apparently took no action. Nor was anyone aware at the time that Ho Leung was also engaged in the extremely hazardous practice of 'kite-flying', meeting obligations by writing cheques on a bank account in London which held funds that were already committed, in the hope (vain as it transpired) that the time lag in clearing the cheques would give him a chance to replenish the account. The outstanding cheques eventually amounted to more than HK$100,000.

On 21 December 1933 Ho Leung gave no hint of his desperation when he agreed to meet his wife for lunch at his sports club. When her husband did not appear, Edna made a number of telephone calls to find him. By seven o'clock that evening she was frantic. According to a statement later made by her brother M. K., it was nearly ten o'clock when she rang him again, to say that a police inspector had just called with the horrifying news that a body dressed in European clothes and found off Taitam Tuk Road (on the south side of Hong Kong Island) was suspected to be that of her husband. An amah and a coolie sent to make the identification confirmed that the dead man was indeed Ho Leung; he had apparently shot himself twice in the chest with his own revolver at a secluded spot on a hillside near his home. He was forty-two years old.

The family now galvanised itself to pull every string available to quash the scandal, beginning with an appeal to the police to report the case as a straightforward case of suicide so that a public coroner's inquest might be dispensed with. No time was lost in arranging for Ho Leung's burial at the Chiu Yuen Cemetery, which took place only a day later. Newspaper reportage was respectful and reticent, but what could not be hushed up was the depth of his recklessness and the extent of the financial calamity.[8] Sir Robert, as Ho Leung's guarantor, had to be told, though no one relished the prospect of passing on the news. In the end it was Lady Margaret who grasped the nettle.

Moments after the fact of the suicide had sunk in, Sir Robert was informed that Jardines was making a claim against him. Only then did it burst upon him how perilously exposed he had been all along. Ho Leung had succeeded his father-in-law, Lo Cheung-shiu, as compradore in 1920. When Sir Robert signed the new guarantee agreement, it never occurred to him that its terms had been altered in any fundamental sense. He was unguarded enough not to have it examined with a fine-tooth comb by his lawyer son-in-law M. K. In fact the clause relating to his liability was no longer precise but ambiguously phrased or, as a lawyer later characterised it, 'not free of difficulties': instead of limiting his liability to $50,000, as he thought, it allowed Jardines to argue that every failed contract could be treated as a claim against him, up to $50,000 for *each* claim. Counsel put it to him this way: 'Suppose a certain firm had concluded three separate contracts and then it went bankrupt. Would there be one claim comprising all three contracts or three separate claims against that firm? You will see the importance of this . . . each contract is about $50,000 in this hypothetical case . . . your liability would be $50,000 or $150,000 depending on what is the meaning of "a claim".'[9]

Sir Robert was aghast, but should he fight the claim? The opinion he obtained from counsel in London was not reassuring. Whatever his own understanding of the agreement—and he was adamant that Ho Leung had shared it, too—a court might find Jardines' contention more compelling. Letters and telegrams went to and fro between England and Hong Kong as auditors unwound Ho Leung's affairs. All Sir Robert's instincts were against litigation; under the auditors' scrutiny, however, the sum of his liability appeared to be escalating daily. He could not bring himself to pay up without a fight.

It was all very distressing and the worry of it was retarding his recovery. By May 1934 he was convalescing in his house at Kew and making plans to return to the clinic at Berne.[10] Perhaps because of its associations with an unpleasant period in his life, Sir Robert was never to spend much time in this house and would put its lease up for sale two years later.

For the time being, he decided, he would concentrate on his health; everything else, particularly the Jardines claim, must be set aside. Katie Archee now proved her devotion, upholding Sir Robert's embargo on further correspondence and taking much of the responsibility for the discussions with Jardines herself. Miss Katie, as she was addressed in the family circle, was a central figure in Sir Robert's life for several reasons. When she looked after him as he languished in bed from 1910 to 1913, patient and nurse had become warmly attached to one another. Sir Robert and Katie, said to be of Guyanese and Chinese ancestry, became lovers, and their son, George Ho, was born in 1918, some three or four years after his recovery. Thereafter Sir Robert came to rely on Katie for more than emotional support. Because she was both highly competent and fiercely loyal, she gradually assumed a multiplicity of roles in his household, from bookkeeper and personal deputy to travelling companion and confidante. She kept the world at bay for him if he wished it.

Autumn saw the convalescent back in Hong Kong. Now the haggling began. Ill-used and misled though he felt, Sir Robert realised he did not have the heart for litigation. He could only hope to settle the claim on terms, and it was at this point that the newly installed taipan, W. J. (Tony) Keswick, took a hand. The auditors' report set Ho Leung's debts to Jardines at a staggering $1.2 million.[11] Large as the sum was, Keswick felt that taking the matter to the courts

Katie Archee

would be no fitting way to end 50 continuous years of very honourable and pleasant association between you [Sir Robert] and the firm. In fact it would be intolerable, especially to me, a member of a family which has been intimately connected
with you for three generations . . .

The other day you suggested that as the firm had indicated when Ho Leung
was alive that we might consider bearing half the losses in import trading to help
him out it would be equitable for the firm now to bear half of such losses claimed
for under your guarantee. Although the guarantee statement . . . specifically states
that the firm may make concessions to the compradore 'without discharging or
impairing the liability of the mortgager under the guarantee', I wonder whether it
is not possible to arrive at some basis of compromise along these lines?[12]

And indeed it was on this basis that the case was finally settled, with Sir Robert
compensating Jardines to the tune of $600,000. He might have remembered
Confucius' saying—'The superior man is dignified, but does not wrangle'—when
he decided to pay up; his sense of injury, however, could not be so easily appeased. It
was only after a concerted effort on the part of Tony and his brother John Keswick
to make amends that the rift was eventually healed. Meanwhile, in the few years
following the case, Sir Robert resigned from the boards of seven Jardines companies in favour of M. K., including the Indo-China Steam Navigation Company,
Canton Insurance, and Hongkong and Kowloon Wharf.

A postscript to this sorry saga is lodged in Sir Robert's correspondence with
David Fortune Landale, chairman and managing director of Jardine Matheson
from 1945 to 1951.[13] For the background to this correspondence, we must scroll
back to 1938, when a portrait of Sir Robert by Oswald Birley was commissioned
and presented to Jardines. After the war, Sir Robert's attempt to locate this portrait was met with a less than prompt response. Irritated, he reminded Landale in a
letter towards the end of 1948 that he still harboured a grievance against Jardines:

> when Ho Leung approached me with the Agreement [naming Ho Tung as his
> guarantor], he told me that I had only to give your firm a further $50,000 as
> personal security; and accepting his word I signed the Agreement without refer-
> ring it to a lawyer, not knowing that the $50,000 was only for each claim. This
> unfortunate Agreement proved beneficial to your firm to the extent of $500,000,
> at my expense; in other words, I paid $600,000.- to Jardine Matheson & Co. for
> the losses which Ho Leung incurred, although I had no interest in the benefits
> which accrued. As a matter of fact, at that time, my solicitors in London were of
> the opinion that I should contest the case in Court and I was given to understand
> that I would win, but because of my long connection with your firm, and because
> of my rather delicate health at the time owing to my two operations in London
> and Switzerland, I refrained from proceeding with the case.[14]

Landale returned quite a detached reply, in which he explained that there was no hope of recovering the painting, for it had been stored in a godown (warehouse), where 'it was wantonly damaged by the Japanese as to be almost unrecognisable, and the frame was completely ruined. The Japanese had occupied the building.'[15] Relations between Sir Robert and David Landale were not as warm as that between him and several generations of the Keswick family. But Sir Robert would not be put off: he was determined to have a replacement painted, and it was to be hung at the very same spot as the previous portrait.

Landale now knew better than to rekindle Sir Robert's sense of ill-usage, so he wrote again more helpfully: not only did he assure Sir Robert that his new portrait would be 'exactly right for the prominent position in which it would be placed in the Private Office', but he would also arrange a ceremony for the presentation. Birley had been reluctant to paint Sir Robert wearing his decorations, but offered the solution of producing a separate painting of them, to hang beneath the portrait.[16] Before the presentation, the portrait was displayed in the Royal Society of Portrait Painters Exhibition in London. It was finally unveiled at Jardines on 23 June 1950.

The combination of illness, mental stress, and financial loss following Ho Leung's suicide in 1933 exacted its toll, and probably induced a wish for a more subdued mode of life. Sir Robert took himself more frequently to his house at Macau, which provided a restful haven from the office. The lull was only momentary, however, though on the surface everyone around him appeared to be occupied, purposeful, and undemanding. Clara was busy with building her temple, a pet project made possible by Sir Robert's gift of $100,000 to each of his wives when he celebrated his golden wedding anniversary with Margaret in 1931. This project was unveiled four years later as the Tung Lin Kok Yuen, a Buddhist centre situated in Happy Valley and comprising the temple, a nunnery, seminary, and school. Clara had installed two halls as a repository for memorial tablets: her first son Henry is remembered in one of them in a portrait. During 1934 Robbie, in pursuit of advanced soldierly skills, took himself and Hesta off to the Staff School at Fort Leavenworth, Kansas. He wanted to prepare himself, he said, for fighting the Japanese in Manchuria and helping Chiang Kai-shek to flush out the Chinese communists from their stronghold in Jiangxi. Eddie was still in Shanghai. Father and son were writing to each other every day, a correspondence brimming with the minutiae of shares bought and sold, market news, property prices, and business done. Cables were exchanged when there were urgent instructions to communicate. But if either felt anything like regret at the rupture which obliged Eddie to live apart, he did not put it in writing. We only know that Eddie's stock went up and down: old-fashioned father that he was, Sir Robert was never fulsome in his praise, and Eddie was more often than not reminded of his debt to his father and put in his place.

Eddie found it a struggle to hold things together in the troubled days of 1934. Following the American stock market crash of 1929, most European currencies had been devalued and China's exports had steadily declined. Japanese encroachments on Chinese territory and economic life continued. Chiang Kai-shek still insisted on winning the civil war against the Communists before confronting the Japanese, and his military expenditure exceeded every other item in the government budget. Despite efforts at establishing a viable financial system, money was always tight, tax revenues were insufficient, and deficit spending was the order of the day. The replacement of the traditional tael by the silver dollar as the medium of exchange in the spring of 1933 was almost immediately undermined by a steep rise in the price of silver on the world market. A result of new American legislation on government purchase of silver internationally, this caused an alarming drain of the metal out of China and a currency crisis. 'The future of China's currency is still very obscure,' wrote Eddie to his father,

> Financial failures are a daily occurrence in Shanghai. Since . . . the 29th two more native banks have failed, one of which is owned by the compradore of the Chartered Bank. I expect there will be a few more today . . . The tragic part about this crisis is that so far no solution is in sight. I am enclosing a clipping 'No Japanese Loan for China'. It seems the Chinese government so far have not been able to make much headway in their game of playing the Americans against Japan. This announcement in the paper is the result of urgent conferences in Nanking when T.V. Soong [ex-finance minister of China] and the Japanese and American ministers were called hurriedly from their beds in the night. Anyhow, short of a huge loan there can be no return of confidence and consequently no solution to the present impasse. At the moment all negotiations regarding a loan have definitely broken off.[17]

Nine months later the government nationalised silver and introduced the *fabi*, a paper currency. This brought financial stability of sorts but the *fabi* would come under extreme pressure when the Japanese stepped up attempts to sabotage China's financial base. Soon a number of incidents unfolded to push the two countries to a devastating confrontation. At the end of 1936 Marshal Zhang Xueliang mutinied with other senior officers at Xi'an, forcing Chiang Kai-shek to join the Communists in a united front against Japan. In the following summer shots were exchanged between Chinese and Japanese troops at the Marco Polo Bridge (Lugouqiao) near Beijing. To stall attempts to open a second front in Shanghai, Chiang Kai-shek's air force dropped several bombs on Japanese warships anchored in the Huangpu River on 14 August 1937. Two stray bombs fell towards the Bund, hitting the Palace and Cathay hotels and killing hundreds of innocent civilians. Through the next two months the city again heroically endured a blitz of shelling. Then its resistance crumbled and, one after the other, Shanghai, Nanjing, and Wuhan fell to the Japanese, forcing Chiang to retreat up the Yangtze to Chongqing.

Three months before he ordered the catastrophic bombing of Shanghai harbour, Chiang was in Nanjing. There he received Sir Robert and Eddie, who were in the capital to attend a national handicrafts exhibition, and Irene, who was working in Nanjing at the time. History does not relate if the visit was made for any other purpose; there was nothing particularly unusual, though, in the Nationalist regime making friendly gestures to rich capitalists like Sir Robert Ho Tung. Mending fences could do no harm, for one thing; it would be understandable, for another, if Sir Robert should wish to distance himself—and by extension Robbie—from their links with Zhang Xueliang, instigator of the Xi'an mutiny against Chiang Kai-shek. In the event, Generalissimo Chiang could not have been more amicable. Sir Robert noted admiringly that his back injury, sustained during the mutiny at Xi'an, did not prevent him from standing for twenty minutes during the meeting. There was time, too, to show off the aeroplane presented by Sir Robert to mark Chiang's fiftieth birthday the previous year; it was flown up specially from Hangzhou for a sensational flying display. Over the fortnight of their visit, Sir Robert and his children were treated to an unceasing round of receptions, dinners, and excursions.[18] Apart from the flying demonstration at the military aerodrome, they were entertained by such luminaries as Sun Fo, the son of Sun Yat-sen; Wu Tingchang, the industry minister; Sir Hughe and Lady Knatchbull-Hugessen, the British ambassador and his wife; and the old warlord Feng Yuxiang.

That autumn Eddie took his family to Hong Kong for safety. They were in time for a party to celebrate Irene's birthday in October, though Mordia is not in evidence in a family photograph taken at Idlewild that day.[19] It was Clara's last family reunion. A few days into 1938, a telegram arrived in Shanghai telling Eddie that his mother had died. The suddenness jolted everyone. On New Year's Eve Clara had contracted a cold, no trivial matter for an asthmatic; within days it had turned into severe bronchitis, and in forty-eight hours she was dead.[20] She was sixty-three. She had died without seeing her favourite son again. For Eddie the loss was extraordinarily great; he would express a wish to be buried next to her Chiu Yuen grave should his father choose to lie alongside Lady Margaret in the Colonial Cemetery.[21]

When debilitated by grief at the sudden death of her first-born son, Henry, in 1898, Clara was warned by her doctor that she was in danger of contracting

Clara Ho Tung's funeral procession, 1938: Sir Robert, in full white mourning clothes, is supported by a nurse, who appears to be carrying a fan and a rug.

tuberculosis or suffering a nervous breakdown if she continued to neglect her own health. Clearly she had never been really strong, and we are told by Irene Cheng that during her last, fatal bout of bronchial asthma, oxygen had to be administered to ease her breathing. A Buddhist master and a number of students from the seminary attached to Tung Lin Kok Yuen, the temple she founded, said prayers at her bedside in her final hours. As she drew her last breath, some of those keeping vigil saw a flash of light pass through the room; several would later wonder if that was sign of Clara' ascendancy to Buddhist sainthood, a manifestation of her liberation from the cycle of birth, death, and reincarnation. Irene offered a more prosaic explanation in her book about her mother: it could have been, she ventured, sunlight refracted from the window or mirror of a car parked in the driveway of The Falls.

The family held off the funeral until Eddie arrived from Shanghai. Chinese custom required any son so unfilial as to have been absent at a parent's death to enter the house and approach the bier on his knees.[22] Just as distressing for Eddie was the fact that, since he had converted to Catholicism, the role of chief mourner at Clara's Buddhist funeral had to be taken by Robbie.

Later that year Eddie and his family returned to a partitioned Shanghai, with its neutral international zone marooned by Japanese-occupied territory. The division of the city reflected the wider breakup of the country itself, for by the end of 1938 the political map of China had been redrawn: a great sweep of territory from Manchuria down the eastern seaboard was held by the Japanese, the northwest was dominated by the Communists, and the central and southwestern interior remained in the hands of the Nationalists. Each zone had its own administration and economic system. The shifting of jurisdictions hardly helped the conduct of commerce, yet Shanghai managed to function, an uneasy co-operation having been forged between the Japanese and the mainly British, American, and French merchants who ran the international parts of the city. With his father's reluctant blessing, Eddie resigned from the stock exchange and began grappling with the problems of the Shanghai Land Investment Company, nearly half of whose shares were held by three leading mercantile lights in Shanghai and Hong Kong: Sir Elly Kadoorie, Sir Victor Sassoon, and Sir Robert Ho Tung. The company had made several loss-making disposals, including the sale of an apartment block, Broadway Mansions, to Japanese interests for considerably less than its original cost. Two million dollars' worth of properties had been destroyed during the hostilities. That, together with looting, poor management, and general inefficiency, had pitched the company into difficulties.

The last years of the 1930s were not a propitious time for owners of real estate in Shanghai. Chinese landlords in Zhabei and Hongkou dared not raise rents for fear of being suspected of pro-Chiang Kai-shek leanings by the Japanese army. One day a sub-agent in the Hongkou district who worked for Eddie, Mr Sasaki, was called before the military police. Charged with profiteering and supporting the enemy, he was not released until he had confirmed that the properties' owner, Sir Robert Ho Tung, was actually a British subject. Not for nothing was Shanghai described as the most dangerous and sinister city in Asia. On top of a vicious criminal underworld, which had long been present, there was now terrorism, for assassinations of Japanese and Japanese collaborators became a weekly occurrence.

If the political confusion was alarming, the influx of thousands of German Jewish refugees was a reminder that, in Europe, Hitler had unleashed a pogrom and embarked on a policy of rearmament and expansion. How all this would affect Asia was difficult to gauge, even when the Allies declared war on Germany on 1 September 1939. Some people in Shanghai thought that, in the event of Japan entering this larger war, property in the international concessions stood in danger of being confiscated as enemy possessions. Others were more optimistic, forecasting a land boom in the city.

By the winter of 1939, Hong Kong, being a British colony, was technically at war and subjected to emergency regulations. Sir Robert was among the first in Hong Kong to observe the directive to surrender foreign currency deposits. This 'loyal example' by 'the largest individual foreign currency holder in the Colony' elicited lavish thanks from the governor:

> As you are so well aware, foreign currency plays a most important part in war economy and the sums you have so willingly transferred to His Majesty's Government at unfavourable rates represent a really considerable share in this Colony's total monetary assistance to the war effort.[23]

As the months ticked by and the uncertainty and tension spread, Lady Margaret began thinking about evacuation. Eddie added his voice to hers, urging his parents to seek temporary asylum in America or Honolulu. Sir Robert, professing himself fatalistic, remained unconvinced. In any case, the sheer impracticality of such a move sapped any desire to leave home. He could not bear the thought of a long sea journey when his delicate digestion and inflexible 'sour milk diet', which required him to take his food 'lying in bed', gave him such trouble.[24] Lady Margaret, he said, was 'already weak and suffering from pains once very twenty-four or thirty-six hours.'[25] In fact, if he was going to search for refuge anywhere, he believed Shanghai safer than either Hong Kong or Macau. Eddie had moved into his father's Shanghai house, but there would still be plenty of room, Sir Robert thought: 'If I come by myself, all your children and your wife can remain where they are, but if Mother also comes, perhaps it may be advisable for your wife to stay outside for a while but the children can stay in the house.'[26]

At the same time that he was entreating his father to leave, Eddie was also urging Sir Robert to sell the properties in Zhabei and Hongkou. Whichever way you looked at it, he said, land values in Shanghai were likely to slump.[27] Sir Robert, however, disagreed with this recommendation, a judgement he would regret just six months later. Far from admitting his mistake, though, he would stubbornly advance several specious arguments to vindicate his decision.

Keeping his forebodings under wraps, Eddie took his children and his secretary, Miss Florence Webb, to Hong Kong a few weeks later, for soon it would be 2 December, the day of a great celebration to mark the diamond wedding anniversary of Sir Robert and Lady Margaret. At first Sir Robert had felt the situation in Europe and China too grave to justify frivolities in Hong Kong. But his friends and children had overcome these reservations, promising to subscribe any expenses they might incur on gifts to charities instead. Everyone was feeling the pinch. Sir Robert himself intended donating only a tenth of the total he gave away on his golden wedding anniversary. Explaining all this to the secretary of Chinese affairs,

Lady Margaret in middle age. Since she is wearing Western dress, this studio photograph may have been taken during one of her trips abroad.

he wrote: 'Owing to the Sino-Japanese war, I have suffered heavy losses in the defaulting of all Customs and Railway Bonds of which I am a big holder, in addition to the heavy depreciation in the Shanghai currency. So much so that during the last two years I have been spending and giving away from my capital in spite of the fact that I received a large amount in rents and dividends.'[28]

Once a celebration was decided upon, the family set to with a will. As usual there was to be a reception conducted on traditional Chinese lines at Idlewild, and one for 'international' friends in the form of a cocktail party at a hotel, this time the Gloucester. In a way the whole of Hong Kong shared in these festivities, providing as they did, however briefly, a talking point among the public, which otherwise felt beleaguered and apprehensive. By now many people thought war inevitable and were bracing themselves to defend the colony. Jean's husband, Billy Gittins, joined the volunteer defence corps as early as 1938; registration of women and children for possible evacuation was ordered in mid-1940. In November 1941 two regiments of Canadian infantry landed to swell the local garrison.

A fortnight before the anniversary, several family members, George She (a Eurasian connection who acted as Sir Robert's secretary for a time), and an employee from the *Kung Sheung* met at Idlewild to settle the final details of the evening reception. It was important to ensure that no blackouts or emergency manoeuvres would mar the day. Ho Wing, Eddie, and Robbie, as hosts, were to receive the guests, and a Filipino string band was instructed to strike up 'God Save the King' on the arrival of the governor.

It was a splendid party, but exhausting for Sir Robert and Lady Margaret. Fortunately they had had the foresight to book themselves into the hotel that night. Three days later Sir Robert went to recuperate in Macau. It is said the Japanese consul had given him a hint of the imminent invasion. When Japan struck on 8 December he was safely on neutral Portuguese territory.

There was never any doubt that Hong Kong, meagrely armed and reinforced, could be held. On the same day as the attack on Pearl Harbor (8 December in Hong Kong), the Japanese bombed the aerodrome in Kowloon and marched into the New Territories from across the Chinese border. Though a valiant stand to delay their advance was made, it took the Japanese only three days to seize control of the peninsula. Of the three Ho Tung daughters who lived in Kowloon, Jean evacuated to the university, where she was secretary of the relief hospital; Grace, married to M. K.'s brother Horace, joined the exodus to unoccupied 'free' China; and Florence, whose husband Dr Yeo Kok-cheang was forced to work under the Japanese in Kowloon, was, with her children, billeted with the rest of the family on the Peak.[29]

The authorities thought The Falls rather too exposed from the air to be safe, however, and moved Eddie; his secretary, Miss Webb; Irene and her husband, Hsiang-hsien Cheng; Florence Yeo; and sundry children and servants to another house lower down the hill, requisitioning The Falls for some of the Canadian infantry. Air raids and the shelling of various positions soon began in earnest, as a prelude to the full capture of Hong Kong Island. The Falls was bombed and looted in the course of the attack. Dunford was similarly wrecked; The Neuk, too, was looted. Nevertheless Eddie, who liked going into the garden to watch the planes through his binoculars, continued to drive himself and his children down to services at the Catholic cathedral every day, an insouciance which horrified his sisters.

Food was becoming desperately short. The Ho Tungs on the Peak, like everyone else, were issued with ration cards. As Eddie was deputed to register on behalf of the household, he duly set off one fateful afternoon with Florence Webb, who had offered to accompany him, and a rickshaw coolie, who was to show them the way. Winter weather in Hong Kong can be bright and cloudless; walking down from the top of Stubbs Road, Eddie and Florence Webb could see the shining sea below and the grey-green hills beyond. According to Eddie's later account, it was quiet except for a distant drone. Suddenly the hum was shattered by an ear-piercing roar. The plane when it appeared out of the clear blue sky was firing hard

Severely damaged in the war, The Falls was repaired and restored several times. Ho Shai-lai lived in an apartment within the building from the 1980s to the 1990s. Subsequently renamed Ho Tung Gardens, The Falls was demolished for redevelopment in 2013. This photograph dates from the intervening period.

and strafing the hillside with its deadly load. Though Eddie and Florence Webb squeezed themselves into the rock and scrub there was no cover. Then he heard an explosion and saw the sky turn black. For a split second he felt unreal and swallowed up in the holocaust—he could hear nothing and see nothing. When his senses returned, he realised that half his right leg and part of his left foot had been blown off. Nearby, Florence was lying motionless, a grotesque shape with truncated limbs and streaked with blood, but still conscious enough to say to him that she didn't think she would pull through.

How Eddie managed to squeeze out the screams from his lungs or the strength in his arms to crawl some distance down the hill remains a mystery, but he did manage to raise help before passing out. Rushed to the War Memorial Hospital, Florence died the same night while Eddie had an operation to amputate his right leg just below the knee. He had sustained more than a hundred shrapnel wounds and lay heavily sedated for the next six days.

The War Memorial Hospital, being on the Peak and subjected to intense shelling, was no place for the wounded. Providentially, as Eddie would say later, he was transferred to the Tung Wah and into the care of Dr Thomas, an old family friend. It was not a moment too soon, for the amputation had been clumsily done and his leg and foot wounds became gangrenous. The result was that not only did Dr Thomas have to unpick the stitches and operate again, but he also had to amputate Eddie's left foot four inches above the ankle. Eddie's fifteen-year-old son Eric had to cram all his growing up into that terrible week. As well as keeping vigil at his father's hospital bedside, he made forays up to The Falls, often braving shellfire, to salvage what he could from the house, from tinned food to wads of cash in small denominations, which the family had carefully hoarded in anticipation of war.

Hong Kong surrendered on Christmas Day. Meanwhile, having found it impossible to stay on the Peak, Irene and her husband, her sister Florence, and the rest of the party moved in with Lady Margaret at Idlewild. Some semblance of order returned as the Japanese occupation forces moved in to take control. The water supply, which had been turned off when the New Territories were seized, was resumed. Luckily Idlewild had a well; even so, the privations took their toll on Margaret, who fell ill with a bout of typhoid fever. It was her nurse, with her smattering of Japanese, who managed to persuade the officers to let the family stay on in the basement. The rooms upstairs were commandeered by a captain and his fifty men.

Eddie returned to Idlewild about a month afterwards, his wounds still raw and needing a change of dressing every day. The Catholic fathers lent him the money to buy streptocide powder, without which his wounds would not heal at all. There were still cooks in the kitchen and servants in the house, but how to secure enough rice to feed them all became an overriding concern. The men-servants claimed to be too weak from hunger to carry Eddie out into the garden, so Eric had to bear his father on his back. They did, however, muster the energy to convey him to mass on Sundays. Jean later said, 'It was heart-rending to see him, a six-footer, now looking so old and shrunken, being carried round by his son Eric. Eddie himself was wonderfully cheerful, confiding in me his plans to go to the United States, as soon as he was able, to have artificial limbs fitted. I was lost in admiration and felt humbled at this truly magnificent display of courage.'[30] He was not a man who whined or complained. His faith undoubtedly helped—perhaps he considered suffering a part of spiritual progress—but mostly he survived his ordeal through will-power and self-control. Down the road, Vic was holding the fort while M. K. was incarcerated for refusing to take part in the military government set up by the Japanese. Jean, with her husband in a prisoner-of-war camp in Kowloon, decided to be counted as British—therefore an 'enemy alien'—and went into civilian internment at Stanley. Eva was not in Hong Kong at all, but working for the Red Cross in China.

There can be no doubt that Sir Robert experienced acute stress and anxiety throughout this period. He had no one to turn to, with Eddie crippled, Robbie at the front in China, and his wife critically ill. His refuge from unbearable pressures invariably lay in a renewed obsession with his digestion; yet, although prices for foodstuffs were rocketing daily, and milk, the staple of his diet, was scarce, his material circumstances were still a great deal better than his family's at Idlewild. Several members of staff had come with him to Macau in early December, including a secretary and a nurse, and his house was commodious and comfortable. He had bought the mansion during the previous war.[31] It stands in a cobbled square redolent of old Portugal, flanked by St Augustine's Church on one side and the charming Dom Pedro V Theatre opposite. Sir Robert's house, no. 3 Largo de Santo Agostinho, rises three balconied storeys above the frangipani and skinny coconut palms at its entrance; with its stuccoed façade and decorated balustrades, it manages to suggest both the Mediterranean and the China Coast. A well at the back provided ample water for the cultivation of a luxuriant garden, where exotic creepers and tumbling roses vied for space with hibiscus and fruit trees. For Sir Robert, the place represented peace and sanctuary, and he was fond of it; he would one day bequeath it to the people of Macau.

He must now call up all his inner resources; fortunately he had in him still a touch of that fixity of purpose which he brought to the management of all practical affairs. The two burning questions of the moment were: how to raise cash to pay all his employees, and should he return to Hong Kong? The occupation force had frozen all corporate bank accounts and imposed withdrawal limits on personal ones. Rents collected by Sang Kee, the company which managed his Hong Kong properties, were dwindling to a trickle. If they needed to borrow funds to tide them over, his personal application might prove more effective than Eddie's. Many clamoured for his return, including the Japanese.

The new year opened on the Japanese making haste to realise their 'Greater East Asia Co-Prosperity Sphere', which was to see their rule extend from Manchuria all the way down to China's southern border. They had set up a puppet regime under Wang Jingwei in Nanjing in 1940; they intended to do something similar in Hong Kong. And as a first step towards assembling a representative council of collaborators to serve under a military legislature, they called a meeting of 131 leading citizens. Sir Robert and M. K. were both on the list. M. K., as we saw, was jailed for refusing to serve. Soon afterwards, they contacted Sir Robert.

A Colonel Sawa called on him in Macau. His message, delivered quietly but ominously, was to the point. As a British subject and enemy national, Sir Robert stood to lose all his property if he did not co-operate with the military administration. Sir Robert replied that he could not be expected to do anything unjust, unrighteous, and detrimental to his good name. If his property were confiscated, he would just have to reconcile himself to not owning a fortune. He said this with his usual graciousness, and the interview concluded with expressions of civility. Two weeks later he returned to Hong Kong. 'To my greatest surprise,' he later recalled, 'three motor cars with a naval officer in uniform were waiting for me at the wharf and took me straight to meet Mr Isaki. After a few formal words with him Mr Isaki escorted me to the ground floor of the Hong Kong Hotel and the navy man motored me home to Idlewild.' Mr Isaki called three days later for an interview punctuated with a great deal of seemingly irrelevant small talk and meaningless promises.[32]

This charade continued for several more hours over the next four weeks. Several Japanese officers and agents called on Sir Robert; they were all unflaggingly polite but pressingly insistent. We should stand together against bullies like Britain and America, they said. Help us with the reconstruction of Greater East Asia for the mutual benefit of all Asiatics. Join our rehabilitation advisory committee and the Chinese representative council; publish sympathetic pieces in your newspaper; give us your opinion on anything you care to discuss. When it was their turn to listen, they were all cordial sympathy. Permits to facilitate Eddie's return to Shanghai? They would pass on the request. Confiscated properties? Perhaps Sir Robert would make a list. Withdrawal of money from local banks? It was not within their power to increase the limit. Rice for family and staff? The authorities were giving their best attention to the matter but for the present the ration had to remain at 6.4 taels. Collection of rents? Rest assured this would be resumed in a few months.[33] Thus they carried on, in courteous, conversational tones, believing him susceptible to their blandishments, and in the end achieving nothing at all. Sir Ronald Campbell, British ambassador in Lisbon, reported as much to the Foreign Office following a telegram from Macau. He disclosed on 16 May 1942 that 'Hotung' had returned to Macau from Hong Kong, where 'he received a good reception which cooled when he refused to join "Rehabilitation Committee" or to make a statement flattering Japan as Sir Robert Kotewall [community leader] and Sir Shouson Chow have done in full measure. He [grp. undec: ? accused] these two of disloyalty whilst protesting his own loyalty ... He is most worried about his current account balance of dollars (Hong Kong) 1,100,000 in Hong Kong and Shanghai Bank.'

Sir Robert did not give in to the Japanese, yet they let him go back to Macau. His age and position probably protected him. Ho Wing was not so lucky. He had allocated funds at the bank to help evacuate employees, but, accused of supplying money to the Chongqing government (it did not help that he had a brother, Robbie, in Chiang Kai-shek's army), he was imprisoned for ten months and tortured. Like Eddie, he would call himself an undutiful son for not being present when Lady Margaret died in February 1944. His warders did, however, release him for half an hour to see her before the end so that he could beg for forgiveness: 'Mother, I am unfilial and am truly sorry that I cannot be by your bedside for long.'[34]

Sir Robert was not there either. He had returned to Macau, where Lady Margaret visited him in 1943. It was the last time he saw her.

Ho Wing and his wife, Kitty, some time before the war (Ho Wing died in 1946).

Link between East and West

Re-established at Idlewild in early 1942, Eddie must often have slipped into despair; he had little time, though, to evade the realities of his situation. As a cripple his first thoughts must have been on various remedies to restore mobility. His wounds were not healing well enough, however, 'even to try on a temporary stump.'[1] And although Sir Robert suggested engaging a special nurse for him, Eddie wished more than anything to go back to Shanghai, where help would be more readily available than in Hong Kong. If only one had the fortune, he said, or, even better, influential friends in the Japanese army or navy, to gain seats on a flight via Canton! He was anxious to see 'what can be done to save something from the wreckage as things in Shanghai do not appear to be normal.'[2] There had been an interval of acute anxiety about how Mordia was coping, especially as communications between Hong Kong and Shanghai broke down for a while. To his relief, a letter reached their son Eric which had been posted to the Catholic mission in Guangzhou and forwarded by the fathers, in which she imparted no news to raise undue alarm.

The Catholic priests were supportive in more ways than one. They propped up his spirits and it is likely that under their encouragement Eddie found a meaning to his suffering through the devotional discipline of confession, mass, and prayer. Father Albert Cooney SJ, who visited him at 8 Seymour Road during his recuperation, would later describe how he 'marvelled at his [Eddie's] courage and fortitude and his deep resignation to God's will. It was edifying to see how he looked forward to the future with such hope. Another man would have considered his life's work finished.'[3]

Another of Eddie's spiritual advisers was Father George Byrne at Hong Kong University, who was instrumental in bringing about help when it was needed. A cleric with a practical streak, Father Byrne knew that, with Florence Webb's death, the burden of running the Shanghai office with only a skeleton staff of inexperienced employees lay too heavily on Eddie's shoulders. Florence Webb needed to be replaced, and soon. The priest was not the person who first introduced Mary

Cheung to Eddie, but when consulted he found he could think of no one more suitable. Mary, a Chinese immigrant from British Guiana, was the cleverest scholarship student Father Byrne had taught at the university. Her father was a Protestant minister, but she had converted to Catholicism about two years before she came to Eddie's notice. She had been teaching at the Italian convent and supporting her parents for some time; a change in the parents' circumstances then freed her to look for work elsewhere. Guided by Father Byrne on the one hand, and urgently in need of support on the other, Eddie became convinced that Mary Cheung was the answer to his prayers. Her theoretical knowledge, he assured his father, 'can easily be put to practical usefulness, because she has had a thorough grounding of advanced accountancy and mathematics besides having a perfect command of the language. The fact that she has been a teacher should not prevent her from going into business and becoming an accountant. Her frugality, her efficiency, and her character, coupled with her knowledge, are just the right qualities I have been seeking to find.'[4]

Mary Cheung became indispensable as a trusted assistant and comrade in the daily fray of keeping the office functioning under the arduous conditions of occupied Shanghai. In April Eddie was issued with permits to return. Mary Cheung either travelled up with the family then or followed later.

The Shanghai Eddie returned to in the spring of 1942 was a war zone. Japanese soldiers, previously a menacing presence on the fringes of the International Settlement, were everywhere. On the very same day as the attack on Pearl Harbor, proclamations had appeared all over the foreign enclave announcing that a state of war existed between the imperial government of Japan and the governments of Great Britain, the United States, and the Netherlands. For all the reassurances that civilians—friend and foe alike—should go about their business as usual, within twenty-four hours the Japanese had taken over the police and raised their flag over the Shanghai Municipal Building. American, British, and other enemy offices were seized and sealed under guard, while the utilities companies found themselves placed under Japanese direction. The city crawled with collaborators whose eyes and ears were picking up every hint of resistance or trouble. Sandbags and barbed-wire barricades sprang up seemingly overnight to check the traffic and clog the roads. Once a glittering scene of neon-lit clubs and bars, the city's famous nightlife faded from the streets as electricity consumption came under restriction. The rapid depletion of rice, cooking oil, and coal was swiftly followed by that inevitable wartime phenomenon, the black market. Over the ensuing months foreign banks such as Chase, Hongkong and Shanghai, and Chartered were systematically stripped of their assets and liquidated.

Through the summer and autumn American and British diplomatic officials were repatriated, assets belonging to enemy aliens were frozen, and the neutrality of the International Settlement became a distant memory. The French Concession was thought to be a safe haven for a time, and there had been a rush to transfer ownership of American and British properties to a Vichy registration to prevent their seizure as enemy assets, but the Japanese military soon exerted its authority there, too.

There was no uniform treatment of Chinese British subjects like Eddie (better known by his Chinese name, Ho Sai-kim, in Shanghai). For a time he and his children had to wear the red armbands issued to enemy aliens. This mark of differentiation became redundant in early 1943 when the Nanjing puppet regime, prodded by Japan, declared war on the Allies. Enemy nationals were rounded up for internment. The very equivocality of Eddie's nationality was in his favour. While foreign assets were appropriated, properties belonging to Ho Tung were not confiscated (Sir Victor Sassoon, whose portfolio spanned hotels, apartment blocks, and office buildings, did not escape so lightly). Eddie and his family were exempt from internment, although they were not entirely immune from the actions of the Japanese military, who periodically descended on 457 Seymour Road and searched the house; Eddie was sure they coveted the property. The Japanese did eventually commandeer most of the house, while Eddie and his family were forced to squeeze into only one corner of it.

Night after night during the bitterly cold winter of 1942 Eddie would be jolted by agonising cramps in his left arm and the stumps of his legs, waking to bouts of giddiness or the eerie silence of a bruised and debilitated city. Shrapnel still lay embedded in his body. He walked with difficulty, and only 'about two blocks each time', he later told his father, as 'any excess would bring about an abrasion of the skin; and if I continue to wear the artificial legs, not only is the first layer of skin broken but also the second layer, and this is very painful. When this happens it takes two to three weeks of rest from wearing the limbs to allow the wound to heal.'[5] Somehow Eddie's iron will held firm through all these tribulations. He is caught in a photograph from those twilight years, before he left Shanghai for good. Despite its pathos, there is a touch of grim humour in the pose—wrapped up in a Chinese padded robe against the cold, he is pictured with his prosthetic legs, all webbing and straps at the top, and fitted with socks and shoes at the 'feet', propped up beside his garden chair. Being 'under Japanese supervision' he ceased doing any business and worked in the garden as often as he could.[6] Anyone lucky enough to have a bit of earth used it to grow food, contriving and improvising, fighting to survive.

Eddie, with his prosthetic legs, in the garden of his house in Shanghai, 1942

For Sir Robert, once the shock of the invasion and his tussle with Japanese officialdom were over, the war years became a test of endurance. As ever, his tactic was to wear people down by his own tenacity and will. Whether it was to squeeze a little more rice for his household from the rationing authorities, or extra oil, kerosene, sugar, and coal from the Macau government, or a higher quota of electricity to run a fan for himself, he waged his own war of attrition on hardship and want.[7] Not that food shortages bothered him as much as the people around him—malnutrition was, after all, his way of life—but he occasionally missed the things he was partial to (once he rather pathetically asked Katie if she had any tins of Quaker oats left). At one point his weight dropped alarmingly to seventy-five pounds. None of the five doctors he consulted over the summer of 1943 and the spring of 1944 agreed on a diagnosis, he noted dismissively, so 'what shall the patient do?' In the autumn he was stricken with dysentery.

He had to take the bad with the good. In Macau there was leisure to put down his reminiscences for a future autobiography (which did not get written), and we hear of him learning Mandarin three times a week in the afternoons. He may have spent time on religious instruction as well, for one day he informed George She, his former secretary and an ordained minister, that he wished to be baptised into the Protestant Church. Whether this interest had anything to do with intimations of mortality and his wish to be buried with Margaret in the Colonial Cemetery can only be surmised. There is certainly no evidence of a dramatic conversion; nor, on the other hand, any indication that he was motivated by purely pragmatic reasons. When questioning Eddie about Catholicism in his letters, he appeared as intrigued by its doctrines as by the outward forms of worship. Perhaps the sight of the Santo Agostinho nearby and the serenity of Christian services, as opposed to Buddhist or Taoist rites, appealed to him.

Reflections on religion did not engross him for long, however. What exercised him particularly through 1944 was the lack of funds to maintain his staff. He sold what he could (a diamond ring, a diamond bracelet, and his only property on Hong Kong's Queen's Road Central, which fetched 110,000 Japanese military yen, as he carefully recorded). It was not enough. His attempts to have funds released from frozen overseas accounts were unavailing.[8] The British government for one ignored his appeals for remittances from his bank in London. It was ironic that he who had made an interest-free loan of £10,000 to the war chest of Britain should now be limited to a paltry £20 a month for his expenses in Macau and Hong Kong. As he complained to the British consul in Macau, he had been put in an impossible position by the high-handed attitude of the authorities in London, 'and I cannot refrain from contrasting the continued proffers of help from the Japanese—which proffers, I would affirm, I never accepted—with those of the British Government, a Government I have always helped.'[9]

On the whole, though, he was much improved in spirits in early 1945, writing cheerfully to Vic that he had succeeded in putting on weight, and offering financial help to his youngest daughter Florence, who was just managing to feed herself and her family by cultivating sweet potato and keeping hens.[10] By 28 August, two weeks after Japan capitulated, his weight had risen to eighty-eight pounds; it was a small personal triumph, though he had lost forty pounds since the invasion. That autumn Robbie, now a lieutenant-colonel in charge of the Japanese surrender of Guangzhou, visited him in the midst of helping Admiral Sir Cecil Harcourt, the British commander-in-chief responsible for Hong Kong, to repatriate Chinese troops from Guangzhou to northern China. (Hesta and their two children had spent part of the war in Kunming.) Highly gratifying was a visit by Major-General Francis Festing, commander of the British landing force, who offered to arrange for his return to Hong Kong on Admiral Harcourt's special launch.

Japanese representatives signing the instrument of surrender at Government House, Hong Kong, 16 September 1945. Ho Kom-tong was among the witnesses standing against the back wall, second left of the soldier carrying a rifle and leaning slightly forward.

'My dear Eddie,' Sir Robert wrote in September, 'I can well realise how happy you and your family, also Bessie[11] and Mary Cheung feel over the news of the complete victory of the Allies against the Japanese.' The return of peace meant, above all, the resumption of business:

> As soon as convenient to you, I should like you to write me fully about our Hongkew [Hongkou] property, all your shares in Shanghai, your American money and your American investments with their present valuation and the rate which you paid for them. What is the present ratio between an American dollar note and a solid gold dollar? Also what is the cross-rate between US$ and sterling?[12]

News of the rest of the family trickled through. Jean came out of Stanley camp on 3 September and had time only to write a note to her father before sailing for Melbourne to collect her children, who had been evacuated to Australia at the beginning of the war. Temporarily quartered in Gloucester Building, she took her meals at the Hongkong Hotel. 'It is a pity,' she said ruefully, 'but now that we have all this food, I have lost my appetite completely.'[13] She would be in Australia before the news of Billy's death was broken to her.

Jean Ho Tung and Billy Gittins were married in Hong Kong with great fanfare in 1929. Billy lost his life before the end of World War II.

Vic sent Sir Robert some papayas from her garden in October; 'in fact I had some bananas, custard apple and papaya trees planted on your top terrace at Idlewild as the ground was lying waste and could benefit all.'[14] Ho Wing had looked well coming out of prison camp, and even walked 'with a firmer step', although he did not survive the war for long, dying in May 1946.[15] Eva, Grace, and Grace's husband, Horace Lo, were safe in southwest China; Irene, who was now widowed, was working at a British-run company, the Kailuan Mining Administration, near Tianjin.

Sir Robert returned to Hong Kong just before Christmas. Of course he was prepared for the worst, but the sight of The Falls, its insides ripped open by bombs, still unnerved him. Seeing the gaunt faces of his servants, he thanked heaven that they were all spared save one, Au Choi, who had served him and Lady Margaret for half a century.[16] Slowly but surely he retrieved what he could. All the ships of the Hongkong, Canton and Macao Steamboat Company, in which he was a controlling shareholder, were lost during the war, and a lighter he owned, the SS *Cheung Ming*, was blown up by a floating mine while travelling from Macau to Guangzhou. When notice came nine months later that reparation claims against Japan would be considered in London, he looked his losses in the face. His houses on the Peak, all six of them, lay in ruins. Four houses on the Wanchai reclamation called Hennessy Road were damaged, not to mention extensive properties from Kowloon to the New Territories. He put his total losses from the war at ten million dollars.

In Shanghai, post-war euphoria was fast giving way to gloom. Eddie could see no silver lining:

If we had optimism at the time of the Japanese surrender, we are very much disheartened now. In the first place, cost of living has gone up an average of about 7 times compared to the peak prices during the Japanese occupation, and in some cases it has reached 10 times. Business prospects are very bad: factories closed, no coal supply; transportation disrupted; winter ahead; influx of American troops and Chungkingites who consider Shanghai prices cheap compared to the interior and have bought manufactured daily necessities in large quantities; local administrations passed laws on price control which are not carried out; conflict between the Central Government and Communists; speculation and hoarding are the principal business. Rents can be increased only to an infinitesimal extent compared to the rise in daily necessities and commodities; and last but not least, unstable currency because as yet no fixed rate of foreign exchange for the fapi has been determined. As yet, foreign banks cannot open; foreign factories and mills are still closed ... Strikes are prevalent everywhere in this town; and yet you cannot get house servants at a reasonable wage ... In the shop, if you want the thing and don't buy immediately and pay whatever price is asked, the next time you decide to buy and go back, the price is already up 2 or 3 times.[17]

The threat communism posed to their prodigious enterprises was felt more palpably by Eddie than his father. It seemed to him that peace had only brought the Nationalists and Communists closer to their final conflict. People now talked about leaving for more tranquil and plenteous shores. Runaway inflation, recurrent strikes, an inept and corrupt government, and privations worse than they had experienced under occupation—all these seemed incontestably good reasons to abandon ship. Post-war Shanghai was being kept afloat by American aid and bounty; it was to the United States that Eddie now looked for a future. Besides, America offered something else which could materially affect his well-being. He had seen a documentary about American amputees. It showed that

> a few months after the first operation they have a second operation called the 'revision' in which the leg is properly trimmed to fit the artificial leg. This is something Shanghai or Hongkong has never seen. It makes walking not so much of an agony as I now go through. I hope someday you [Sir Robert] will let me go to the States and have my legs properly attended to and fitted up so that I can walk properly and comfortably and at least reduce the pain that I now suffer all the time. The trip could also be combined with business in that I could see what prospects [there are] for investments in the USA for our frozen funds there.[18]

Before he could do so, two more blows would fall. At home a strained domestic peace, now no longer maintained by the exigencies of war, finally shattered with the departure of Mordia. Nobody was having an easy time of it, but she had borne the ebb and flow of terrible events for too long. Ever since that fateful day in London when she had plunged into marriage, Mordia had had to devote all her energies to the triple task of steeling herself against coldness from Eddie's parents, bringing up a family and, from 1932 onwards, enduring the anxieties of an extraordinarily stressful time. She was utterly spent and desperately needed a change. Eddie, too, accepted that their marriage had run its course. Since divorce was out of the question for Roman Catholics, they legally separated in May 1946, after which she returned to England, leaving the children behind. Eddie would suffer a setback on the work front, too. In October, just before his departure for the States, his father asked him to hand over the management of a block of houses to Robbie. Sir Robert might have done this entirely to be useful to both his sons; Eddie was overworked, and Robbie now had time to interest himself in a significant facet of the family business. Besides, there was no saying what good Nationalist connections might achieve in the Shanghai property scene, especially if a little municipal muscle was needed to evict defaulting tenants in Hongkou. Sir Robert's way of making his wishes known was, however, less than delicate or tactful: he sent his instructions to 457 Seymour Road by Hesta. All this was tantamount to a vote of no confidence as far as Eddie was concerned. Fraternal relations were never very good; this latest gesture, suggestive as it was to Eddie of favouritism, would only widen the breach.

We may well ask if Sir Robert was really so blind to the undercurrents of rivalry between his sons. It seems he was. Hesta, on the other hand, had more than an inkling; as she explained to him, 'In temperament, character and political outlook and everything else, Eddie and Robbie are as diverse as the North and South Pole. Therefore it is plain that they can never be friends nor can they ever co-operate. It is most unfortunate but this sort of thing between two brothers is not uncommon.'[19] Eddie was understandably bitter:

> I have spent a great deal of time studying real estate problems in Shanghai and during the years of Japanese occupation went through a great deal of hardship and suffering because I had your Hongkew properties on my hands . . . Now that the war is over and after a lot of trouble with the Chinese authorities to get the properties returned to my management and things are beginning to get straightened out, it is very discouraging to me to find that you have given full instructions to Hesta to negotiate with me on this property . . . It is not good policy to take a block out from a property that has been under my management . . . since the time of the Ezras. I would not care to see it split into different managements as it would imply a reflection on my management in consequence of which my reputation must suffer . . . If . . . you wish to bring him [Robbie] into real estate dealings then surely you have other properties elsewhere that would serve the purpose. I have never asked you for any share in the *Kung Sheung Pao* or Tung Lok cinema or other enterprise which you have delegated to him. Now that I have settled my family troubles I would have more time and energy to attend my business . . . One of the objects of my trip to America is to study real estate developments there with a view to future redevelopments since we cannot sell it . . . From the time I took over . . . I can conscientiously say that I have done my best for you and the position now is very much better than eleven years ago. Anyway, ever since I became a Catholic I have tried to do everything I could to please you to make up for the past. In spite of my forebodings that the war was coming soon in November 1941, I came down to your diamond wedding and got caught. I am now badly handicapped but I am not complaining. Hesta says that your instructions are that I should hand a part of the Hongkew properties to Robbie's management. Though it hurts me very much I am ready to do so if you say that it would please you to have me do so, although I would ask you to please weigh and consider the matter again and then send me definite instructions and I will act accordingly.[20]

Actually it was rather too late to be thinking of management changes or redevelopment. Within three years the very idea of private ownership of land and capital would be swept away by the Communist victory, which rolled across China like a cleansing flood, turning the familiar world topsy-turvy and delivering everything into the hands of the proletariat. By then Eddie was in Hong Kong. In 1947 he had as planned made an extended tour of America, where his father visited him in 1948. When he returned briefly to Shanghai in April the following year the city he knew was vanishing before his very eyes. Beijing and Nanjing having already fallen to the Communists, Shanghai bulged with refugees. Nationalist armoured vehicles patrolled the streets. Western residents were being evacuated, though many Shanghailanders still regarded the latest troubles as no more than a local war, apt to blow over sooner or later, after which they could resume their wheeling and dealing and carry on the good life they had known. If it came to it, they would chance their luck with the city's new masters. Eddie was much less sanguine; indeed, he had returned to Shanghai to settle his affairs, taking the precaution of picking up the title deeds to his father's properties before the city's surrender to the Communists, which he believed inevitable.

News of the Communist takeover of Shanghai in late May caused more than a ripple in Hong Kong, but like many businessmen who chose to stay on, Sir Robert expected things to settle down again. Whether it was out of bravado or real conviction, he remained adamant that Hong Kong was safe. Its immediate retrocession was highly unlikely, in his opinion, even if the Communists were to gain control of the whole of China.[21] How insouciant he felt can be readily inferred from the long holiday he took in 1949, when he made a jaunt to Europe five months before the People's Republic was established.

This expedition, the first lap of which involved a marathon flight to London via Bangkok, Calcutta (where he stayed a few days), New Delhi, Karachi, Damascus, Istanbul, and Brussels, would stand out among his most pleasurable experiences. A visit to the zoo in London's Regent's Park was also interesting enough to be recorded in his diary. His preoccupation with diet extended even to the animals, for he made notes of what some of them were eating. What pleased him most, though, was his marked success in gathering up a host of prominent people during his peregrinations. He later recalled being 'received by kings'—and indeed he was, by the crowned heads of Denmark, Sweden, and Norway. From Grosvenor House, London, he wrote to the ninety-three-year-old Bernard Shaw suggesting lunch or tea in town or a visit to Ayot St Lawrence. The last time they had corresponded, in 1946, Shaw had described himself at ninety years old as 'finished and considerably decayed'. Sir Robert himself felt far from 'finished' and longed to see his old friend

Sir Robert Ho Tung and Bernard Shaw at Shaw's home, Ayot St Lawrence, 1949

again. He was engaged on several sittings for his portrait by Sir Oswald Birley, he explained, and friends had invited him to the Henley Regatta, but any time before the middle of July, when he planned to leave for the Continent, would be at Shaw's disposal.

'Your invitation is very tempting;' Shaw replied, 'but London is beyond my reach: I doubt whether I shall ever see it again. I am an impossible guest anyhow with my peculiar meals and incessant work and business. I am working all the time when I am not sleeping or hobbling round the garden for a pennyworth of exercise.'[22] The mountain must therefore go to Mohammed. The meeting is forever enshrined in the photographs taken when Bernard Shaw, wearing a Chinese robe, presented an autographed copy of his play *Buoyant Billions* to Sir Robert.

Meanwhile Hong Kong, transformed by events across the border, had become a refugee camp. Transients, from rich Shanghainese industrialists to destitute Cantonese peasants, jostled for a foothold on the colony's streets. Squatter huts were mushrooming across the hillsides, thrown up by people who thought they were the lucky ones; the less fortunate slept on pavements and in doorways. Shortly after the dawn of the new year, Sir Robert accidentally sprained a ligament in his thigh, so he was confined to bed when he heard the news of Britain's official recognition of Red China. The intelligence brought relief, but by spring there was a tension and the shadow of fear again, as Hong Kong buzzed with rumours of worsening relations between North and South Korea.

On 25 June 1950 North Korean troops invaded South Korea, and America went to war. Confusion reigned in Hong Kong as China's anti-American campaigns gathered intensity and the Communists talked of delivering their Asiatic brothers from the yoke of white imperialism. The price of gold shot up while stock prices plummeted. It was once again a time for exodus from the colony. We find Eddie, convinced that Hong Kong 'would be handed back to China on a platter',[23] leaving for the States that year, to be joined by Mary Cheung in due course. In July Sir Robert was confiding his worries to Bernard Shaw:

> I dare say you must have read about the political situation in China. The latest
> development in Korea has made it worse. Local stocks have dropped 30% in value
> . . . The money position is very tight and the banks refuse to advance money
> against real estate. Under these circumstances you can well imagine how much
> worry I have to go through. Fortunately, I still have the fighting spirit in me . . .
> Many of my friends and relatives advise me to get out from this place and go to
> the States for my personal safety. Up to the moment of writing I still feel that I
> should remain behind and die with the city.[24]

It was his last letter to the playwright. Four months later Shaw was dead. Sir Robert, who had identified closely with the other 'sage', found the news deeply upsetting. The year before, he had read a typical epigram from Bernard Shaw in a newspaper: asked if he was well, Shaw had said to his interlocutor, 'At my age, young man, you are either well or dead.' Along with this quotation, Sir Robert noted other 'thoughts' he liked. One, headed simply 'Power to control others, etc.'[25] certainly chimed with his own disposition to lead and dominate; the recommended mantra was: 'I have the power to control others, the ability to bring to pass that which I desire and the capability of enjoying life to its utmost.' A second 'thought' was 'Take time to eat meals'; still another, 'Be calm, cool, collected. Anger harmful'.

Sir Robert was six years younger than Shaw and still had many things to accomplish before he laid down his own burdens. As long as his health held, he continued ceaselessly to work; his secretaries tottered under the weight of typing and memoranda and letters that issued from him. A donation towards the relief

Sir Robert received several celebrities on their way through Hong Kong. Besides Bernard Shaw, he was visited by the American actor William Holden, who was on location to shoot the film Love Is a Many Splendored Thing *(1955).*

of flood victims in the Yangtze and Yellow river valleys in 1949, which he hoped would conciliate the Communists and put him in the way of a meeting with Mao Tse-tung at some future date;[26] $250,000 to found a school and Chinese library in Macau; a hall of residence for women undergraduates at the university[27]—such were the gifts and projects of his last years. To accumulate the money so he could more readily give it away, he transacted and contrived as indefatigably as ever. Nothing was too trivial or beneath his notice. He would plan a chain of restaurants like the Lyons Corner Houses one day, and run a cinema the next.[28] All the nuts and bolts of business continued to be put before him at Idlewild: rent reviews, redevelopment proposals, architectural plans, directors' reports, lists of staff salaries and bonuses, not to mention social correspondence and invitations. Nearly ninety years old, he no more questioned his own incessant involvement with these affairs than he would complain about their demands on him.

There had been, nevertheless, a change in his relations with Eddie. His desire to impose his will, still strong despite his waning vigour, was increasingly checked by evidence of mature judgement in his son. Eddie had become his confidant, his adviser, his deputy. There was still a certain decorum in their contacts with each other (though it has to be said that Sir Robert's other children observed the same conventions). It was as though Idlewild had become a palace in which deferential courtiers revolved round its overlord and obeyed an elaborate etiquette. Both when Eddie was in America[29] and while he was living in the same house, every topic of discussion between father and son from business matters to social engagements was conducted by letter. Sir Robert remained crystal clear about Eddie's financial obligations, accepting a monthly interest on the loan he had given his son all those years ago. Eddie for his part was always punctilious, for instance applying to his father in writing for permission to use the drawing room and dining room at Idlewild when he wished to give a tea or dinner party. At these occasions a guest list would be submitted, and Sir Robert was always courteously invited, though we may assume he seldom attended.

When Eddie returned to Hong Kong for Sir Robert's ninetieth birthday, he could see that old age had at last laid its touch upon even his father. The eyes were still keenly alert but the features in that remarkably fine, rosy-cheeked face had mellowed. Sir Robert's hearing was worse and he moved more stiffly, the suppleness of his fragile, wasted figure dissolving in the creeping advance of arthritis. There was indecisiveness where previously he was quick to settle and to act. His assets in China were a case in point: he simply did not know what to do about them. Though he had held them through years of political chaos, this time the rules of the game were fundamentally different. In the end he paid for his hesitation, for he lost them to the People's Government of Shanghai, which relieved him of all his properties for a nominal compensation.

His fixation on health and well-being continued. A typical diary entry for 26 May 1952 (a few months before his ninetieth birthday) 'is concerned with the meticulous, but totally unembroidered enumeration of the day's events':[30]

> Weight 100 ¾ - same. Slept 4 hours the whole night. Sweated a great deal all night and changed sleeping attire 5 times. Felt tremors in the legs and pains in the head several times . . . colour of urine deep yellow, quantities small.
>
> 8.15 a.m. got up. Bowel movement. Washed face. During the entire night urinated 3 times – 1.00, 3.15 and 5.10 – altogether 3 ½ ounces.

There follows a list of exact quantities of medication, water, sour milk, digestion tablet and vitamin B (? illegible) tablet he took from 8.15 p.m. to 8.15 a.m.

Did he, in his ninety-first year, have a sense of his own life drawing to its conclusion? In 1953 he wrote to his half-brother in England, Alec Bosman, enquiring about suppliers of tombstones in England.[31] Some time earlier the half-brothers had made contact and entered into correspondence. C. H. M. Bosman had married Mary Agnes Forbes, an American, in 1877. They settled in London and had four sons and a daughter: Alexander (Alec) was their eldest son. Judging from letters exchanged, relations between Sir Robert and Alec were cordial; Irene Cheng recalled a tea party given in 1932 by Sir Robert in London, at which Alec was present. One of Alec Bosman's daughters, Barbara Holmes, wife of a Royal Air Force officer, visited Hong Kong in 1953. While Sir Robert showed her every courtesy, her exact relationship to himself was too delicate a subject for him to invite her to stay at Idlewild.

Sir Robert was punctilious in keeping his last will and testament up to date, leaving instructions in 1955 that he should be buried next to Margaret in the Protestant Cemetery in Happy Valley, and making a bequest to his trustees to maintain not only his and Margaret's graves but also the graves of Hector MacLean and Frederick Stewart. It had been his intention for a very long time to have a Christian burial: instructions were included in an even earlier will in 1913: 'I direct that my burial shall take place in the Protestant Cemetery, Hongkong, according to the rites of the Church of England and I desire that my relations and friends shall in no way mourn for me or worry themselves on account of my death.' A clear signal of his wish to reclaim a part of his European heritage, which he had publicly denied for most of his life, he pondered about being received into the Anglican church but did not act, for he was still declaring his *intention* to become a Christian as late as 1941. He also discussed his wish to be christened with George She during the

A formal photograph, probably taken before or after their presentation to King George V and Queen Mary in 1924: Sir Robert and Lady Ho Tung appear entirely at home in the dual aspects of their heritage, as represented by their Chinese robe and Western dress.

war, as we saw. Did he then have a deathbed baptism? While it seems unlikely that he would have left it that late, no official record of his baptism (perhaps privately by George She) has been found. Margaret, it seems, was less well prepared. Said to be following Sir Robert's wishes in the matter of burial with him in the Protestant Cemetery, she would have been christened when she lay dying by John Chung Yan Laap, a member of the wartime clergy at St John's Cathedral. Although his 'widow', Margaret, and Clara Ho Tung (still his 'cousin-in-law') were named executors in Sir Robert's 1913 will, along with his brothers Ho Fook and Ho Kom-tong, all his executors predeceased him. The Hongkong and Shanghai Bank was the executor and trustee of his will of 1955.

Besides legacies to his children and others related to him, Sir Robert remembered members of his staff, his rent collectors, former nurses, and long-serving domestic servants. Under the will generous donations were to go to the Welfare League, Clara's Tung Lin Kok Yuen for the education of 'poor Chinese girls', St Joseph's Home for the Aged run by the Little Sisters of the Poor, St Francis' Hospital, the Sisters of St Paul de Chartres, and the Society of St Vincent de Paul. He made a gift of £10,000 to the 'Prime Minister of England' for the benefit of orphaned children of British servicemen who had lost their lives in World War II, 'as Her Majesty the Queen shall in her pleasure direct'. The governor of Macau was to exercise similar discretion in the distribution of HK$50,000 to schools and orphanages, both Portuguese and Chinese, in Macau. Not forgetting the needy in China, he set up two funds—backed by property and shares in one of his companies—to relieve those facing loss of land and livelihood through devastation by floods in both the north and the south of the country. As mentioned in the Preface, he bequeathed a Qianlong-era ivory screen to the British Museum.

Over the years he had thought about death from time to time, even going so far as to dictate instructions for his funeral. His cortège, he said, should wind its way through Bonham Strand, site of the old offices of Canton Insurance and Hongkong Fire; after that it could go through Queen's Road or Des Voeux Road straight to the Monument, where his European friends might join the procession if they so wished. Tellingly, he asked his mourners to wear black instead of white, the colour of mourning for Chinese. And in yet another renunciation of traditional Chinese practice, he said, 'It is my intention to become a Christian before my death . . . I have selected a burial place in the Colonial Cemetery not far from the grave of Sir Paul Chater.'[32] 'As for the three-week memorial service so much accustomed to by Chinese, I do not think it necessary,' the note continues, 'On the other hand if there should be a memorial service in the church I will not object.'

He left no stone unturned. To commemorate his long association with the firm, and to show the respect he thought was his due, would Jardines do him the honour to fly its flag at half-mast upon his death? He raised this request most politely, of course, but made it evident he would not brook a refusal. John Keswick at last sent a confirmation of his promise: 'Jardine's flag will be flown at half-mast as requested and the portrait of you, which now hangs in the Board Room, will be placed in the front hall of the building. This is, I am glad to learn, what you would like.'[33]

A year before he died, the British government finally decided that the moment had come to bestow another honour on him. It had long rankled with Sir Robert that he had remained a knight bachelor; not for nothing had he again and again brought his philanthropic acts to the attention of those in authority. J. H. Thomas, secretary of state for the colonies at the time of the first Wembley Exhibition, had initially sown the seed of hope, hinting in 1924 that a second knighthood might be forthcoming in the New Year honours. This promise—if it was a promise—came to naught. In the ensuing years Hong Kong governors Sir Reginald Stubbs and Sir Geoffry Northcote both pressed his claim, the former actually recommending him for the order of Knight of the British Empire, and he himself lobbied his high-ranking friends when in England in 1949.

When at last a KBE was conferred, what could be more understandable than that he should wish to receive the insignia from Queen Elizabeth in person? Not surprisingly Eddie thought the plan unwise, given Sir Robert's age and health, though he fell in with it readily enough. Nothing daunted, Sir Robert took two nurses, his secretary Elsie Cheung, and two maidservants on the forty-hour flight, travelling first class by a Pan American Airways clipper and keeping his wheelchair, medicine chest, and 'sour-milk basket' with him as cabin luggage. The day of the investiture at Buckingham Palace, 12 July 1955, dawned warm and sunny. By prior arrangement Sir Robert was wheeled into the presence of the queen. Not being able to reach far enough to hang the insignia ribbon round his neck, she stepped down from the dais to do so. A medal was pinned on his black silk jacket with jade buttons, which he had put on over a blue, silk-lined robe and padded leggings. He was, as the press remarked, 'a picture of Chinese benevolence'. The queen, Elsie observed from the gallery, was wearing a cream-coloured afternoon frock, white shoes, a three-strand pearl necklace, and no hat or gloves.[34]

Sir Robert's part in the ceremony—he left before the end—took no more than an hour. Even so, his attendance had been a bold and magnificent gesture. The British press loved it: 'Sir Longevity',[35] they had called him on his arrival in London, recounting in detail his dreary diet—sour milk and mashed potatoes with a little yeast extract and sometimes a bowl of chicken soup—but also commenting on how well he looked on it ('pink and white complexion of a child' and sparkling eyes).[36] Inevitably, letters of appeal poured into Grosvenor House, where he stayed, as a result of this publicity. As if this were not fatiguing enough, lack of sleep and an upset stomach left him even more strained and fretful. He loved the attention, but his constitution could no longer stand the excitement and he was forced to cut short his visit.

That autumn Eddie returned to New York to attend his daughter Mary's wedding and resume his negotiations with the Treasury, which had frozen his American assets since the Korean War. He was still there the following spring, cheerfully writing to Elsie: 'I am heartened to hear that he [Sir Robert] gives himself 10 to 15 years. The way to keep alive is to have the will to live, however I think he should be persuaded to eat more solid food.'[37] This might well have been in response to Elsie's report on Sir Robert's state of health: after a spell of illness, his condition took a turn for the better at the beginning of April. Optimism and good spirits were evident in a record he dictated on 3 April: 'I slept very well last night. When I woke this morning, I smiled. I had not smiled like this for several days.'[38] But Eddie's letter had barely reached Hong Kong when a relapse followed, and while there would be some better days, then bad, then good again, everyone at Idlewild could see that Sir Robert was withdrawing into his own private universe of aches and pains, temperature fluctuations, weight loss, and insomnia. He sensed the bitterness of fearing to die, consulting doctors almost daily for reassurance and comfort. A bout of bronchial pneumonia was the *coup de grâce*. On 22 April Katie cabled Eddie in New York: 'Condition very serious'. Embarking immediately on a flight via Manila, Eddie arrived in Hong Kong on 26 April 1956, the day Sir Robert died. The grieving son did not know it then, but it was nearly the end of the road for him as well, for he was to outlive his father by less than fifteen months. Eddie died at Idlewild of a sudden heart attack on 2 July 1957, aged fifty-five years. There had been few years in Eddie's life when his world was not darkened by illness, violent change, tumultuous war, or personal anguish. He had needed to call up all his perseverance and courage to survive. But even with his great staying power, his heart could not remain long immune to the attrition of his body and spirit.

The public eulogies and press reports on Sir Robert's demise said it all: 'Grand Old Man of Hongkong', 'the Colony's most eminent and respected citizen', 'commercial and financial magnate, industrialist, philanthropist ... Hongkong's greatest individual benefactor'. His death marked the end of an era, for his whole life had been bound up with the spirited British and Chinese adventure that conjured up the colony and made it prosperous. He was a man completely in tune with his place and time, a pioneer whose fortunes ran parallel to the astonishing development of Hong Kong. No wonder he became the inspiration of writers and the stuff of fiction: few men could have so perfectly realised the rags-to-riches fantasy or held a mirror up to more exciting times. But the fable had its sober side, too. Harnessing his talents to supreme advantage for himself, he was yet a greater benefactor to the city of his birth. His endowments and donations aside, he made himself useful to the community in other ways. Casting aside his European ancestry, he took on an intolerant colonial system to champion a fairer deal for the Chinese of Hong Kong. Tilting at racial exclusiveness, he set a precedent by moving his family to the Peak. While never giving anyone cause to doubt his probity as a loyal British subject, and always wary of expressing any ideology or credo—oscillating niftily between political leaders and factions, for example—he nonetheless involved himself in the reunification of China; a man of peace, he tried to exert his influence on the side of reconciliation and reform, at the same time relieving—with timely help where it was needed—some of the vast suffering of the poor in that populous country. Achieving so much, he was yet without the slightest touch of arrogance, keeping his faith in the decency and charity of his fellow men intact to the end.

The graves of Sir Robert and Lady Ho Tung, Hong Kong Colonial Cemetery (later Hong Kong Cemetery)

Sir Robert Ho Tung was interred in Happy Valley beside Lady Margaret, their graves marked by two white marble crosses. His epitaph could not be simpler—

Sacred to the Everlasting Memory of
SIR ROBERT HO TUNG, K.B.E., L.L.D., J.P.
Born 22-12-1862   Died 26-4-1956

The headstone is also inscribed with his name and title in Chinese. It is an apposite memorial to what he symbolised. Beyond the richest man in Hong Kong, beyond the great philanthropist, beyond the public-spirited colonial citizen, and beyond the Chinese patriot, he was, as the London *Times* put it, a 'Link between East and West'.[39] *The New York Times* made a similar point, mentioning his knighthood and describing him as a 'go-between'.[40] One needs no imagination to find his last resting place redolent of that link. No man is free of his history: he was from first to last a creation of the encounter between two cultures.

Family Trees

Family Tree 1: SZE Shi 施氏

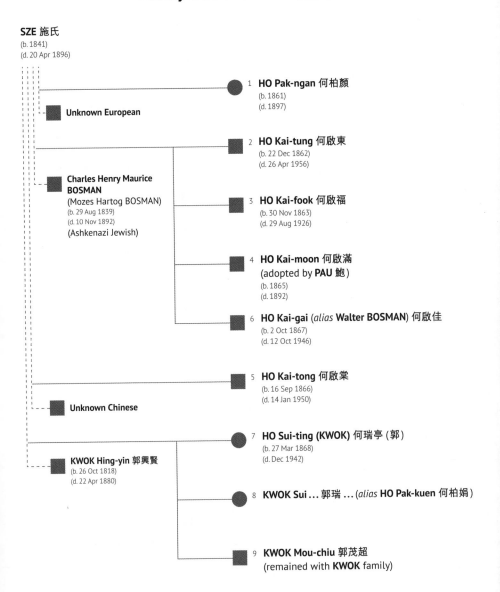

SZE 施氏
(b. 1841)
(d. 20 Apr 1896)

Unknown European

Charles Henry Maurice BOSMAN
(Mozes Hartog BOSMAN)
(b. 29 Aug 1839)
(d. 10 Nov 1892)
(Ashkenazi Jewish)

Unknown Chinese

KWOK Hing-yin 郭興賢
(b. 26 Oct 1818)
(d. 22 Apr 1880)

1 **HO Pak-ngan** 何柏顏
(b. 1861)
(d. 1897)

2 **HO Kai-tung** 何啟東
(b. 22 Dec 1862)
(d. 26 Apr 1956)

3 **HO Kai-fook** 何啟福
(b. 30 Nov 1863)
(d. 29 Aug 1926)

4 **HO Kai-moon** 何啟滿
(adopted by **PAU** 鮑)
(b. 1865)
(d. 1892)

6 **HO Kai-gai** (*alias* **Walter BOSMAN**) 何啟佳
(b. 2 Oct 1867)
(d. 12 Oct 1946)

5 **HO Kai-tong** 何啟棠
(b. 16 Sep 1866)
(d. 14 Jan 1950)

7 **HO Sui-ting (KWOK)** 何瑞亭 (郭)
(b. 27 Mar 1868)
(d. Dec 1942)

8 **KWOK Sui ...** 郭瑞 ... (*alias* **HO Pak-kuen** 何柏娟)

9 **KWOK Mou-chiu** 郭茂超
(remained with **KWOK** family)

Family Tree 2: HO Tung 何東

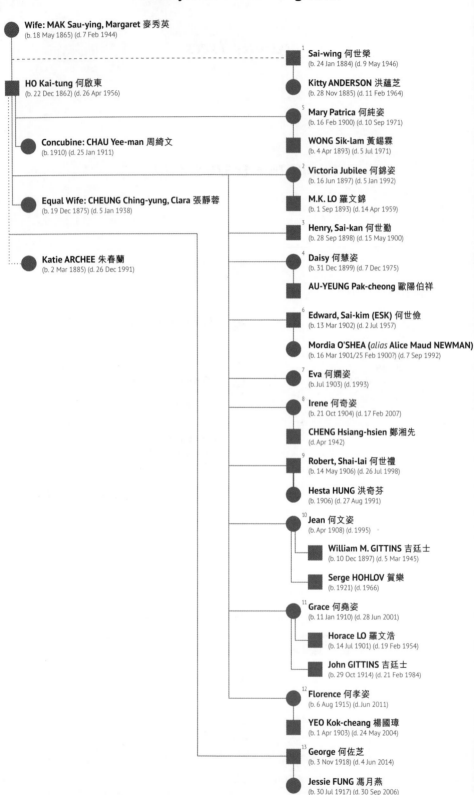

Wife: MAK Sau-ying, Margaret 麥秀英
(b. 18 May 1865) (d. 7 Feb 1944)

HO Kai-tung 何啟東
(b. 22 Dec 1862) (d. 26 Apr 1956)

Concubine: CHAU Yee-man 周綺文
(b. 1910) (d. 25 Jan 1911)

Equal Wife: CHEUNG Ching-yung, Clara 張靜蓉
(b. 19 Dec 1875) (d. 5 Jan 1938)

Katie ARCHEE 朱春蘭
(b. 2 Mar 1885) (d. 26 Dec 1991)

1 Sai-wing 何世榮
(b. 24 Jan 1884) (d. 9 May 1946)

Kitty ANDERSON 洪蘊芝
(b. 28 Nov 1885) (d. 11 Feb 1964)

5 Mary Patrica 何純姿
(b. 16 Feb 1900) (d. 10 Sep 1971)

WONG Sik-lam 黃錫霖
(b. 4 Apr 1893) (d. 5 Jul 1971)

2 Victoria Jubilee 何錦姿
(b. 16 Jun 1897) (d. 5 Jan 1992)

M.K. LO 羅文錦
(b. 1 Sep 1893) (d. 14 Apr 1959)

3 Henry, Sai-kan 何世勤
(b. 28 Sep 1898) (d. 15 May 1900)

4 Daisy 何慧姿
(b. 31 Dec 1899) (d. 7 Dec 1975)

AU-YEUNG Pak-cheong 歐陽伯祥

6 Edward, Sai-kim (ESK) 何世儉
(b. 13 Mar 1902) (d. 2 Jul 1957)

Mordia O'SHEA (*alias* Alice Maud NEWMAN)
(b. 16 Mar 1901/25 Feb 1900?) (d. 7 Sep 1992)

7 Eva 何嫻姿
(b. Jul 1903) (d. 1993)

8 Irene 何奇姿
(b. 21 Oct 1904) (d. 17 Feb 2007)

CHENG Hsiang-hsien 鄭湘先
(d. Apr 1942)

9 Robert, Shai-lai 何世禮
(b. 14 May 1906) (d. 26 Jul 1998)

Hesta HUNG 洪奇芬
(b. 1906) (d. 27 Aug 1991)

10 Jean 何文姿
(b. Apr 1908) (d. 1995)

William M. GITTINS 吉廷士
(b. 10 Dec 1897) (d. 5 Mar 1945)

Serge HOHLOV 賀樂
(b. 1921) (d. 1966)

11 Grace 何堯姿
(b. 11 Jan 1910) (d. 28 Jun 2001)

Horace LO 羅文浩
(b. 14 Jul 1901) (d. 19 Feb 1954)

John GITTINS 吉廷士
(b. 29 Oct 1914) (d. 21 Feb 1984)

12 Florence 何孝姿
(b. 6 Aug 1915) (d. Jun 2011)

YEO Kok-cheang 楊國璋
(b. 1 Apr 1903) (d. 24 May 2004)

13 George 何佐芝
(b. 3 Nov 1918) (d. 4 Jun 2014)

Jessie FUNG 馮月燕
(b. 30 Jul 1917) (d. 30 Sep 2006)

Glossary of Chinese Names

Archee, Katie 朱春蘭
Au choi (*alias* Au Shing-cheung) 區成璋

Beidaihe 北戴河
Beijing 北京
Beiping 北平

Canton, *see* Guangzhou
Cao Kun 曹錕
Chang Hsueh-liang, *see* Zhang Xueliang
Chang Tso-lin, *see* Zhang Zuolin
Chan Kai-ming 陳啟明
Chiang Kai-shek 蔣介石
China-Western Daily News, see *Zhongxi ribao*
Chinese Club 華商會所
Chinese Recreation Club 中華游樂會
Chiu Yuen Cemetery 昭遠墳場
Choa Chee-bee 蔡紫薇
Choa Leep-chee 蔡立志
Chow Shouson 周壽臣
Chung, John Yan Laap 鐘仁立
Chung Sai Yat Po, see *Zhongxi ribao*
Cixi, Dowager Empress 慈禧太后

Dairen 大連 (Dalian, formerly Lüda)
Dalian 大連
dujun 督軍

fabi 法弊

fapi, see *fabi*
Fengtian 奉天
Feng Yuxiang 馮玉祥
Fuzhou 福州

Guangdong 廣東
Guangxi 廣西
Guangxu, Emperor 光緒帝
Guangzhou 廣州
Guomindang 國民黨
Guo Songtao 郭嵩濤

Hankou 漢口
Henan 河南
Heung Shan 香山
Ho A-mei 何亞美
Ho Leung 何亮
Hongkew, *see* Hongkou
Hongkou 虹口
Hong Xiuquan 洪秀全
Ho Yow 何祐
Hsu Shih-ch'ang, *see* Xu Shichang
Huangpu 黃浦
Hung Kam-ning 洪錦寧

Jiangsu 江蘇
Jiang Suzhen 蔣素珍

Kailuan Mining Administration 開灤礦
務局

Kang Guangren 康廣仁
Kang Youwei 康有為
K'ang Yu-wei, *see* Kang Youwei
Kien Lung, *see* Qianlong
Koo, Wellington 顧維鈞
Kung Sheung Yat Po (*Industrial and Commercial Daily Press*) 工商日報
Kunming 昆明
Kwok Chung (*alias* Kwok Hing-yin) 郭松 (郭興賢)

Lau Chu-pak 劉鑄佰
Lee, Bruce 李小龍
Lee Hoi-chuen 李海泉
Lee Yuen Sugar Refinery 利園煉糖廠
Leong On 梁安
Li Chai-sum, *see* Li Jishen
Li Hongzhang 李鴻章
Li Jishen 李濟深
Li Yuanhong 黎元洪
Lo Cheung-shiu 羅長肇
Lo Cheung-ip 羅長業
Lo Hok-pang 羅鶴朋
Lo Shui-choi, Lucy 羅絮才
Lüda 旅大
Lugouqiao (Marco Polo Bridge) 盧溝橋
Luoyang 洛陽
Lu Yongxiang 盧永祥

Macao, *see* Macau
Macau 澳門
Manchuria 滿洲
Mao Tse-tung 毛澤東
Mei Lanfang 梅蘭芳
Mingshan youji 名山遊記
Mukden, *see* Shenyang

Nanjing 南京
Nanking, *see* Nanjing
Ng A-Wei (*also* Ng Wei) 吳亞煒
Ng Choy, 伍才, *see* Wu Tingfang
Ningbo 寧波

paijiu 牌九
paikau, *see paijiu*
Peitaiho, *see* Beidaihe
Po Leung Kuk 保良局
Puyi 溥儀

Qianlong 乾隆
Qingdao 青島
Qi Xieyuan 齊燮元

Samshui, *see* Sanshui
Sang Kee 生記
Sanshui 三水
Shanghai 上海
Shanhaiguan 山海關
Shantou 汕頭
Shanxi 山西
She, George 施玉麒
Shenyang 沈陽
Sichuan 四川
Sin Tak-fan 冼德芬
Sun Cheong Fat 新昌發
Shunde 順德
Soong, T. V. 宋子文
Sun Fo 孫科
Sun Tai-tseung 孫帝象
Sun Yat-sen 孫逸仙
Su Zhaozheng 蘇兆徵

taipan 大班
Taiping Heavenly King 太平天王
Taiping Rebellion 太平天國運動
Taipingshan 太平山
Taiping Theatre 太平戲院
Tai Tam Tuk 大潭篤
Tai Yau Bank 大有銀行
Tang Caichang 唐才常
Tang Jiyao 唐繼堯
Tianjin 天津
Tianzuhui 天足會
Tung Lin Kok Yuen 東蓮覺苑
Tse, Francisco 謝詩屏

Tse Ka-po, Simon 謝家寶
Tse Tsan-tai 謝讚泰
Tsoi Sing-nam 蔡星南
Tung Lok (cinema) 同樂戲院
Tung Wah Hospital 東華醫院

Wanchai 灣仔
Wang Jingwei 汪精衛
Wei Yuk 韋玉
Wu Dingchang 吳鼎昌
Wu Peifu 吳佩孚
Wutai shan 五台山
Wu Tingchang, see Wu Dingchang
Wu Tingfang 伍廷芳

Xiamen 夏門
Xi'an 西安
Xingzhonghui 興中會
Xu Shichang 徐世昌

Yantai 煙台
Yan Xishan 閻錫山

Yangtze 長江
Yellow River 黃河
yici 義祠
Yuan Shikai 袁世凱
Yuen Fat Hong 元發行
Yunnan 雲南

Zhabei 閘北
Zhang Xueliang 張學良
Zhang Zuolin 張作霖
Zhejiang 浙江
Zhifu (now Yantai) 芝罘
Zhili 直隸
Zhili Clique 直隸系軍閥
Zhongxi ribao (China-Western Daily News)
    中西日報
Zhu Gang 祝鋼
Zhu Pu (Sze) 祝普

Notes

Preface

1. Eric Peter Ho, *Tracing My Children's Lineage*, 96–97.

Chapter 1

1. The photograph may have been taken the day before. A note from Irene Cheng suggested this as a more practical time. Hotung Papers.
2. M. K. Lo to Sir Robert, 16 October 1952; Hotung Papers.
3. Sir Robert to John Keswick, 24 December 1952, Hotung Papers.
4. *South China Morning Post*, 22 December 1952.
5. Sir Robert to L. N. Shaw, executive vice president and manager of the overseas division of the National City Bank of New York, 26 July 1953, Hotung Papers. On one side of the medallion is the single word, 壽; on the other, under the dates, are 期頤記念.
6. Sir Winston Churchill to Sir Robert, 29 May 1953; Winston Churchill Archive Trust, CHUR 2/409B. Runhua Wu kindly brought the documents to my attention.
7. *South China Morning Post*, 22 December 1952.
8. Charles Ford (1844–1927) was a botanist and gardener. He was recommended to Governor MacDonnell by Sir Joseph Hooker, director of the Royal Botanic Gardens at Kew, for his appointment as 'Superintendent of Gardens and Plantations at Hongkong'. He arrived in Hong Kong in 1871 and stayed till his retirement in 1902. He was also a plant collector; several species of trees and flowering plants were named after him, including *Rhododendron fordii*.

Chapter 2

1. Translated from the Chinese by the author.
2. Bruner, Fairbank, and Smith, *Entering China's Service*, 230.
3. E. J. Eitel, *Hongkong Government Gazette 1880*, cited in Fisher, 'Eurasians in Hong Kong', MPhil thesis, University of Hong Kong.

4. Medical Missionary Society of China Reports 1838, 1848, cited in Smith, *A Sense of History*, 295.

5. *Hong Kong: Return to an address of the House of Lords, dated 22nd March 1889, for copy of report of the Commissioners appointed by the Governor of Hong Kong to inquire into the working of the Contagious Diseases Ordinance of 1867.*

6. Jiang Suzhen. Zhu Pu and Sze Tai's sister had three sons; one of their grandsons, Zhu Gang, married a schoolteacher, Jiang Suzhen, who wrote a long note on the Zhu–Ho relationship in 1995. Zhu Gang's connection to the Ho family, particularly to Ho Shai-lai, an officer in the Nationalist Army, counted against him during the Cultural Revolution. Criticised and imprisoned, he was one of countless victims at that time; his health was affected and he died in 1980.

7. Will of Sir Robert Ho Tung, 15 September 1947. Copies of the following wills were found among the Hotung Papers: wills dated 1 March 1913, 26 April 1918, 8 April 1932, 15 September 1947, and 4 July 1955. Fourteen codicils were added in the years 1947, 1948, 1949, 1951, and 1955.

8. Carl T. Smith, 'Protected Women in Nineteenth-Century Hong Kong', in *Women and Chinese Patriarchy*, ed. Jaschok and Miers, 226–27.

9. *China Directory*, 1861 and 1862.

10. Ho, *Tracing My Children's Lineage*, 26. It is not known whether 'Maurice' was adopted in place of 'Mozes'.

11. Sinn, *Pacific Crossing*, 116.

12. Circular, Koopmanschap & Bosman to Jardine, Matheson & Co., 20 October 1862; Jardine Matheson Archives, Cambridge University Library.

13. Bosman & Co. to Jardine, Matheson & Co., 20 October 1862; Jardine Matheson Archives.

14. Sinn, *Pacific Crossing*, 354n84.

15. Jarrett, 'Old Hong Kong' by 'Colonial', 507; *South China Morning Post*, 22 September 1933.

16. *Hongkong Daily Press*, 2 March 1868. In his toast to the governor, Bosman referred to the many public works launched or completed within the last couple of years, from the foundation-laying of the new city hall to the opening of the Seamen's Hospital. He alluded to the serious financial difficulties the Hotel Company had passed through, and said he saw about him many who had doubted the hotel could ever be built, or who thought it could never be used except as a lunatic asylum, in which the shareholders and directors might be confined (this joke was greeted by applause and laughter). He was happy to say, he continued to his audience's amusement, that no such arrangement was at present contemplated, and probably the only people who would ever be locked up in the hotel would be the juries sent over from the Supreme Court. Bosman himself had been on the jury list since 1859, and was a special juror in 1863–1869.

17. Barth, *Bitter Strength*, 192–93.

18. *Hongkong Daily Press*, 16 April 1869.

19. Cheng, *Clara Ho Tung*, 7. In *Tracing My Children's Lineage*, 97, Eric Peter Ho recounts a story that suggests Ho Tung was first named 何冬—as in 'winter'; teased by his schoolmates, who dubbed him 冬瓜 (winter melon), he changed his given name to the phonetically identical 東, as in 'east'.

20. *Chicago Times*, 7 December 1869, and *New York Herald*, 9 December 1869; I am grateful to Runhua Wu for bringing these reports to my attention.

21. He lived first at 8 Redcliffe Square, and later at 42 Bramham Gardens, South Kensington, London. His death was reported in *Hongkong Daily Press*, 21 December 1892; noted in the files of Carl T. Smith.

22. Information provided by Eric Hotung.

23. *Hongkong Government Gazette 1880*, cited in Fisher.

24. Noted in the files of Carl T. Smith.

25. Frodsham, ed., *The First Chinese Embassy to the West*, 6.

26. Stokes and Stokes, *Queen's College*, 232.

27. Ibid.

28. Sir Robert's notes for his memoirs [undated]; Hotung Papers.

29. Cited in Bickley, *The Golden Needle*, 146.

30. Stokes and Stokes, *Queen's College*, 232; 'memoriter writing' involves writing down memorised pieces of text, probably in classical Chinese.

31. Bickley, *The Golden Needle*, 165.

32. Will of Sir Robert Ho Tung, 4 July 1955; Hotung Papers.

33. Sir Robert to K. Ashdowne, Commissioner of Chinese Customs, Kowloon and District, 18 March 1946; Hotung Papers.

34. Sir Robert's notes for his memoirs; Hotung Papers.

35. Cited in Spence, *To Change China*, 104.

36. Ibid., 112.

Chapter 3

1. Drage, *Servants of the Dragon Throne*, 70.

2. Keswick, ed., *The Thistle and the Jade*, 35.

3. Returning to London after three decades in the East, William Keswick put his broad knowledge of China to good use, guiding the firm's fortunes through its conversion into a limited company in 1906 and as its managing director until his death six years later. His brother James, son Henry, grandsons Tony and John (who one way or another perpetuated the association with Sir Robert Ho Tung), and great-grandsons all followed in his footsteps.

4. Coates, *Whampoa*, 158.

5. Information provided by Eric Hotung.

6. MacLean died on 24 March 1894.

7. The story probably originated from Ho Tung himself.

8. *China Mail*, 19 June 1871; cited in Carl T. Smith, *Chinese Christians*, 155.

9. The source for the two amounts of savings is Sir Robert Ho Tung himself. He mentioned $2 million in the notes for his memoirs, and $600,000 in a few undated carbon copies of a typescript recording his recollections, which may have been set down in 1940 (see Chapter 2 and the account of his schooling); Hotung Papers.

10. Edward Fleet Alford (1850–1905), youngest son of Bishop Alford of Victoria, Hong Kong; employee of Jardine, Matheson & Co. from 1867; partner, 1894–1899; retired from business and returned to England, 1899; served on government committees to enquire into Chinese indemnity question, 1901–1902; created knight for work in connection with the MacKay Customs Treaty after the Boxer War, 1902; records at Matheson & Co. Ltd., London.

11. Jardine, Matheson, General Agents of Canton Insurance Office, to The Chief Manager, Hongkong & Shanghai Banking Corporation, 15 September 1880; Jardine Matheson Archives.

12. Canton Insurance Office to Messrs Arnhold Karberg & Co., agents for Str. *Aegean*, 26 September 1882; Jardine Matheson Archives.

13. Eitel, *Europe in China*, 528.

14. E. F. Alford to W. Humphrey, [?] 1878; Jardine Matheson Archives.

15. *Hongkong Telegraph*, 31 March 1882.

16. John Bell-Irving (1846–1915), whose mother was a niece of William Jardine, went to China in 1872, was a partner of Jardine Matheson, 1875–1891; returned to Britain, 1889. Three brothers were partners of the firm, and his son, also called John, became a director in 1919; records at Matheson & Co. Ltd, London.

17. Sir Robert's notes for his memoirs; Hotung Papers.

18. Quoted in *South China Morning Post*, 17 July 1933.

19. Wotton & Deacon, Solicitors & Notaries, 35 Queen's Road, Hong Kong to Messrs Jardine, Matheson & Co., 10 December 1888; Jardine Matheson Archives.

20. Choa Leep-chee was Choa Chee-bee's nephew and his successor to the compradoreship of the China Sugar Refining Co.

21. Details of the purchase and sale of R.P. of M.L. 10 and R.P. of M.L. 12 between 1888 and 1899, when the Ho brothers sold to a consortium of four Hong Kong traders, are based on notes from Land Registry Office records taken by Carl. T. Smith.

22. SO 1477, Hong Kong Public Records Office, see Ho, *Tracing My Children's Lineage*, 65.

23. Liu, *Ho Kom-tong*, 97.

24. Sir Charles Addis to Sir Robert, 14 November 1941; Hotung Papers. For more on Addis, see Shiona M. Airlie, 'Addis, Sir Charles Stewart', in *Dictionary of Hong Kong Biography*, ed. Holdsworth and Munn, 1.

25. *China Mail*, 19 October 1899.

26. Cited by Ho Tung in his draft contribution to Braga, ed., *Hong Kong Business Symposium: A Compilation of Authoritative Views on the Administration, Commerce*

and Resources of Britain's Far East Outpost, Hotung Papers. The compilation was started in 1955 but not published until 1957, after Sir Robert's death.

27. See Hong Kong Public Records Office: HKRS 149-2-1700; and the Land Registry Memorial UB21250. Lo Cheung-ip and Lo Cheung-shiu were also Eurasians, the latter an assistant compradore at Jardines and brother-in-law of Ho Fook. The family ties were strengthened further when two of Lo Cheung-shiu's sons married Ho Tung's daughters Victoria and Grace.

28. Private letter, Sir Robert Ho Tung to Mrs Li Ho Huen Man, 21 July 1951. Mrs Li's relationship to Sir Robert is unclear. She may have been a trusted assistant at one time; Hotung Papers.

29. Cheng, *Intercultural Reminiscences*, 309; see also Gittins, *Eastern Windows—Western Skies*, 19.

30. James Jardine Bell-Irving (John's brother) to Ho Tung, 4 June 1900; Hotung Papers.

Chapter 4

1. Yeo, *My Memories*, 12. Ho, *Tracing My Children's Heritage*, 14. The 'Spanish-Portuguese great-grandfather' on Clara's mother's side is noted in a handwritten 'genealogical tree of E. S. K. Hotung showing foreign blood ancestry', undated; Hotung Papers.

2. Translation from the Chinese by the author; for the original, see Cheng, *Clara Ho Tung*, 12. The Three Dependences of a woman are dependence first upon her father, then her husband, and finally her son; the Four Virtues are right behaviour, right speech, right demeanour, and right employment. As for the Three Imperishable Qualities of the superior man, the other two are establishing his merit and his words. The *Yijing* is the *Book of Changes*, a Confucian classic of philosophy. Eric Ho believed the date of Margaret's letter was Sir Robert's birthday in 1894, when he was thirty-two years old.

3. Reported in *Hongkong Telegraph*, 3 December 1931.

4. Document dated 13 June 1895; Hotung Papers.

5. Cheng, *Clara Ho Tung*, 16.

6. Cheng, *Intercultural Reminiscences*, 28–37; but it should be noted that her memories were of the house in more recent times, not as it was at the turn of the century.

7. *Hongkong Daily Press*, 1 August 1900.

8. Cheng, *Intercultural Reminiscences*, 1.

9. Stokes and Stokes, *Queen's College*, 251.

10. *New York Times*, 16 April 1901.

11. Stokes and Stokes, *Queen's College*, 31.

12. This account is from a copy of Ho Tung's letter to his brother, date illegible; Hotung Papers.

13. 'Return to Hong Kong: Extracts from Captain Walter Bosman's account of his overland journey from Europe, 1937'; Stokes and Stokes, *Queen's College*, 454.

14. Report attached in letter from W. G. Parminter, Political Secretary, South Africa House, Trafalgar Square, London WC1, to the Under Secretary of State, Dominion Office, Downing Street, London SW1, 6 June 1939; F6166/28/10. Enclosures also include letter from the Honorary Trade Commissioner for the Union of South Africa, 110 Hankow Road, Shanghai, reporting on information gleaned about W. Bosman's background and his well-known family in Hong Kong, in particular his brother Sir Robert Ho Tung. Runhua Wu kindly brought these documents to my attention.

15. *Hongkong Daily Press*, 10 October 1902.

16. Smith, *Chinese Christians*, 154. Hung Kam-ning switched to using his English name, Henry Graham Anderson, after retiring from government service (he had been an interpreter at the Magistracy). His daughter was later known as Catherine (or Kitty) Anderson.

17. Stokes and Stokes, *Queen's College*, 252.

18. Not including children by Ho Fook's concubine. See Hall, *In the Web*, 180. Cheng, *Intercultural Reminiscences*, 8, gives the number of children as ten.

19. Gittins, *Eastern Windows—Western Skies*, 20.

20. Ibid., 15.

21. Ibid., 20–21.

22. Sir Henry May to the Rt. Hon. Lewis V. Harcourt, M.P., Secretary of State for the Colonies, 22 April 1914; Hong Kong Public Records Office: CO129/410, 360–63.

23. Cheng, *Intercultural Reminiscences*, 70.

Chapter 5

1. Cited in Smith, 'A Sense of History (Part I)', *Journal of the Hong Kong Branch of the Royal Asiatic Society (JHKBRAS)*, Vol. 26, 1986, 235.

2. Ibid., 239.

3. Ibid., 243.

4. Elizabeth Sinn, 'Ho A-Mei', in *Dictionary of Hong Kong Biography*, ed. Holdsworth and Munn, 184–86.

5. 'The Night Pass Crusade', *Hongkong Telegraph*, 4 December 1895.

6. Extracts from speeches by Ho A-mei and Ho Tung at the meeting are taken from the detailed report, 'The Chinese Protest', in *Hongkong Telegraph*, 23 December 1895.

7. Cited in Smith in 'A Sense of History (Part II)', *JHKBRAS* 27 (1987): 138.

8. Ibid., 142.

9. Po Leung Kuk Board of Directors for 1977–1978, *Centenary History of the Po Leung Kuk Hong Kong, 1878–1978*, 214.

10. Tung Wah Board of Directors 1970–71, *One Hundred Years of The Tung Wah Group of Hospitals 1870–1970*, 66.

11. Sinn, *Power and Charity*, 205.

12. Paterson, *A Hospital for Hong Kong*, 16. Ho Kai, doctor of medicine from the University of Aberdeen and barrister-at-law of Lincoln's Inn, lost his wife, Alice Walkden, to typhoid fever in Hong Kong in 1884.

13. Carroll, 'Ho Kai: A Chinese Reformer in Colonial Hong Kong', in *The Human Tradition in Modern China*, ed. Hammond and Stapleton, 61; Carroll, 'Ho Kai', in *Dictionary of Hong Kong Biography*, ed. Holdsworth and Munn, 188.

14. *Hongkong Telegraph*, cited by Jarrett, 'Old Hong Kong' by 'Colonial', 376; *South China Morning Post*, 22 June 1934.

15. Ibid., 545; *South China Morning Post*, 13 September 1934.

16. Registrar-General, A. W. Brewin, and Inspector of Schools, Edward A. Irving to Officer Administering the Government of Hong Kong, Major-General Sir William Gascoigne, 28 January 1902; CO 129/311.

17. Ho Tung to Colonial Secretary, J. H. Stewart Lockhart, 17 February 1902, cited by Jarrett, 'Old Hong Kong' by 'Colonial', 917.

18. Lugard to the Earl of Crewe, 4 June 1908; CO129/347.

19. Cited by Sinn, 'Tse Tsan Tai', in *Dictionary of Hong Kong Biography*, ed. Holdsworth and Munn, 438.

20. *Hongkong Daily Press*, 6 June 1902.

21. *Hongkong Telegraph*, 10 June 1902.

22. *Hongkong Daily Press*, 10 June 1902.

23. Cited by Eric P. Ho, 'Ho Fook', in *Dictionary of Hong Kong Biography*, ed. Holdsworth and Munn, 188.

24. *New York Times*, 29 September 1908.

25. Wright and Cartwright, eds., *Twentieth Century Impressions of Hongkong, Shanghai, and Other Treaty Ports of China*, 751.

26. Correspondence, 1914–1919; Hotung Papers.

27. Cheng, *Intercultural Reminiscences*, 75.

28. War Office to Hon. Secretary and Organiser of the Overseas Club, London, 17 January 1916; copy, Hotung Papers.

29. Tsai, *Xianggang ren zhi Xianggang shi*, 103.

30. *Hongkong Daily Press*, 8 March 1922.

31. Carroll, *A Concise History of Hong Kong*, 98.

32. Letter, Luk King Fo, Delegate from Commissioner's Office of Foreign Affairs, Canton, *Hongkong Daily Press*, 8 March 1922.

33. *Hongkong Daily Press*, 8 March 1922.

34. Chan Wai-kwan, *The Making of Hong Kong Society*, 189–91.

35. Notes on correspondence, Hotung Papers.

36. *Hongkong Daily Press*, 22 January 1926. undated letter from Sir Robert to the Colonial Secretary, headed 'Seamen's (1922) Strike Settlements'; Hotung Papers.

Chapter 6

1. *Hongkong Telegraph*, 4 September 1895.
2. Ibid.
3. Cited in Spence, *The Gate of Heavenly Peace*, 32.
4. Lo, *K'ang Yu-wei*, 95.
5. Sir Robert's notes for his memoirs; Hotung Papers.
6. Ibid.
7. *Hongkong Telegraph*, 4 March 1900.
8. Ho Yow or Ho Shan-yow was a brother of Dr Ho Kai and the brother-in-law of Ng Choy.
9. Ho Tung, San Francisco, to Wu Tingfang, Washington, 11 January 1901; Hotung Papers.
10. *New York Times*, 16 April 1901.
11. Ibid.
12. Schiffrin, *Sun Yat-sen and the Origins of the Chinese Revolution*, 305–6. According to Schiffrin's footnote, a copy of the secret enquiry conducted by a Chinese government agent, which cast suspicion on Ho Tung, was leaked to the governor, Sir Henry Blake. Blake's dispatch to the Foreign Office was dated 18 June 1903: National Archives, FO-17-1718. Lau Chu-pak was for a time compradore to the Hong Kong company A. S. Watson's; he was also a businessman and community leader who, like Ho Tung, was both galvanised by China's republican revolution but also disappointed by the factionalism and political disintegration that ensued.
13. Sir Robert's notes for his memoirs; Hotung Papers.
14. Sir Robert, 3 Shih Lao Niang Hutung, Peking, to Dr Wu Tingfang, 30 May 1921; Hotung Papers.
15. Wu Tingfang, Ministry of Foreign Affairs, Canton, to Sir Robert, 15 June 1921; Hotung Papers.
16. Carroll, 'Ng Choy', in *Dictionary of Hong Kong Biography*, ed. Holdsworth and Munn, 337.
17. Sir Robert, Peking, to Wu Tingfang, Canton, 2 July 1921; Hotung Papers.
18. *Peking Daily News*, 28 September 1921.
19. Sir Robert's notes for his memoirs; Hotung Papers.
20. Wilbur, *Sun Yat-sen*, 143.
21. Sir Robert's contribution to Braga, *Hong Kong Business Symposium*, 27.
22. *North China Daily News*, 14 December 1923.
23. *China Mail*, 15 January 1923.
24. *China Mail*, 30 July 1923.
25. Sir Robert's notes for his memoirs; Hotung Papers.
26. *China Mail*, 8 August 1923.

27. Sun, Canton, to Sir Robert, 29 September 1923, cited in *China Mail*, 5 October 1923.
28. *North China Daily News*, 14 December 1923.
29. Sir Robert's notes for his memoirs; Hotung Papers.
30. Bonavia, *China's Warlords*, 89.
31. Nathaniel Peffer, 'Currents and Characters in China', *Asia*, January 1922, cited in Bonavia, *China's Warlords*, 90.
32. *North China Daily News*, 14 December 1923.
33. Extracts from Sir Miles Lampson's report on his tour in China, [undated, ? May 1928], CO 129/510/10, National Archives.
34. Cipher telegram from Foreign Office to Sir Miles Lampson, 29 June 1928, CO 129/510/10, National Archives.
35. *China Mail*, 27 November 1923, reporting Sir Robert's statement to the press in Shanghai.

Chapter 7

1. Sir Robert to Dr Harston, 11 August 1919; Hotung Papers.
2. Stokes and Stokes, *Queen's College*, 304.
3. Gittins, *Stanley*, 14.
4. Cheng, *Intercultural Reminiscences*, 58.
5. Catharine L. Hartshorn, Cheshire, to Lady Ho Tung, Hong Kong, 18 July 1915; Hotung Papers.
6. *Hongkong Daily Press*, 5 April 1918.
7. Letter, Mother Eliza Superioress to Sir Robert Ho Tung, 9 June 1939; Hotung Papers.
8. Memos re Daisy: Vic to Sir Robert, 26 May 1940 and 27 May 1940; Hotung Papers.
9. Gittins, *Eastern Windows—Western Skies*, 43.
10. Cheng, *Intercultural Reminiscences*, 120. Cheng refers to Ho Cheuk as the seventh son.
11. R. F. Johnston, 46 Tsai-ch'ang Hutung, Peking, to Sir Robert Ho Tung, 17 January 1922; Hotung Papers.
12. Sir Robert to R. F. Johnston, 22 March 1922: Hotung Papers.
13. Gittins, *Stanley*, 18. Jean was married to Billy Gittins on 19 March 1929. He did not survive the war but died in a prisoner-of-war camp in Japan in early 1945.
14. Cheng, *Intercultural Reminiscences*, 121.
15. *South China Morning Post*, 19 December 1922. A 1947 statement of rents received lists also twenty-four properties on Bubbling Well Road; Hotung Papers.
16. The elegant Hotung Pavilion in the Shanghai Museum was created with a donation by Eric Hotung. Opened in 1996, it consisted of a cunningly lit courtyard filled with trees and shrubs, and two side halls. The halls were furnished with traditional Chinese furniture and carried the names 'Sai-kim' (Eddie) and 'Mordia Alice Ho-Tung'. It is not known whether the pavilion remains intact.

17. Robbie to Sir Robert, 14 December 1934; Hotung Papers.

18. Robbie to Sir Robert, 17 June 1935: Hotung Papers.

19. Robbie to Sir Robert, 14 November 1925: Hotung Papers.

20. CO 129/503/4.

21. Robbie to Sir Robert, 2 June 1926: Hotung Papers.

22. Sir Robert's notes, undated typed transcript, possibly for an article for Reuters in 1955. Hotung Papers.

23. I. Ho Tung to the Home Office, 12 December 1927; CO 129/503/4.

24. Handwritten notes, CO 129/503/4.

25. Sir Robert to Robbie, 13 December 1927: Hotung Papers.

26. Transcript of a radio broadcast made in Mukden, 29 August 1929; Hotung Papers.

27. Bonavia, *China's Warlords*, 74.

28. Listed in the Shanghai Directory of 1930 as 157 Seymour Road (later renumbered as 457 Seymour Road). His neighbours were Anna Stunzi, the Ohel Rachel Synagogue, and A. E. Hardoon, among others.

29. *All About Shanghai: A Standard Guidebook* reprint, 11.

30. Sir Robert to Hesta, 22 March 1932; Hotung Papers.

31. Robbie, Hotel Keining, Mukden, to Sir Robert, 7 October 1930: Hotung Papers.

32. The *Kung Sheung* was not Sir Robert's first venture into newspaper publishing. In 1900 he was a member of the syndicate that bought the afternoon paper *Hongkong Telegraph*. (Its one-time manager, the Portuguese J. P. Braga, proposed the motto 'From Trial to Triumph' for Sir Robert's coat of arms.) Ho Tung and Ho Fook, two of the *Telegraph*'s shareholders, offered to sell their paper to the new *South China Morning Post* on its launch but the asking price proved too high; see Hutcheon, *SCMP*, 24. Though the offer was declined, the interests of the *Telegraph* did eventually merge with *Morning Post* some twenty years later.

33. Will of Sir Robert Ho Tung, 8 April 1932; Hotung Papers. Included in the pecuniary bequests was the sum of $500,000 'to my son Robert in recognition of my apprecia-tion of his self-sacrifice in serving the Chinese Army with such honesty, tenacity and earnestness of purpose'. There was no similar bequest to Eddie, who was left only his share of the income from trusts established for all the Ho Tung children.

Chapter 8

1. Sir Robert visited Bernard Shaw at his home in Ayot St Lawrence on 4 July 1949. Shaw liked Sir Robert's present, a Chinese padded gown, so much that he asked to be photographed in it.

2. Shaw sent Sir Robert a copy of the photograph with the message 'From one sage to another'. He described himself as 'a groggy old skeleton (93 1/2)' to another corre-spondent in early 1950; Hotung Papers.

3. Cited in Laurence, *Bernard Shaw*, 764. A temple based on Clara's shrine was used in a scene in *Buoyant Billions: A Comedy of No Manners*, Shaw's last play, which he wrote when he was ninety-two years old.

4. Shaw, *Buoyant Billions: A Comedy of No Manners* (1948), in *The Complete Plays of Bernard Shaw*. See also http://gutenberg.net.au/ebooks03/0300421h.html.

5. Sir Robert to Eva, 30 July 1929; Hotung Papers. By then Eva had qualified in medicine and was in Europe pursuing postgraduate studies.

6. John Fleming of Lowe, Bingham & Matthews, Chartered Accountants, to Jardine Matheson, 22 June 1934, reported shortages on freight carried by the Indo-China Navigation Company and other claims for goods amounting to more than a million dollars; copy, Hotung Papers; Leung, *Lady Victoria Jubilee Lo*, 80.

7. Ho Leung to Jardine Matheson, 14 July 1932; copy, Hotung Papers.

8. The accounts in the *South China Morning Post* of 22 and 23 December 1933, for example, mentioned neither the suicide nor Ho Leung's financial troubles.

9. Lo & Lo Solicitors to Sir Robert, 26 June 1934; Hotung Papers.

10. In the previous year Sir Robert had put this house, 18 Mortlake Road, at the disposal of Sir Reginald Johnston for a nominal rent; see Reginald Johnston to Irene, 25 February 1933; Hotung Papers. Sir Reginald, his glorious term as imperial tutor having ended in 1931, was teaching at the London School of Oriental Studies and writing his memoirs, *Twilight in the Forbidden City*.

11. At a very rough guess about $80 to $90 million in today's money.

12. Tony Keswick to Sir Robert, 12 October 1934; Hotung Papers.

13. David Fortune Landale (1905–1970) was born in Shanghai. His father, David Landale, also ran Jardines. The mother of the senior Landale was a Jardine and thus distantly related to the founder of the firm, Dr William Jardine. He is remembered in the name of a street in Wanchai, Hong Kong—Landale Street. The career of the junior Landale (D. F. Landale) in Jardine Matheson was a long one. He was at the helm during the Second World War—joining the Royal Naval Volunteer Reserve and later serving in the Middle East—and throughout the tumultuous period culminating in the Communist takeover of China in 1949, as well as the outbreak of the Korean War in 1950. He served on Hong Kong's Legislative Council as senior unofficial member (1946–1950).

14. Sir Robert to David Landale, 17 December 1948; Hotung Papers.

15. David Landale to Sir Robert, 31 March 1949; Hotung Papers.

16. David Landale to Sir Robert, 21 January 1950; Hotung Papers. The new portrait remains in Jardines' offices in Hong Kong. Eric Hotung commissioned a copy, which differs from the original in the shade used for the background. This copy is reproduced on the book cover.

17. Eddie to Sir Robert, 2 February 1935; Hotung Papers.

18. An account of this visit, 11–24 May 1937, was typed up by Sir Robert's secretary. It includes the transcript of a speech he broadcast from the capital, in which he praised the government's adoption of a managed currency system, and noted the progress

made in railway construction and the salutary effect this had had on the price of railway bonds; Hotung Papers.

19. This photograph appears in Cheng, *Clara Ho Tung*, 164. In *Intercultural Reminiscences*, 228, Cheng states that Mordia was then still in Shanghai. But according to her son Eric, Mordia was evacuated with him and, being cold-shouldered by her in-laws, had to stay at a hotel. Since it was the Peninsula in Kowloon she must at least have been more comfortable than at Idlewild.

20. Gittins, *Eastern Window—Western Skies*, 106; Cheng, *Clara Ho Tung*, 153; Cheng, *Intercultural Reminiscences*, 236.

21. He was actually buried in the Christian cemetery in Happy Valley and later re-interred in London with Mordia after her death.

22. Cheng, *Clara Ho Tung*, 160.

23. Governor Sir Geoffry Northcote to Sir Robert, 28 May 1941; Hotung Papers.

24. Sir Robert to Eddie, 6 May 1941; Hotung Papers.

25. Ibid. What caused the pain is not known. Irene Cheng, referring to a uterine tumour as a possible cause of Margaret's infertility, says 'it caused her considerable suffering' during the final years of her life; see *Intercultural Reminiscences*, 1.

26. Sir Robert to Eddie, 6 May 1941; Hotung Papers. This reference to Eddie's wife suggests that Sir Robert's objections to Mordia had softened but that Lady Margaret's had not.

27. Eddie to Sir Robert, 1 November 1941; Hotung Papers.

28. Sir Robert to the Honourable Mr R. A. C. North, 29 September 1941; Hotung Papers.

29. K. C. Yeo, a government doctor, was medical officer of health for the New Territories. He was imprisoned for a time.

30. Gittins, *Eastern Windows—Western Skies*, 134.

31. Bought by Sir Robert in 1918, it was eventually donated to the government of Macau on condition that it would be turned into a library for Chinese books.

32. Sir Robert kept notes of these interviews; Hotung Papers.

33. Ibid.

34. Cheng, *Intercultural Reminiscences*, 291.

Chapter 9

1. Eddie to Sir Robert, 6 February 1942; Hotung Papers.

2. Ibid.

3. The Rev. Father Albert Cooney, SJ, Colegio S. Luiz Gonzaga, 63 Praia Grande, Macao, to Sir Robert, 29 July 1943; Hotung Papers.

4. Eddie to Sir Robert, 8 April 1942; Hotung Papers.

5. Eddie to Sir Robert, 16 November 1945; Hotung Papers.

6. Eddie to Sir Robert, 23 February 1947; Hotung Papers.

7. Sir Robert to Servicios Municipais de Electricidade, Macao, 4 June 1943; Hotung Papers.
8. Sir Robert to C. Y. Kwan, solicitor, asking for a wire to be sent to Arthur Morse of the Hongkong and Shanghai Bank, London, about remitting £10,000 through Lisbon to Macau. He was 'badly in need of financial help to keep myself and my household staff in Macao.' Hotung Papers.
9. Sir Robert to J. P. Reeves, His Majesty's Consul, Macao, 28 March 1945; Hotung Papers.
10. Sir Robert to Vic, 9 January 1945, and Florence to Sir Robert, 18 February 1945; Hotung Papers.
11. Bessie Lum was Sir Robert's secretary. She was sent to Shanghai to help Eddie during the war.
12. Sir Robert, 3 Largo de Santo Agostinho, Macao, to Eddie, 23 September 1945; Hotung Papers.
13. Jean to Sir Robert, 16 September 1945; Hotung Papers.
14. Vic to Sir Robert, 2 October 1945; Hotung Papers.
15. Sir Robert's notes on an interview with Mrs John Litton, 2 September 1945; Hotung Papers. Ho Wing's death was reported in *South China Morning Post*, 6 May 1946.
16. Au Choi is buried at the foot of Lady Margaret's grave in the cemetery at Happy Valley.
17. Eddie to Sir Robert, 16 November 1945; Hotung Papers.
18. Ibid. The 'frozen funds' mentioned were freed after the war, only to be blocked by the US Treasury again in the wake of the Korean War.
19. Hesta to Sir Robert, 8 October 1946; Hotung Papers.
20. Eddie to Sir Robert, 15 October 1946; Hotung Papers.
21. Interview, *China Mail*, 2 May 1949.
22. Bernard Shaw to Sir Robert, 24 June 1949; Hotung Papers.
23. So Eddie surmised when invited to tea by Sir Alexander Grantham, the governor, at a race meeting in March, see his report to Sir Robert, 14 March 1950; Hotung Papers.
24. Sir Robert to Bernard Shaw, 6 July 1950; Hotung Papers.
25. Typed note, possibly from 1954; Hotung Papers.
26. In early 1949 Sir Robert, touched by newspaper reports of children dying from the cold in Shanghai, offered HK$20,000 to any charitable organisation devoted to the poor. This sum was held back in view of the unsettled political conditions until the summer, when Sir Robert asked for it to be diverted to flood victims. By August, in the aftermath of the *Amethyst* incident, the Colonial Office was advising him to withdraw his donation altogether. It was refunded to him in mid-1950.
27. The Lady Ho Tung Hall, built with a million-dollar donation from Sir Robert, was opened by Lady Grantham; see *South China Morning Post*, 17 March 1951.
28. The restaurant chain, based on England's Lyons Corner Houses, never got off the ground, but cinemas, including the Princess Theatre in Kowloon ('the most expensively built theatre in the Far East', according to Eddie in 1956), became quite an active interest for Sir Robert at one time.

29. Eddie dealt in exchange and remittance between New York and Hong Kong from late 1950 to October 1952, and was also engaged in a long-running negotiation with the US Treasury to convince its officials that he was not a Chinese Communist agent and to retrieve his frozen assets there.

30. An article by Lt. Colonel D. M. Roberts, MD, of the Royal Army Medical Corps, who was probably in Hong Kong in the 1980s, seems to have been commissioned by Eric Hotung—'The Great Obsession: An Oriental Riddle'. The doctor was asked to try and make a retrospective diagnosis of Sir Robert Ho Tung's medical condition from the few diaries spanning 1941 to the end of Sir Robert's life (with a gap of six years during and after the Second World War) that were shown to him. Not surprisingly, the only conclusion drawn was that Sir Robert suffered from an intestinal disorder, and that the recurring symptoms became a 'great obsession' as he aged; Hotung Papers.

31. Alexander Rudolph Forbes Bosman, born to C. H. M. Bosman and his wife, Mary, on 11 October 1878; see Ho, *Tracing My Children's Lineage*, 34.

32. 'Funeral Instructions', undated. A separate memorandum on the same subject is marked 3 August 1941; Hotung Papers.

33. John Keswick to Sir Robert, 8 September 1955; Hotung Papers.

34. 'Investiture at Buckingham Palace on 12th July 1955' by Elsie Cheung; Hotung Papers.

35. *Daily Express*, 7 July 1955.

36. *Daily Telegraph*, 8 July 1955.

37. Eddie to Elsie Cheung, 12 April 1956; Hotung Papers.

38. Typed note, 3 April 1956; Hotung Papers.

39. Obituary, the *Times*, 27 April 1956.

40. *The New York Times*, 27 April 1956.

Sources and Bibliography

Unpublished Material

This biography draws most heavily on what are referred to in the endnotes as 'Hotung Papers'. The nature and source of these documents are described in the Preface, and I shall not repeat the details here.

Over a period of three decades the doyen of historians of Hong Kong, the Rev. Carl T. Smith, built up a unique card index file of public records in the colony. This included a note on every mention of the Ho Tungs in the local newspapers. Apart from making this file available, Carl Smith also generously shared his research into C. H. M. Bosman with me. Sir Robert's father seemed a rather shadowy figure then, but some light was cast by the more recent researches of Andrew Tse, Eric Peter Ho, and Elizabeth Sinn—their works are mentioned below. Runhua Wu, an independent scholar in Foshan, China, trawled several online archives to track Bosman's footprints after he left Hong Kong, and she generously forwarded her findings to me. Those traces do not, however, detract from the impression of Bosman as a smooth, plausible man whose most remarkable achievement in the end was to have fathered Sir Robert Ho Tung and some of his brothers. After his stint in Asia, Bosman lived as an ordinary businessman in London where he married and settled.

The Public Records Office of Hong Kong and the National Archives at Kew, London, were founts of interesting material, while the Jardine Matheson Archive at Cambridge University Library provided useful background information on sugar trading and the insurance companies' operations during Ho Tung's compradore years. I visited the Jardine Matheson Archive long ago, years before its catalogue went online, so the discovery of a series of letters between Jardines and Bosman & Co. was entirely serendipitous. Those letters concern shipments of quicksilver and gold bars from San Francisco between 1861 (the year before Sir Robert's birth) and 1865 (the beginning of one of Bosman's extended absences from Hong Kong).

References on 'protected women' were drawn from Eitel, *Europe in China* (see below), and *Hong Kong: Return to an address of the House of Lords, dated 22nd March 1889, for copy of report of the Commissioners appointed by the Governor of Hong Kong to inquire into the working of the Contagious Diseases Ordinance of 1867.*

Over the years Andrew Tse painstakingly put together family tress of the extended Ho family as well as a collection of photographs and film. His *Genealogy of the Ho Family, Volumes 1, 2, 3* and *4*, a digital compilation, is an indispensable resource. The family trees at the back of the book are adapted from this genealogy. Andrew also gave me a copy of 'Zhushi he He Dong jiazhu guanxi jianshu' (祝氏和何東家族關係簡述), a handwritten note on the Zhu–Ho family connection, which provides a little more information on Ho Tung's mother and her life in Chongming and Shanghai.

I have also cited from an MPhil thesis submitted to the University of Hong Kong in 1975, 'Eurasians in Hong Kong: A Sociological Study of a Marginal Group', by Stephen Frederick Fisher.

Published Material

As the obituary in *South China Morning Post* of 27 April 1956 succinctly put it, 'Sir Robert's history was that of the Colony'. Many of the publications consulted and listed below are therefore those about the development of colonial Hong Kong. I must also single out the personal memoirs of Jean Gittins and Irene Cheng, whose books are invaluable sources of information on the family life of the Ho Tungs.

Several books germane to this biography have been published since an earlier version of it was completed over two decades ago. Bibliographic details of these titles, by Elizabeth Doery (Jean Gittins's daughter), Eric Peter Ho (Sir Robert's great-nephew), Leung Hung Kee (a granddaughter of Ho Sai-wing), Frances Tse Liu (a descendant of Ho Kom-tong), Elizabeth Sinn, and Zheng Hongtai and Wong Siu-lun, are included below.

All About Shanghai and Environs: A Standard Guide Book, 1934–35 edition. Shanghai: The University Press. Reprinted with an introduction by H. J. Lethbridge. Hong Kong: Oxford University Press, 1983.

Barth, Gunther. *Bitter Strength: A History of the Chinese in the United States, 1850–1870.* Cambridge, MA: Harvard University Press, 1964.

Bickley, Gillian. *The Golden Needle: The Biography of Frederick Stewart (1836–1889).* Hong Kong: David C. Lam Institute for East-West Studies, Hong Kong Baptist University, 1997.

Bonavia, David. *China's Warlords.* Hong Kong: Oxford University Press, 1995.

Braga, J. M., ed. *Hong Kong Business Symposium: A Compilation of Authoritative Views on the Administration, Commerce and Resources of Britain's Far East Outpost.* Hong Kong: South China Morning Post, 1957.

Bruner, Katherine F., John K. Fairbank, and Richard Smith, eds. *Entering China's Service: Robert Hart's Journals, 1854–1863.* Cambridge, MA: Harvard University Press, 1986.

Cameron, Nigel. *The Hongkong Land Company Ltd: A Brief History.* Hong Kong: The Hongkong Land Company Ltd, 1979.

Carroll, John M. *Edge of Empires: Chinese Elites and British Colonials in Hong Kong*. Cambridge, MA: Harvard University Press, 2005.

Carroll, John M. *A Concise History of Hong Kong*. Hong Kong: Hong Kong University Press, 2007.

Chan Wai-kwan. *The Making of Hong Kong Society: Three Studies of Class Formation in Early Hong Kong*. Oxford: Clarendon Press, 1991.

Cheng, Irene. *Clara Ho Tung: A Hong Kong Lady, Her Family and Her Times*. Hong Kong: The Chinese University Press, 1976.

Cheng, Irene. *Intercultural Reminiscences*. Hong Kong: David C. Lam Institute for East-West Studies, Hong Kong Baptist University, 1997.

Coates, Austin. *Whampoa: Ships on the Shore*. Hong Kong: South China Morning Post, 1980.

Doery, Elizabeth. *Golden Peaches, Long Life*. Victoria, Australia: Daracombe House, 2010.

Drage, Charles. *Servants of the Dragon Throne: Being the Lives of Edward and Cecil Bowra*. London: Peter Dawnay, 1966.

Eitel, E. J. *Europe in China*. Hong Kong: Kelly and Walsh, 1895. Reprinted with an introduction by H. J. Lethbridge. Hong Kong: Oxford University Press, 1983.

Endacott, G. B. *A History of Hong Kong*. Hong Kong: Oxford University Press, 1958.

England, Vaudine. *Fortune's Bazaar: The Making of Hong Kong*. New York: Simon & Schuster (forthcoming).

Frodsham, J. D., ed. *The First Chinese Embassy to the West: Journals of Kuo Sung-t'ao, Liu Hsi-hung and Chang Te-yi*. Oxford: Clarendon Press, 1974.

Gittins, Jean. *Eastern Windows—Western Skies*. Hong Kong: South China Morning Post, 1969.

Gittins, Jean. *Stanley: Behind Barbed Wire*. Hong Kong: Hong Kong University Press, 1982.

Hall, Peter A. *In the Web*. Third edition. Heswall: Peter Hall, 2012.

Hammond, Kenneth J., and Kristin Stapleton, eds. *The Human Tradition in Modern China*. Lanham, Maryland: Rowman & Littlefield Publishers, 2008

何張靜蓉。《名山遊記》。香港：東蓮覺苑，1934。[Ho Cheung Ching-yung (Clara). *Mingshan youji*. Hong Kong: Tung Lin Kok Yuen, 1934.]

Ho, Eric Peter. *Tracing My Children's Lineage*. Hong Kong: Centre of Asian Studies, University of Hong Kong, 2010.

Holdsworth, May, and Christopher Munn, eds. *Dictionary of Hong Kong Biography*. Hong Kong: Hong Kong University Press, 2011.

Hutcheon, Robin. *SCMP: The First Eighty Years*. Hong Kong: South China Morning Post, 1983.

Jarrett, Vincent H. G. 'Old Hong Kong' by 'Colonial', a series of articles from *South China Morning Post*, 17 June 1933 to 13 April 1935, arranged alphabetically by subject and typed; photocopy. Hong Kong: Public Records Office of Hong Kong.

Jaschok, Maria. *Concubines and Bondservants: A Social History*. Hong Kong: Oxford University Press, 1988.

Jaschok, Maria, and Suzanne Miers, eds. *Women and Chinese Patriarchy: Submission, Servitude and Escape*. Hong Kong: Hong Kong University Press, 1994.

Keswick, Maggie, ed. *The Thistle and the Jade: A Celebration of 150 Years of Jardine, Matheson & Co*. London: Octopus Books, 1982. Revised and updated by Clara Weatherall, *The Thistle and the Jade: A Celebration of 175 Years of Jardine Matheson*. London: Frances Lincoln, 2008.

Laurence, Dan H., ed. *Bernard Shaw: Collected Letters 1926–1950*. London: Max Reinhardt, 1988.

Lee, Vicky. *Being Eurasian: Memories across Racial Divides*. Hong Kong: Hong Kong University Press, 2004.

梁雄姬。《中西融合：羅何錦姿》。香港：三聯書店（香港）有限公司，2013。 [Leung Hung Kee. *Lady Victoria Jubilee Lo*. Hong Kong: Joint Publishing (HK), 2013.]

Little, Mrs Archibald. *In the Land of the Blue Gown*. London: Everett & Co., 1912.

Liu, Frances Tse. *Ho Kom-tong: A Man for All Seasons*. Hong Kong: Compradore House, 2003.

Lo Jung-pang. *K'ang Yu-wei: A Biography and a Symposium*. Tucson: University of Arizona Press, 1967.

Lo, T. S. *A Family Album*. Hong Kong: Green Pagoda Press, undated.

Paterson, E. H. *A Hospital for Hong Kong: The Centenary History of the Alice Ho Miu Ling Nethersole Hospital*. Hong Kong, undated.

Po Leung Kuk Board of Directors for 1977–78. *Centenary History of the Po Leung Kuk, Hong Kong 1878–1978*. Hong Kong: Po Leung Kuk. undated.

Schiffrin, Harold Z. *Sun Yat-sen and the Origins of the Chinese Revolution*. Berkeley: University of California Press, 1968.

Shaw, George Bernard. *The Complete Plays of Bernard Shaw*. London: Oldhams Press, 1934.

Sinn, Elizabeth. *Power and Charity: The Early History of the Tung Wah Hospital, Hong Kong*. Hong Kong: Oxford University Press, 1989.

Sinn, Elizabeth. *Pacific Crossing: California Gold, Chinese Migration, and the Making of Hong Kong*. Hong Kong: Hong Kong University Press, 2013.

Siu, Helen F., ed. *Merchants' Daughters: Women, Commerce and Regional Culture in South China*. Hong Kong: Hong Kong University Press, 2010.

Smith, Carl T. *Chinese Christians: Elites, Middlemen, and the Church in Hong Kong*. Hong Kong: Oxford University Press, 1985.

Smith, Carl T. *A Sense of History: Studies in the Social and Urban History of Hong Kong*. Hong Kong: Hong Kong Educational Publishing, 1995.

Smith, Carl. T. 'A Sense of History (Part I)'. *Journal of the Hong Kong Branch of the Royal Asiatic Society* 26 (1986): 144–265 (reprints of a series of articles first published in *South China Morning Post*, 1977–79).

Smith, Carl T. 'A Sense of History (Part II)'. *Journal of the Hong Kong Branch of the Royal Asiatic Society* 27 (1987): 117–253 (reprints of a series of articles first published in *South China Morning Post*, 1977–79).

Snow, Philip. *The Fall of Hong Kong: Britain, China and the Japanese Occupation*. New Haven and London: Yale University Press, 2003.

Spence, Jonathan. *To Change China: Western Advisers in China 1620–1960*. Harmondsworth: Penguin Books, 1980.

Spence, Jonathan. *The Gate of Heavenly Peace: The Chinese and Their Revolution 1895–1980*. Harmondsworth: Penguin Books, 1982.

Stokes, Gwenneth, and John Philip Stokes, *Queen's College: Its History 1862–1987*. Hong Kong: Queen's College Old Boys' Association, 1987.

Sweeting, Tony. 'Hong Kong Eurasians', ed. Peter Cunich. *Journal of the Royal Asiatic Society Hong Kong Branch* 55 (2015): 83–113.

Teng, Emma. *Eurasian: Mixed Identities in the United States, China, and Hong Kong, 1842–1943*. Berkeley: University of California Press, 2013.

Teng, Emma. 'Hong Kong's Eurasian "Web" Viewed through the Lens of Inter-Asian Studies'. *Journal of Asian Studies* 76, no. 4 (November 2017): 1–9.

蔡榮芳。《香港人之香港史1841–1945》。香港：牛津大學出版社，2001。[Tsai Jung-fang. *Xianggang ren zhi Xianggang shi, 1841–1945*. Hong Kong: Oxford University Press, 2001.]

Tung Wah Board of Directors 1970–71. *One Hundred Years of The Tung Wah Group of Hospitals 1870–1970*. Hong Kong: The Tung Wah Group of Hospitals, undated.

Wasserstein, Bernard. *Secret War in Shanghai: Treachery, Subversion and Collaboration in the Second World War*. London: Profile Books, 1998.

Wesley-Smith, Peter. *Unequal Treaties 1898–1997: Great Britain and Hong Kong's New Territories*. Hong Kong: Oxford University Press, 1980.

Wesley-Smith, Peter. 'Sir Francis Piggott: Chief Justice in His Own Cause'. *Hong Kong Law Journal* 12 (1982): 260–313.

Wilbur, C. Martin. *Sun Yat-sen: Frustrated Patriot*. New York: Columbia University Press, 1976.

Wright, Arnold, and H. A. Cartwright, eds. *Twentieth Century Impressions of Hongkong, Shanghai, and Other Treaty Ports of China: Their History, People, Commerce, Industries, and Resources*. London: Lloyd's Great Britain Publishing Company, 1908.

Yeh, Wen-hsin, ed. *Wartime Shanghai*. London: Routledge, 1998.

Yeo, Florence. *My Memories*. Pittsburgh: Dorrance Publishing, 1994.

鄭宏泰、黃紹倫。《香港大老：何東》。香港：三聯書店（香港）有限公司，2007。[Zheng Hongtai, and Wong Siu-lun. *Xianggang dalao—He Dong*. Hong Kong: Joint Publishing (HK), 2007.]

鄭宏泰、黃紹倫。《香港將軍：何世禮》。香港：三聯書店（香港）有限公司，2008。[Zheng Hongtai and Wong Siu-lun. *Xianggang jiangjun—He Shili*. Hong Kong: Joint Publishing (HK), 2008.]

鄭宏泰、黃紹倫。《何家女子：三代婦女傳奇》。香港：三聯書店（香港）有限公司，2010。[Zheng Hongtai and Wong Siu-lun. *He jia nüzi: san dai funü chuanqi.* Hong Kong: Joint Publishing (HK), 2010.]

Zheng, Victor, and Sui-lun Wong. 'The Mystery of Capitalism: Eurasian Entrepreneurs' Socio-Cultural Strategies for Commercial Success in Early 20th-Century Hong Kong'. *Asian Studies Review* 34:4 (2010): 467–87. https://doi.org/10.1080/10357 823.2010.527919.

Index

Sir Robert Ho Tung is indexed as Ho Tung throughout.